The Price Advantage

Founded in 1807, John Wiley & Sons is the oldest independent publishing company in the United States. With offices in North America, Europe, Australia, and Asia, Wiley is globally committed to developing and marketing print and electronic products and services for our customers' professional and personal knowledge and understanding.

The Wiley Finance series contains books written specifically for finance and investment professionals, sophisticated individual investors and their financial advisors, and senior business executives. Book topics range from portfolio management to e-commerce, risk management, financial engineering, valuation, financial instrument analysis, and pricing strategy, as well as much more.

For a list of available titles, visit our Web site at www.WileyFinance.com.

The Price
Advantage

MICHAEL V. MARN
ERIC V. ROEGNER
CRAIG C. ZAWADA

WILEY

John Wiley & Sons, Inc.

Published by John Wiley & Sons, Inc., Hoboken, New Jersey.
Published simultaneously in Canada.

For general information on our other products and services, or technical support,
please contact our Customer Care Department within the United States at 800-
762-2974, outside the United States at 317-572-3993 or fax 317-572-4002.

Wiley also publishes its books in a variety of electronic formats. Some content that
appears in print may not be available in electronic books.

For more information about Wiley products, visit our web site at www.wiley.com.

Library of Congress Cataloging-in-Publication Data:
Marn, Michael V.
    The price advantage / Michael V. Marn, Eric V. Roegner, Craig C.
Zawada.
        p.   cm.
    Includes bibliographical references and index.
    ISBN 0-471-46669-7 (CLOTH)
    1. Pricing.   I. Roegner, Eric V.   II. Zawada, Craig C.   III. Title.
    HF5416.5.M365   2004
    658.8'16—dc22

                                                            2003017896

Printed in the United States of America.

10   9   8   7   6   5

For
Nancy, Kristina, and Gail

Contents

Preface   xi

Acknowledgments   xv

PART ONE
Pricing Fundamentals

CHAPTER 1
  Introduction   3

CHAPTER 2
  The Three Levels of Price Management   13

PART TWO
Exploring the Levels

CHAPTER 3
  Transaction   23

CHAPTER 4
  Product/Market Strategy   43

CHAPTER 5
  Industry Strategy   74

PART THREE
Special Topics

CHAPTER 6
  New Product Pricing   93

CHAPTER 7
   Solutions, Bundles, and Other Packaged Offerings   **112**

PART FOUR
Unique Events

CHAPTER 8
   Postmerger Pricing   **127**

CHAPTER 9
   Price Wars   **143**

PART FIVE
Expanding the Boundaries

CHAPTER 10
   Technology-Enabled Pricing   **161**

CHAPTER 11
   Legal Issues   **177**

PART SIX
Bringing It Together

CHAPTER 12
   Pricing Architecture   **193**

CHAPTER 13
   Driving Pricing Change   **207**

CHAPTER 14
   The Monarch Battery Case   **220**

CHAPTER 15
   Epilogue   **237**

APPENDIX 1
Sample Pocket Price and Pocket Margin Waterfalls   239

APPENDIX 2
Antitrust Issues   253

APPENDIX 3
List of Acronyms   278

About the Authors   279

Index   280

Preface

When we conceived the idea of writing a book on pricing, we asked ourselves—as our readers should too—several basic questions. Why a book on pricing? Why a book by McKinsey & Company on pricing? Why a book on pricing now? Let us begin by addressing these basic questions.

WHY A BOOK ON PRICING?

Pricing, although one of the most critical management functions, remains one of the most misunderstood and undermanaged functions at many companies that are otherwise high performers. Pricing is far and away the most sensitive profit lever that managers can influence. Very small changes in average price translate into huge changes in operating profit.

The universe of pricing concepts and knowledge has advanced significantly over the past several decades, with business and academic journals regularly featuring articles on the topic. That said, few businesses have successfully tapped into the incredible potential that improved pricing holds. Even thoughtful general managers feel helpless to make real progress on the pricing front. They do not even know where to begin to get a handle on identifying—much less capturing—the exciting performance upside that pricing so often holds.

This book is not designed to be an exhaustive review of the considerable body of pricing theory that has accumulated over the years. To the contrary, this book has been written as a practical pricing guide for that thoughtful general manager who has been tempted by the unrealized promise of improved pricing and, perhaps, frustrated by attempts to translate pricing theory into bottom-line impact for his or her business. It is intended to provide a logical and structured approach for identifying where the most precious sources of untapped pricing opportunity reside in a business, along with practical, case-illustrated guidance on how to capture that opportunity.

WHY A BOOK BY McKINSEY ON PRICING?

Over the past 20 years, pricing has become one of the most frequent areas in which we have helped businesses across Europe, the Americas, and the Asia Pacific region to improve their performance. These companies represent a rich and diverse range of industries, including industrial goods, consumer packaged goods, consumer durables, banking, telecommunications, chemicals, retailing, high-tech products, basic materials, insurance, pharmaceuticals, and transportation. To support our service to clients, McKinsey has invested more than $20 million in developing practical knowledge in pricing over the past five years alone. We are credited with having developed and advanced a majority of the most useful contemporary pricing frameworks—the pocket price waterfall and the value map are just two examples.

WHY A BOOK ON PRICING NOW?

Over the past decade, we have published more than 20 full-length journal articles on specific topics in pricing. These articles have often followed our investments in developing fresh knowledge in the pricing space and have covered a range of issues, including transaction price management, price wars, making pricing change happen, postmerger pricing, and pricing strategies for integrated solutions. The breadth of our knowledge in pricing has grown to the point where presenting a holistic and integrated perspective in a single volume seems appropriate and timely.

In addition, conditions may be more favorable than ever for companies that try to create what we call the price advantage. In the early 1990s, many businesses tried to improve pricing performance and capability, but despite the best intentions, most failed to create real pricing improvements. Changes in organizations and information technology (IT) have increased the chances of success for companies trying to create the price advantage.

Based on our experience, less than a third of the major companies around the world had functional departments professionally dedicated to pricing ten years ago. When general managers mounted initiatives to upgrade the discipline and professionalism with which pricing was executed, they were often handicapped by an organization that lacked resident core skills in pricing. Now, however, more than four-fifths of these companies have created or begun to create dedicated pricing departments. Today, more and more companies have the horsepower to drive and execute pricing excellence throughout their organizations.

Also in the early 1990s, many companies simply did not have effective, enterprise-wide information systems that could allow fast access to accurate data on customers, transactions, and markets. Successful pricing is a game of knowledge and information, and such systems are necessary to support effective pricing judgment. Furthermore, well-developed pricing application and decision support software was virtually unavailable. Even businesses with viable enterprise data systems had to write their own pricing decision support and performance reporting software, often adding years to the implementation of thoughtful price improvement programs.

These IT constraints are by and large no longer major obstacles. Most companies now have functioning enterprise information systems that can provide at least the core data required to support pricing excellence. And a robust variety of commercial pricing software applications has been developed in recent years that further ease the development of pricing excellence in organizations.

Beyond these IT and organizational shifts, pricing is also capturing a higher priority on management agendas. It is one of the few performance improvement areas that remain essentially untapped for many companies today. With the easiest cost cutting already accomplished in most businesses and with demand growth slowing in many markets, superior pricing stands out as one of the few powerful and unexploited levers available to managers today.

Given that the intrinsic priority of the pricing function is on the rise and the organizational and IT hurdles are mostly behind us, now may be the best of times for businesses to get serious about improving their pricing capability and performance—and to have at their disposal a practical handbook to help guide that improvement.

STRUCTURE OF THE BOOK

This book is organized into six main sections. Part One describes the price advantage and explains why it is worthwhile for businesses to pursue that rare but valuable advantage. It then lays out our overarching framework for identifying and ultimately capturing pricing opportunity. This framework, the three levels of price management, provides the integrating thread that weaves through the book and is applicable to most business situations. Part Two explores each of these three levels in considerable detail.

Parts Three, Four, and Five address in turn special pricing topics, unique pricing events faced by companies, and themes that open a wider field of pricing opportunities. Part Six is devoted to the practical enablers and constraints to making enduring and positive pricing change happen, including a detailed case study and some final thoughts. In addition, the Appendixes are designed to provide some useful examples of the application of core frameworks discussed in the book and an overview of key points in pricing law.

This book contains a number of disguised cases to illustrate pricing concepts, frameworks, and insights. These cases are rooted in McKinsey's extensive client work in pricing, and client identities are heavily disguised to assure protection of confidential client information and strategies. The location and nature of opportunities identified are consistent with the underlying cases, and the magnitude of improvements shown by these examples is real.

Unless otherwise noted, when we talk about a company's "product," we are referring to that company's comprehensive product, service, and support offering to customers. This convention allows for more economical word usage throughout the book.

Acknowledgments

When you spend more than a year of your life writing and rewriting, planning and drafting, editing and redoing, it is difficult to express your appreciation for those who accompanied you on the journey. But we will do our best to recognize the efforts of those who inspired us, toiled with us, and supported us throughout the writing of this book.

First, we must acknowledge that this book represents the culmination of more than 25 years' experience in pricing. This experience was gained from hundreds of engagements involving hundreds of McKinsey & Company consultants. We want to thank all the clients who allowed us to be a part of their transformation, and all the consultants who contributed to our knowledge over the years.

Next, it is appropriate to recognize the contribution of the "godfathers" of pricing, those who first recognized the power of pricing—Kent B. Monroe, Tom Nagle, Dan Nimer, and Arleigh Walker—and those who supported the development of the pricing discipline within McKinsey: David Court, Tom French, Robert Garda, Philip Hawk, Ralf Leszinski, Andrew Parsons, and Rob Rosiello. They created the foundation on which this book is built and continue to support the continuing evolution of our knowledge.

Once we decided the time had come to commit our knowledge to paper and write this book, there were two people who made the entire journey with us, from blank screen to printed book. Cheri Eyink served as our ever-persistent project manager. Besides managing the schedules and deadlines, she acted as a thought partner on the content of the book, pushing our thinking and challenging us on what our readers want to know. Roger Malone was our trusty editor throughout the process. From the beginning, he guided us through this daunting task, not only acting as our sounding board and editor, but also pushing us to deliver the best of the Firm and ourselves to our readers. We want to thank both of them for their input and support.

In addition, eight people were instrumental in developing key concepts included in this book and sharing that knowledge through the written word. For their contributions in these areas, we would like to thank John Abele (postmerger pricing), Scott Andre and Robert Musslewhite (industry strategy), Walter Baker (value profiling), Daniel G. Doster (solutions pricing), Dieter Kiewell (pricing tools and implementation), John Voyzey (price wars), and Gene Zelek, chair of the Antitrust and Trade Regulation Group at Freeborn & Peters in Chicago (legal issues). There were also a number of people who made significant contributions to the knowledge we present here: Kevin Bright, Hugh Courtney, David Dvorin, Kristine Kelly, Andy Kincheloe, Michal Kisilevitz, Eric Lin, Glenn Mercer, Jamie Moffitt, David Sackin, Mike Sherman, Philippe Stubbe, and Lynda Martin Alegi, head of the Global Antitrust Group at Baker & McKenzie in London.

Additional editorial support was also provided by our colleagues at *The McKinsey Quarterly*, in particular Don Bergh, Stuart Flack, and Allan Gold, and by Bill Falloon and his team at John Wiley & Sons. We are grateful for their involvement.

As everyone knows, projects of this magnitude are not accomplished without the support of professionals who take care of the many details. We would particularly like to thank Mary Turchon for her assistance with organizing meetings, printing manuscripts, and generally taking care of the administrative issues. We would also like to thank Danica Reed for her research assistance. Finally, we would like to recognize Janet Clifford and Mary Ann Brej for their work on the exhibits, formatting and reformatting them to help us get our message across.

To all those identified above and those who supported us over the years, we offer a heartfelt thank you. Although the words do not seem to capture our gratitude, please know they are offered in sincere appreciation and recognition of your contributions.

Pricing Fundamentals

CHAPTER 1

Introduction

What's your advantage? What capability distinguishes your company from its peers, allows your business to perform better than your competitors, provides the foundation for superior returns to your shareholders? Is it a cost advantage—do you purchase better and manufacture more efficiently than your competition? Is it a distribution advantage—are your products sold through the best wholesalers, retailers, and locations in your markets? Is it a technology advantage or an innovation advantage? Or is yours a brand advantage or a capital structure advantage or a service advantage?

For all of the advantages that businesses pursue, there is one powerful advantage that is accessible to virtually every business, but actually pursued—much less achieved—by very few. That advantage is *the price advantage*.

Setting prices for goods and services is one of the most fundamental of management disciplines. It is unavoidable. Every product and every service sold since the beginning of time has had to have a price assigned to it. And setting that price is among the most crucial, most profit-sensitive decisions that all companies have to make. Ironically, very few companies price well. For a host of reasons, few ever develop anything resembling a superior, businesswide, core capability in pricing. In other words, few companies build pricing into the distinctive business advantage that it can be.

In this book, we will discuss the details of creating and sustaining a price advantage, where pricing excellence generates superior returns to shareholders. But first, let us look at why getting pricing right is so important, and why so few companies realize this advantage.

THE POWER OF 1 PERCENT

Why is it so vital to get pricing right? Because pricing right is the fastest and most effective way for companies to grow profits. The right price will boost profits faster than increasing volume; the wrong price can shrink profit just as quickly. As shown in Exhibit 1-1, the power of pricing is dramatic. Using the average income statement of the Global 1200 (an aggregation of 1,200 large, publicly held companies from around the world), the exhibit illustrates just how quickly the right price can create profit.

Starting with price indexed to 100, we see that fixed costs (items like overhead, property, and depreciation that do not vary when volume changes) amount to an indexed average of 24.5 percent of price. Variable costs (expenses like labor and materials that shift in tandem with volume) account for another 66.4 percent. This leaves an average return on sales (ROS) of 9.1 percent.

Now, against these average Global 1200 economics, how much is it worth to improve your price by 1 percent? Assuming volume remains steady, price will rise to 101, fixed costs by definition are unchanged, and, since there is no change in volume, variable costs are also constant.

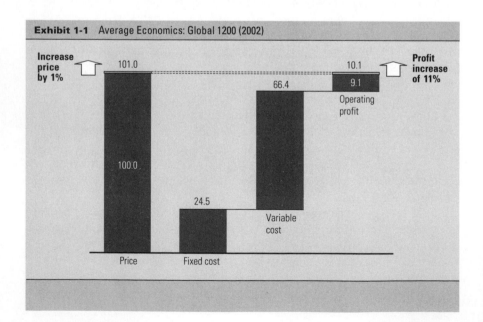

Exhibit 1-1 Average Economics: Global 1200 (2002)

Operating profit, however, rises to 10.1 percent from 9.1, a relative increase of 11 percent.

The clear message is that very small improvements in price translate into huge increases in operating profit. When you talk about creating a pricing advantage, you may have to recalibrate your thinking about the significance of very small change. Pricing initiatives that increase average prices by only a quarter or a half percent are important because they bring disproportional increases in operating profit. A 1 or 2 percent price improvement is a major victory with significant profit implications. Find 3 percent—and many companies can, once they start looking—and operating profit can jump by more than 30 percent, using average Global 1200 economics.

Pricing is far and away the most powerful profit lever that a company can influence. Continuing with average Global 1200 economics, Exhibit 1-2

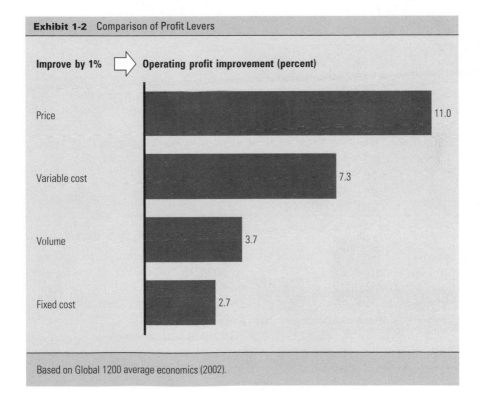

Exhibit 1-2 Comparison of Profit Levers

Improve by 1% ⇨ Operating profit improvement (percent)

Price — 11.0

Variable cost — 7.3

Volume — 3.7

Fixed cost — 2.7

Based on Global 1200 average economics (2002).

illustrates what happens to operating profit when each of the other levers is improved by 1 percent, while the other factors stay constant.

A 1 percent decline in variable costs results in a 7.3 percent increase in operating profit. Though not as powerful as a change in price, this is still significant. However, most companies have pushed the variable cost lever quite hard in recent years through purchasing and supply management initiatives, labor productivity improvements, and other measures. Continued improvement in variable cost structure has become increasingly difficult.

Changes in fixed costs have an even smaller effect on operating profit. A 1 percent improvement generates only a 2.7 percent operating profit increase. While making other cost-cutting efforts, companies in the 1990s were also busy trimming these fixed costs, such that, as with variable costs, further improvements are becoming more and more elusive.

The profit sensitivity to a change in volume can be a real surprise to many. A 1 percent increase in unit sales volume, while prices and per-unit costs are held constant, results in a 3.7 percent increase in operating profit. This is about a third of the impact of a 1 percent improvement in pricing. But which lever gets the majority of the attention and energy from marketing and sales people? The volume lever, despite its profit impact being so much lower than improving price.

Unfortunately, the pricing lever is a double-edged sword. No lever can increase profits more quickly than raising price a percentage point or two, but at the same time nothing will drop profits through the floor faster than letting price slip down a percentage point or two. If your average price drops just a single percentage point, then assuming your economics are similar to the Global 1200 average, your operating profits decrease by that same 11 percent.

THE PRICE/VOLUME TRADEOFF

This inevitably leads us to the age-old question of the price/volume/profit tradeoff: If I lower my price, can I increase volume enough to generate more operating profit? Exhibit 1-3 explores how that tradeoff works—or, more accurately, does not work. If a business takes steps that effectively reduce average prices by 5 percent, how much of a volume increase would be necessary to break even on an operating profit basis?

With economics similar to the Global 1200 average, a 5 percent price decrease would require a 17.5 percent volume increase, not to increase operating profits but just to break even. Such an increase is highly unlikely. For a 5 percent drop in price to generate a 17.5 percent volume

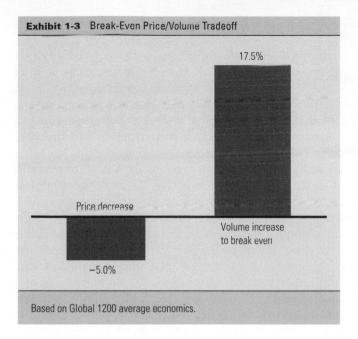

Exhibit 1-3 Break-Even Price/Volume Tradeoff

17.5%

Price decrease

Volume increase
to break even

−5.0%

Based on Global 1200 average economics.

rise would require a price elasticity of −3.5:1. That is, every percentage point drop in price would have to drive unit volume up by 3.5 percent. Our experience in real markets shows price elasticities commonly reach a maximum of only −1.7:1 or −1.8:1. On rare occasions, usually for consumer items purchased on impulse, it might be as high as −2.5:1. In the real world, −3.5:1 price elasticity is *extremely* rare. Thus, the basic arithmetic of decreasing price to increase volume to increase profits just does not add up. Note that you should do this calculation using the economics of your own business to confirm how the price/volume/profit tradeoff works for you.

So the first reason pricing is so important is that profits are extremely sensitive to even minute changes in prices. Each percentage point of price is a precious nugget of profit that should be held tight to the chest and never given up without a hard fight. Unfortunately, sales reps, propelled by their incentive systems, routinely negotiate away five percentage points at a time through discounts, special offers, and other inducements to complete a contract. Companies with a superior pricing capability—with the price advantage—consistently let fewer of those nuggets slip away.

MARKET FORCES ADD PRESSURE

The second reason managing pricing is so important is because even if nothing changes internally, most companies, whether selling to consumers or to businesses, face unprecedented downward pressure on prices. If nothing is done, these external forces will depress prices and erode profits quickly.

Prices in consumer markets are being squeezed by a combination of fundamental changes in the business environment and demographic shifts, as illustrated in Exhibit 1-4. Discount retailers such as Wal-Mart, Home Depot, and Costco are growing larger, and the industry is becoming increasingly concentrated. These giants are using their market power to extract ever lower prices from consumer goods suppliers. The growth of the Internet, as well as increased use of price advertising by these discounters, has made it easier for shoppers to find and compare prices of consumer products. Meanwhile, private-label packaged goods, usually sold under a retailer's brand name, have also witnessed quality improvements that put added pressure on traditional brands in many product categories.

Generational shifts are leaving their mark on the consumer market as well. The baby boomers who fueled much of the rampant consumer spending through the 1990s are throttling back on their purchases now

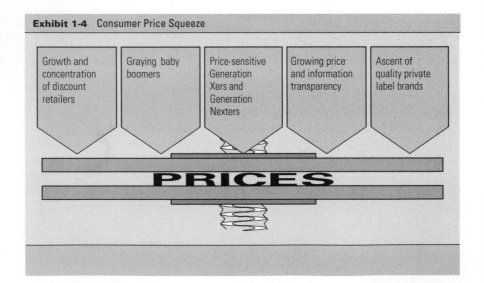

Exhibit 1-4 Consumer Price Squeeze

that they are helping children through college, supporting aging parents, preparing for their own retirement, and carrying other new financial burdens. The generations behind the baby boomers have been notably more price sensitive, having grown up surrounded by discount retailers of every stripe.

Business-to-business (B2B) companies are also feeling price pressure from changes in the market environment, as shown in Exhibit 1-5. Buyers are tougher and more skilled than ever in extracting every last penny of price from suppliers. Efficiency programs during the 1990s have unleashed newfound excess capacity into many markets. Supplier base reduction programs tend to concentrate a large volume of a customer's purchases onto a decreasing number of suppliers, thereby raising the stakes and the negotiating power of the customers over the suppliers. Open-book costing, in which powerful buyers insist on knowing the details of a supplier's costs for each component of a product, including individual component materials costs, direct labor, and overhead, has become more common. With this greater visibility into suppliers' costs, buyers gain leverage in negotiating prices.

Furthermore, many industrial suppliers have significantly cut their own costs—have themselves become leaner and meaner—and thus generally feel more confident to compete more aggressively on price to secure business. Also, global companies are increasingly shopping the world for

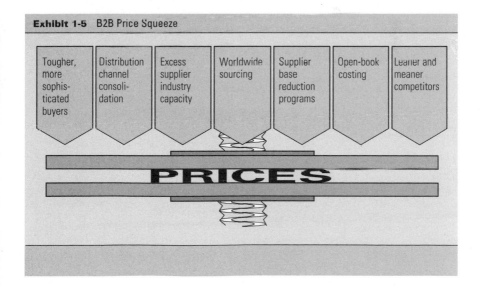

Exhibit 1-5   B2B Price Squeeze

the best prices, and then insisting on those unified low prices for all their buying locations. And finally, just as in consumer distribution, B2B distribution channels are becoming more concentrated and more powerful relative to suppliers.

The forces that are putting pressure on companies that serve consumers and businesses alike are gathering strength and are not likely to subside in the foreseeable future. A company that neglects pricing, that does not actively develop an enhanced pricing capability and a price advantage to combat this onslaught, will inevitably find prices crumble away under the weight of these prevailing forces.

THE NOBILITY OF PRICING EXCELLENCE

The last reason why building a price advantage in your business is so important goes beyond profit economics or market forces to the spirit, heart, and pride of an organization. There is a genuine nobility to pricing done well. Individuals responsible for setting prices hold a sacred trust. They assure that a business gets fairly rewarded in the marketplace for products and services superior to its competitors—that there is a real payoff for being better.

The price advantage is not about gouging customers or employing tricks to gain undeserved revenues. Quite to the contrary, the real price advantage is a source of organizational pride. The highest compliment a customer can pay a supplier is to knowingly pay more for that company's goods and services. In doing so, the customer is saying, "You are higher priced, but you are worth it; you are superior to my other supplier alternatives." Businesses that, lacking the pricing advantage, fail to have their superiority rewarded with higher prices often lose their drive—and even their ability—to continue to be superior.

WHY THE PRICE ADVANTAGE IS SO RARE

The reasons for pursuing a price advantage are compelling, but very few companies have achieved a level of competence in pricing that could be described as a price advantage. While many may attribute much of the double-digit profit growth that was so common in the 1990s to improved pricing practices, in fact the bulk of this growth can be traced to cost cutting and increased demand. Pricing had little to do with the profit growth during this period and remains a largely untapped opportunity.

A number of factors explain why companies undermanage the opportunities inherent in pricing and why so few businesses have ever developed a pricing advantage.

- Under past buoyant economics brought on by strong demand and sharp cost cutting, many companies sensed little need to develop advanced pricing skills and to pursue pricing as a source of increased profits.
- Companies often did not believe that pricing was manageable. They saw prices as set by the market, by customers, or by unreasonable competitors.
- Data to support pricing decisions was either not available or not current enough to help with real-time pricing decisions.
- Price differentiation and other pricing actions were misperceived as always illegal, and therefore degrees of pricing freedom were internally limited.
- Pricing mistakes and errors were hard for most companies to detect. If your sales representative in Scotland negotiated a price that was 5 percent lower than it could have been, it was unlikely to raise a red flag at headquarters.
- Frontline pricers often had virtually no incentive to stretch for an additional percent in price.
- Senior managers often had little, if any, involvement in pricing.

As we will show in later chapters, the obstacles outlined here are real but can be overcome with some effort. Indeed, these barriers to building pricing capabilities are not trivial, and creating a price advantage is hard work. But the payoff is so large that knocking down these barriers is well worth the effort.

* * *

The price advantage is a powerful advantage worth pursuing and is achievable by each and every business, but fully realized by very few. It deserves pursuit because pricing is such an extremely sensitive profit lever, with small swings in price levels generating huge swings in bottom-line profitability. As we have shown, a 1 percent increase in price can increase your profit by 11 percent or more; a 1 percent slip in price can erode profits by that same 11 percent or more. And rare are the circumstances where decreasing price can generate nearly enough additional sales volume to offset the effects of a price cut and produce incremental profitability.

Furthermore, the price advantage deserves pursuit because of prevailing market forces—both in consumer and business markets—that are putting unprecedented downward pressure on industrywide price levels and showing no signs of subsiding. Failure to take real initiative in pricing today virtually assures that percentage points of price will slip through your hands annually—and that huge chunks of operating profit will drop off your bottom line. Finally, achieving the price advantage can be a source of organizational pride as employees are reassured that their hard work to create superior products and services does not go unrewarded.

CHAPTER 2

The Three Levels of Price Management

The reasons, economic and otherwise, to pursue the price advantage are compelling, as we have seen. But the sheer breadth of pricing issues in most companies can make even determining where to start a real challenge.

Pricing issues are seldom simple and isolated; they are intricate and linked to multiple aspects of a business. Even pricing decisions that seem entirely tactical often have strategic implications—effects on other prices, on other customers, even on competitors. The missed opportunities illustrated by the three cases described below help highlight the inherent breadth and diversity of issues in pricing.

- A specialty wire company failed to recognize that the closing of a competitor's large European factory had created industrywide shortages. Prices could have been justifiably raised by at least 10 percent, but were not.
- A consumer electronics firm underpriced an innovative compact disc (CD) player because it did not realize that customers really valued the new model's special features and design.
- An automobile parts supplier inadvertently sold items to some of its smallest accounts at net realized prices lower than those charged to its largest accounts. Why? The supplier's off-invoice price structure, which included items like cash discounts and program rebates, had gotten out of control.

While each of these cases clearly demonstrates issues in pricing, the underlying problems somehow feel fundamentally different—and they are. One of the real challenges of making progress in pricing is defining the territory. When you say "price," it means different things to different people.

Depending on their points of view (their training and their jobs, among other factors), thoughtful business people will understand the topic in a variety of different ways.

For the economists, the word *price* fosters images of intersecting supply and demand curves and price indices that rise and fall. They focus on overall industry price levels, using microeconomics to project market price trends. Economists would be most intrigued with the pricing opportunity missed by the specialty wire manufacturer that failed to capitalize on the wire shortage caused by a competitor's plant closure.

Marketers are also in the game, but they view the field quite differently. For them, the primary force in play is customer perception, or, more to the point, how customers weigh their product's benefits against a competitor's offerings. If a product or service is superior to a competitor's, the marketer's pricing concern is about determining the overall price premium that the product deserves in the marketplace. If the product is inferior, the marketer worries about figuring out either the price discount required relative to the superior competitor or how to improve the product offering to allow it to command a higher price. The marketer, of course, would be attracted to the pricing issues of the consumer electronics company that somehow underestimated the market's positive reaction to its innovative new CD player.

And finally, while savvy sales representatives may appreciate the concepts of microeconomics and market positioning, their concern is usually much more about getting the price right for individual customer transactions—negotiating the right invoice price, discounts, allowance, terms, and conditions, among other items, deal by deal. Most salespeople could readily relate to the dilemma of the auto parts supplier whose differences in transaction prices between customers did not seem to make sense.

So who has the correct perspective on pricing? Economists, with their focus on industry prices that are driven by supply-and-demand balances? The marketers, who focus on getting the right price relative to competing products? Or the sales reps, who concentrate on coming up with the correct transaction price for each specific customer?

AN INTEGRATED APPROACH

On the surface, each constituent group seems to address diverse and unrelated issues across the pricing spectrum. But are they really at odds with each other? No, they are not. Each viewpoint is an integral part of the broad pricing dynamic. They reinforce each other and define the levels at which companies that truly excel at pricing address pricing issues, opportunities, and threats. Understanding the *three levels of price management*, as illustrated in Exhibit 2-1, is a first step in getting a handle on the challenge of pricing.

We will discuss each level in more detail in later chapters, but first let us take the executive tour of the structure.

INDUSTRY STRATEGY

The first level of price management considers overall industry price levels. The main question centers on how myriad factors—supply, demand, costs, regulations, technological shifts, and competitor actions, among others—shift industrywide prices. Companies that excel at this level have a better understanding of industry trends and their underlying drivers than does the competition. They invest in gaining rich insights into the near- and longer-term direction that industry prices are heading. They develop a fact-based understanding of available industry supply and the variables that can change it and of industry demand and the market factors that can move it.

Excellence in industry pricing requires not only in-depth knowledge of your own company and how your actions will affect market prices, but also of the competition. Capacities, costs structures, capital investments, research and development (R&D) expenditures, and growth aspirations of

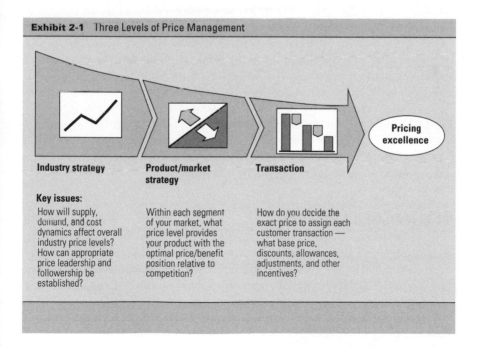

Exhibit 2-1 Three Levels of Price Management

Pricing excellence

Industry strategy

Product/market strategy

Transaction

Key issues:

How will supply, demand, and cost dynamics affect overall industry price levels? How can appropriate price leadership and followership be established?

Within each segment of your market, what price level provides your product with the optimal price/benefit position relative to competition?

How do you decide the exact price to assign each customer transaction — what base price, discounts, allowances, adjustments, and other incentives?

other companies must be a part of the overall picture. In addition, the potential for new market entrants must also be weighed.

Bringing all this knowledge together, companies can anticipate industry price trends and become proactive rather than just a pawn of the market's invisible hand. They can adjust their tactics to take advantage of this superior understanding, for instance by avoiding long-term, fixed-price deals just ahead of an expected upturn in market prices. And finally, they know how to influence constructive price behavior across their industry—when the time is right to lead price up (or to follow faithfully a competitor) and when it is not.

More careful monitoring at this level would have enabled the specialty wire company to spot the industrywide shortage earlier—and to have raised its prices quickly to new industry levels. Its lack of vigilance at the industry strategy level of price management cost the wire company three percentage points of price over the year and a missed opportunity to increase its operating profits by 36 percent.

PRODUCT/MARKET STRATEGY

At the second level of price management, the primary issue is price positioning relative to competitors—that is, within each market segment that you serve, what price level positions you optimally, in customers' eyes, on a price/benefit basis. Price actions at this level tend to be quite visible to the market—both to customers and competitors. At this level, you are setting, for instance, list prices, base prices or target prices in a very public way, telling the marketplace what you think your product is worth relative to competitive offerings. The key phrase here is *customer perceptions*. Unless you can figure out how potential customers perceive the benefits of your product compared with those of the competition, you cannot go much beyond a guessing game in setting list prices or base prices. You will not know what list price premium to seek or list price discount to take relative to competitors. There are plenty of research tools that can help determine and measure these customer perceptions, which we will discuss in later chapters.

Companies that shine at this level are obsessive about understanding customers' perceptions of both their products and their price. They continually research and update their understanding of how customers perceive competitors as well as themselves, and how that all varies by customer segment. Armed with this understanding, these companies seek justifiable price premiums, move to optimal price/benefit positions for each customer segment, and avoid destructive price competition.

The consumer electronics company failed at the product/market strategy level when it launched its new CD player. Had it understood customer perceptions of the benefits the new player offered, it could have set a list price 4 percent higher without sacrificing unit sales volume.

TRANSACTION

The focus at this third level of price management is deciding on the exact price to assign to each and every customer transaction—in other words, from a list price, base price, or target price set at the product/market strategy level, what discounts, allowances, payment terms, volume bonuses, and other inducements to apply. For most companies this is the most detailed, most time-consuming, most systems- and energy-intensive level of pricing. It is the level that generates the price the customer sees and ultimately the net revenue that a company realizes. At most companies, it entails hundreds, even thousands, of individual pricing decisions daily, usually made at multiple organizational levels.

The best companies at the transaction level break through the complexity and gain a superior understanding of the full economics of every transaction and customer. They fully account for every discount and cost-to-serve item that swings the attractiveness of transactions. They know the types of customers and transactions that are best for them and aggressively seek their business. They know which current customers and transactions are underperforming, they know why, and they actively take steps to improve them (or even drop them).

If the auto parts supplier had greater discipline at the transaction level, the overdiscounting to small accounts would have been readily apparent and corrected. More rigorous monitoring and control on a transaction-by-transaction basis, with a full accounting of all discounts after the invoice, would have effectively increased the average realized price by 5 percent with minimal loss of unit sales.

AN INTERDEPENDENT HIERARCHY

There is a natural hierarchy to the three levels of price management. The industry price level is the most general, with its orientation around pricing issues that have an impact across the entire industry. The product/market strategy level entails a tighter scope that focuses on value specific to customer segments, particularly on setting list or base prices by segment. The transaction level is the most detailed, with its microscopic focus on individual transactions and customer pricing.

These three levels are not independent but, rather, interrelated. The industry price level provides a constant backdrop against which product/market strategy price decisions are made, and in turn the product/market strategy level defines the starting point for pricing at the transaction level, often providing the list prices from which on- and off-invoice items are subtracted.

Companies that have created the price advantage for themselves are typically more skilled than their competitors at each of the three levels. Furthermore, they do a better job of orchestrating pricing moves across the three levels, assuring that actions taken at one level reinforce objectives at the others. For example, when prices are generally expected to rise (industry strategy), they do not introduce a low-priced product (product/market strategy) that could put downward pressure on the market, or they would be careful not to discount heavily (transactions) when launching a new product targeted to premium market segments (product/market strategy).

Their interrelationships notwithstanding, the three levels help break the broad and sometimes daunting range of pricing issues that businesses face into more manageable subcategories. When a challenging pricing issue arises, asking which pricing level is most relevant can focus the discussion and provide a useful context for finding a solution. An issue that has industry pricing implications would be considered in a much different light than one with only specific transaction implications.

PINPOINTING THE OPPORTUNITY

Where across the three levels is your pricing opportunity? Each business will have different priorities based on its unique situation. Below are questions that can help managers pinpoint the untapped pricing opportunity waiting to be discovered.

INDUSTRY STRATEGY

- Do you have a fact-based projection of overall pricing trends in the industry for the near, medium, and long term? Is that view shared across your organization so that market pricing behavior is consistent with those projections? How accurate have these projections been historically?
- Do you have a mechanism in place to assess specific market events, such as technological shifts, capacity additions and reductions, changes in component and raw material costs, and demand shifts, and their likely impact on industry prices?
- Have you tried to lead price in your industry upward? If so, how did you decide when and how much? How successful were you? Did competitors follow? Has there been a pattern of price leadership/followership in your industry?

PRODUCT/MARKET STRATEGY

■ Do you research customer attitudes in detail or rely on hunches and anecdotes from the sales force? Has the research led to an understanding of customer segments and of what attributes each segment values most, how each segment compares to others, and how each grades the available products against the attributes it desires most? Has your company changed prices recently based on this understanding?

■ Do you collect and synthesize competitive price data routinely, both in situations where you won business and lost?

■ Have you pinpointed the premium or discount that is justified in relation to competitors' prices? Do you understand how this varies by customer segment, and is this reflected in price levels and structure?

TRANSACTION

■ Do you monitor price performance for each transaction, including all discounts, allowances, rebates, and other incentives, whether or not they are reflected on the invoice? Are these price performance metrics at an aggregate level or can they also be viewed by transaction, customer, or segment?

■ Do you understand how widely net realized prices vary? Do you know which customers or segments regularly pay the highest and lowest net prices? Are there programs in place to attract more of the best and to fix or drop the worst?

■ Have you clearly defined and limited discounting authority, and are the rules rigorously enforced?

■ Do your sales and marketing forces have incentives, monetary or otherwise, to stretch for higher transaction prices?

The chapters in the next section are organized around the three levels of price management. We will explore each level in greater depth, introduce key analytic tools to apply at each level, and provide a number of real business cases to bring the approaches at each level to life. The levels will be addressed in reverse order, starting with the transaction level. This is the level that has broadest applicability across businesses and industries, and often results in the quickest positive impact on price performance. Many of these cases will be disguised to protect confidential information, but they all represent real efforts by companies to capture the price advantage.

*   *   *

The range of issues that falls under the umbrella of *pricing* can be so broad and daunting that many companies with a sincere desire to create the price advantage have difficulty sorting out the issues and gaining any real traction. The *three levels of price management* can help logically categorize the broad range of issues in pricing that exist in most companies into more manageable and addressable components.

The three levels—industry strategy, product/market strategy, and transaction—progress from broad, industrywide pricing issues to very specific customer and transaction issues. Businesses that have achieved the price advantage, when considering a pricing issue, first determine under which of the three levels that issue falls. They then employ the appropriate analytic frameworks, approaches, and mindset for that level in addressing each specific pricing issue.

Exploring the Levels

Transaction

The transaction level is the most granular level of price management. At this level, the critical issue is how to manage the exact price charged for each transaction—that is, from a list price or target price, what discounts, allowances, rebates, conditions, terms, bonuses, and other incentives to apply. Where concern at the industry and product/market strategy levels is directed toward the broader issues of overall industry price levels and relative price position within an industry, focus at the transaction level is almost microscopic—customer by customer, deal by deal, transaction by transaction.

The objective of transaction management is to achieve the right and best realized price for each order or transaction. Transaction pricing is a game of inches where each day hundreds or even thousands of customer-specific (and even invoice line-specific) pricing decisions determine success or failure, where companies capture or lose percentage points of profit margin one transaction at a time. But high transaction volume and complexity, top management neglect, management reporting shortfalls, and lack of aligned incentives all contribute to missed transaction pricing opportunities.

The sheer volume and complexity of transactions tend to create a smoke screen that makes it difficult if not impossible for the rare senior manager who shows an interest to understand what is really going on at the transaction level. Management information systems all too often do not report on transaction price performance or report only average prices that shed no real light on pricing opportunities missed transaction by transaction. And rarer still is the incentive system that genuinely rewards sales and marketing individuals for achieving deal-by-deal pricing excellence. In fact, many incentive approaches, with their emphasis on total sales volume, discourage salespeople from taking the risk required to prevent percentage points of price from slipping away at the transaction level.

THE POCKET PRICE WATERFALL

At the transaction level, all too many companies focus on an incorrect or incomplete measure of price. Most concentrate management energy on either the list price or the invoice price and fail to manage the full range of components that contribute to the final transaction price. Exhibit 3-1 shows the price components for a manufacturer that sells large rolls of linoleum to national, regional, and local flooring retailers, who in turn resell them to residential and commercial customers. The starting point is the dealer list price, $6 per square yard for this particular product. From that list price, an order-size discount (based on the total dollar volume in that order) and a "competitive discount" (a discretionary discount negotiated before the order is taken) are subtracted to arrive at the invoice price of $5.78 per yard. This is the price that is printed on the billing invoice sent to the retailer for that order. For companies that monitor price performance, this invoice price is the most commonly used measure.

OFF-INVOICE DISCOUNTS

But in almost all B2B businesses and most consumer businesses, the pricing story does not stop at invoice price. There are usually a number of pricing

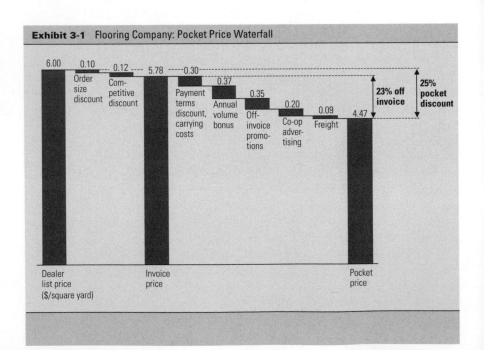

Exhibit 3-1 Flooring Company: Pocket Price Waterfall

components that occur after invoice price that substantially affect revenues resulting from a customer transaction (see box).

When you subtract these transaction-specific, off-invoice items from the invoice price, what is left is called the *pocket price*—the revenues that are actually left in a company's pocket from a transaction to cover costs and contribute to profit. Pocket price—not invoice price or list price—is the right measure of the pricing attractiveness of a transaction.

TYPICAL OFF-INVOICE ITEMS

The list of off-invoice items that reduce the pocket price realized by a supplier can be long. Some of the common elements include the following:

- Annual volume bonus: an end-of-year bonus paid to customers if preset purchase volume targets are met.
- Cash discount: a deduction from the invoice price if payment is made quickly—for instance, within 15 days.
- Consignment costs: the cost of funds when a supplier provides consigned inventory to a retailer or wholesaler.
- Cooperative advertising: an allowance usually paid as a percentage of sales to support local advertising of a manufacturer's brand by a retailer or wholesaler.
- End-user rebate: a rebate paid to a retailer for selling a product to a specific customer, often a large or national customer, at a discount.
- Freight: the supplier's costs of transporting goods to a customer.
- Market-development funds: a discount to promote sales to a specific market segment.
- Off-invoice promotions: a marketing incentive that would, for example, give retailers an additional rebate for each unit sold during a specific promotional time period.
- Online order discount: a discount offered to customers ordering over the Internet or an intranet.
- Performance penalties: a discount that the seller agrees to give buyers if the seller misses performance targets, such as quality levels or delivery times.
- Receivables carrying cost: the cost of funds from the moment an invoice is sent until payment is received.
- Slotting allowance: an allowance paid to retailers to secure a set amount of shelf space and product positioning.
- Stocking allowance: a discount paid to wholesalers or retailers to make large purchases into inventory, often just before a seasonal increase in demand.

Exhibit 3-1 shows the series of off-invoice discounts and allowances that dropped the invoice price down to the pocket price for the flooring manufacturer. The company gave dealers a payment terms discount of 2 percent of invoice price if they paid an invoice within 30 days, and also incurred carrying costs on receivables as it awaited payment. It offered an annual volume bonus, paid at the end of the year, of up to 8 percent of a dealer's total invoice purchases. Retailers received promotional funding to support in-store promotions, as well as cooperative advertising allowances of up to 4 percent of invoice price if they featured the flooring manufacturer's products in local newspaper and broadcast advertising. And the company paid freight and delivery costs on all orders exceeding a preset dollar value. Taken individually, none of these off-invoice discounts significantly affected transaction economics. Together, however, they amounted to a 23 percent additional drop in revenues from invoice price down to pocket price. As Exhibit 3-1 shows, this product, which was listed at $6.00 per yard, ends up generating an *average* pocket price of only $4.47 per yard, less than 75 percent of the starting list price. This 25 percent reduction from the dealer list price to the pocket price is called the *pocket discount*.

Pocket price can be a difficult number for even competent and well-intended managers to get a handle on. Accounting systems often fail to collect many of the off-invoice discounts on a customer or transaction basis. For example, payment terms discounts get buried in interest expense accounts, cooperative advertising is often included in companywide promotional and advertising line items, and customer-specific freight gets lumped in with all other business transportation expense. Since these items are often collected and accounted for on a companywide basis, it is difficult for managers to think about them—let alone manage them—on a customer-by-customer or transaction-by-transaction basis. (See Chapter 10 for a discussion of recent technological advances that have made tracking transaction pricing easier.)

THE POCKET PRICE WATERFALL VIEW

The overall picture in Exhibit 3-1, which shows revenues cascading down from list price to invoice price to pocket price, is called the *pocket price waterfall*. Each element of the pocket price waterfall, both on and off the invoice, represents a revenue leak. The 23 percent drop from invoice price down to pocket price for the flooring company may seem large, but it is not at all uncommon. In recent McKinsey client situations, the average decline from invoice price down to pocket price was 24 percent for a breakfast cereal company, 38 percent for a data communication service company, 47 percent for a furniture manufacturer, and 72 percent for an electrical controls supplier. Of course, the structure and components of the pocket price waterfall vary across companies and industries. (Appendix 1 shows sample pocket price waterfalls from a variety of businesses.)

Pricing becomes a lot more interesting for companies that take on this pocket price waterfall view of pricing. All of a sudden, pricing is more than just setting list prices and standard discounts. Pricing degrees of freedom expand to managing each and every component of the pocket price waterfall. Recall our earlier discussion of the impact of a 1 percent improvement in price. With the pocket price waterfall view, companies have a lot more places to look for that precious 1 percent. If you can find a 1 percent improvement in any of the items in the pocket price waterfall, either on or off the invoice, it will have that same dramatic effect on bottom-line profitability. Companies that do not actively manage the entire pocket price waterfall, with its multiple and often highly variable revenue leaks, miss all kinds of opportunities to enhance price performance.

THE POCKET PRICE BAND

The elements of the pocket price waterfall are not the same for all customers. Different starting point list prices are used for different customer sets. Order size and total annual purchase volume affect discount and rebate levels. How and when customers pay their invoices affects both cash discounts and receivables carrying cost. The result is that at any given point in time, no item generates the same pocket price for all customers. Rather, items sell over a range—often a very wide range—of pocket prices. The distribution of sales volume of a product over the range of pocket prices that a company realizes is called the *pocket price band* for that product.

Exhibit 3-2 shows the flooring company's pocket price band for the single product represented in the previous pocket price waterfall. The horizontal axis is pocket price in dollars per square yard. The height of the bars represents the percentage of volume that is sold within each pocket price range. The graph shows that some transactions for this product are generating a pocket price as high as $5.80, while others are as low as $3.80. The largest chunk of volume (15 percent) is sold in the $4.41 to $4.60 range, which is near the average of $4.47. At one extreme, 2.7 percent of the volume has a pocket price of $5.80; at the other, 3.1 percent of the volume has a pocket price of $3.80 per square yard.

Note that the difference between the lowest priced transactions and the highest is 53 percent. Although the width of this pocket price band may appear quite large, much wider price bands are commonplace. We have seen pocket price bands with a range of 65 percent for an electrical controls manufacturer, 80 percent for a medical equipment supplier, 170 percent for a specialty metals company, and 500 percent for a fastener supplier.

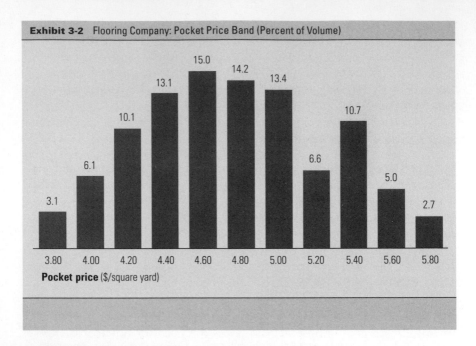

Exhibit 3-2   Flooring Company: Pocket Price Band (Percent of Volume)

Pocket price ($/square yard)

(Values shown on bars: 3.1, 6.1, 10.1, 13.1, 15.0, 14.2, 13.4, 6.6, 10.7, 5.0, 2.7)

(X-axis: 3.80, 4.00, 4.20, 4.40, 4.60, 4.80, 5.00, 5.20, 5.40, 5.60, 5.80)

UNDERSTANDING THE POCKET PRICE BAND'S WIDTH

So there are wide pocket price bands in most businesses and industries. Price bands happen. They are a fact of business life. Most managers either do not know that they exist or, if they do know, they just let them happen. Companies that excel at pricing understand their pocket price band and make actively managing it one of the core disciplines in marketing and sales.

Understanding the variations in pocket price across customers and transactions is critical to capturing pricing opportunity at the transaction level. If a manager can identify a wide pocket price band and comprehend the underlying causes of the band's width, then that band can be managed to the company's benefit. Recall the huge operating profit payoff from a 1 percent increase in average price. When, as in the case of the linoleum flooring manufacturer, pocket price varies over a 53 percent range, it is not hard to imagine how changing the distribution along the price band slightly through more deliberate management might yield percentage points of price improvement and the rich operating profit awards that accompany such improvement.

The width and shape of a pocket price band often tell a fruitful story. When managers see their pocket price band for the first time, they are invariably surprised along several dimensions. They are surprised by the width of the pocket price band, often realizing for the first time the combined effect of all on- and off-invoice discounts on transaction economics. They are further surprised by the identity of customers at the extremes of the pocket price band. Customers perceived by managers as very profitable (based on high invoice price) can end up at the low end of the band, driven there by excessive off-invoice discounting that is not always transparent to managers. And some customers perceived as unprofitable end up on the high end of the pocket price band because of relatively light discounting and revenue leaks off the invoice.

WIDE BANDS SUGGEST OPPORTUNITY

Managers are often dismayed by the width of their price bands and perceive wide price bands as absolute negatives. Nothing could be further from the truth. Wide price bands almost always indicate significant pricing opportunity that can be captured. Wide pocket price bands mean that there is potentially manageable heterogeneity in markets. They indicate differences in customers: how they value a product, how they order, how sophisticated they are, how costly they are to serve. They indicate differences in competitive situations: segments or regions where there are many versus few competitors, situations where a single competitor's strength varies widely. And they may indicate variability within the supplier itself: markets where it is stronger or weaker, segments where a supplier's products and services are a better fit with customers' needs, sales representatives whose price negotiating skills vary widely.

So wide pocket price bands should not be seen as negative, nor should they be perceived as needing to be aggressively narrowed. They should be seen as a positive sign of rich variability and texture in the markets served—variability and texture that can ultimately be managed to your advantage. And when price bands are very wide, small changes in the shape of the bands—for instance, a few more transactions at the high end of the band or a modest improvement in pricing for a few transactions at the low end—can readily move the average price for the entire band up by multiple percentage points. When price bands are narrow (indicating less texture and grain in a market being served), such changes tend to be more difficult and have less impact on average pocket price.

Furthermore, the shape of the pocket price band provides the astute manager with a graphic profile of the business, depicting, among other things, what percentage of volume is being sold at deep discounts, what groups of customers are inherently willing to pay higher prices to you, and how appropriately field discounting authority is being exercised.

So what do you do if you discover that you have a wide price band? As the case that follows will show, the key to finding opportunity in your price bands is to gain a detailed understanding of why your pocket price bands are so wide. That understanding will unlock the pricing and profit opportunity inherent in wide price bands.

THE SOUNDCO RADIO COMPANY CASE

The Soundco Radio Company makes aftermarket automobile radios and CD players. A car owner would purchase a Soundco radio either to replace an existing malfunctioning radio or to upgrade to higher performance. The following case shows how Soundco used the pocket price waterfall and pocket price band to identify profit leaks and regain control of its pricing system. It illustrates one way in which the basic price band and waterfall concepts can be applied and, if a company does not manage its entire pocket price waterfall and the pricing policies around the waterfall, how experienced customers can use your pocket price waterfall to their own advantage.

As background, Soundco sells its radios directly to regional and national electronics retailers, several automotive stereo catalog retailers, and electronics wholesalers who then resell Soundco radios to smaller auto stereo retailers and installers. Exhibit 3-3 shows Soundco's economics and profit structure. With return on sales (ROS) of 6.8 percent, Soundco's profitability is very sensitive to even small improvements in price. A 1 percent price increase with no volume loss would increase operating profit by 15 percent. As Exhibit 3-3 shows, that is almost three times the impact of a 1 percent increase in volume (assuming no decline in average price).

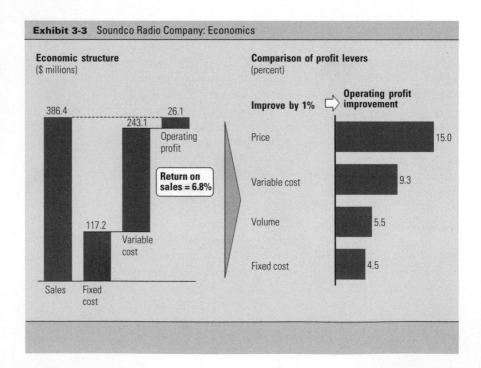

Exhibit 3-3   Soundco Radio Company: Economics

The automotive replacement radio industry was in a state of overcapacity driven by the installation of increasingly high-quality original-equipment radios in many automotive brands. Gradual commoditization had made it more and more difficult for Soundco to distinguish its products from competitors. So Soundco senior management was skeptical that there was much, if any, potential for price improvement. However, Soundco managers had entirely overlooked lucrative pricing opportunities at the transaction level.

SOUNDCO'S POCKET PRICE WATERFALL

Exhibit 3-4 shows the average pocket price waterfall for one of Soundco's most common radio models, the CDR-2000. From a dealer base price of $109, Soundco deducted up to four specific discounts to arrive at invoice price. There was a standard dealer/distributor discount that varied by account channel category and averaged $15.45 per radio. Soundco ran frequent on-invoice promotions to stimulate sales of particular products which, in the case of the CDR-2000, averaged 90 cents per unit sold. Soundco also paid a discount of up to 4 percent off base price, based on

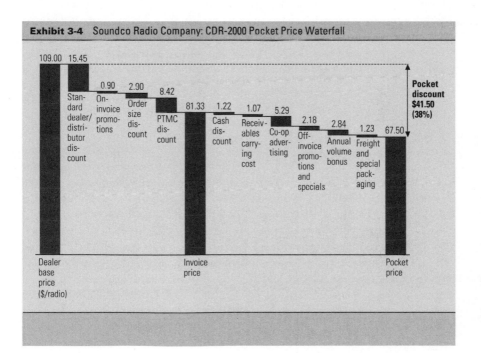

Exhibit 3-4 Soundco Radio Company: CDR-2000 Pocket Price Waterfall

the total dollar value of an order. On average, it was $2.90 per radio. Additionally, many transactions also included an on-invoice price-to-meet-competition (PTMC) discount, negotiated on a customer-by-customer basis, to meet competitor prices offered to accounts. With these on-invoice discounts, the average invoice price for the CDR-2000 model was $81.33. The minimal consideration Soundco paid to transaction pricing focused almost entirely on that invoice price.

With that invoice price focus, Soundco management overlooked a major part of the total pricing picture: all the discounting and revenue leaks occurring off of invoice price. Soundco paid a cash discount of 2 percent for payment of invoices within specified time periods. In addition, Soundco also granted extended terms (payments not required until 75 or even 90 days after receipt of an invoice) to a handful of distributors and high-volume retail accounts. The extra cost of carrying these extended receivables averaged $1.07 per radio. Miscellaneous off-invoice promotions and specials (cash rebates to end customers, awards for retailer sales personnel) cost an average of $2.18 per unit sold. Cooperative advertising, where Soundco provided partial funding for local and regional advertising of Soundco products, cost an average of $5.29. An annual volume bonus, based on the total volume purchased from Soundco over the course of a year, represented $2.84 in additional off-invoice discounting per radio. Finally, freight and special packaging expenses paid by Soundco for shipping the radios to retailers and distributors cost an average of $1.23.

When this long list of off-invoice discounts, allowances, and costs is subtracted from invoice price, the average pocket price is only $67.50, a full 17 percent less than invoice price. The total revenue drop from dealer base price down to pocket price, the pocket discount, was on average 38 percent.

SOUNDCO'S POCKET PRICE BAND

As one would expect, not all transactions for the CDR-2000 had the same pocket price. Accounts of different types qualified for different standard dealer and distributor discounts. Quantities ordered by accounts varied widely, which resulted in variations in order-size discounts. And the PTMC discounts were negotiated with each deal. Even more variability extended into the off-invoice items. Not all accounts paid invoices promptly, resulting in major differences in cash discounts and receivables carrying costs; and not all accounts utilized all of the cooperative advertising allowance for which they were qualified. Wholesalers and retailers took advantage of off-invoice promotions and specials at different levels, with some not participating at all. Account size (and resulting cost-to-serve efficiencies) drove the level of annual volume bonus, and freight and packaging paid by Soundco varied widely based on retailer location, order pattern, and special packaging needs such as information printed in multiple languages.

These differences in on- and off-invoice discount elements resulted in the very wide pocket price band shown in Exhibit 3-5. The average pocket price was $67.50, but units sold for a pocket price as low as $45 and as high as $95, resulting in a 111 percent difference between the lowest and highest pocket prices. A pocket price band like this should trigger immediate questions: What are the underlying drivers of the price band's shape and width? Does this pocket price variability make good management sense and align with Soundco's market strategy? Why are pocket prices so variable, and can that variability be positively managed?

Managers at Soundco were at first quite surprised at the width of the price band for their CDR-2000 model but, on reflection, concluded that it was all due to and justified by differences in account sizes. Soundco had a clearly stated market strategy of rewarding account volume with lower prices, rationalizing that cost-to-serve would decrease with higher account volume.

To test the assumption that variability in pocket price was explained

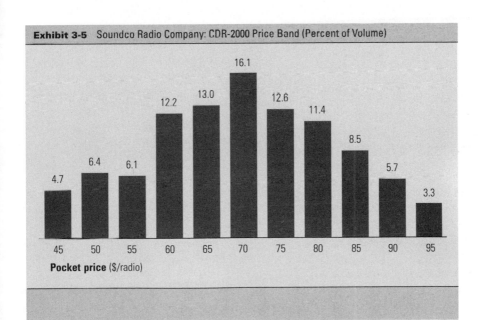

Exhibit 3-5 Soundco Radio Company: CDR-2000 Price Band (Percent of Volume)

Pocket price ($/radio)

by account size, the company plotted discounts against account size and created the analysis shown in Exhibit 3-6. Each numbered point on this chart represents a single Soundco retail or wholesale account. The horizontal axis shows annual dollar volume of sales through each account. The vertical axis shows pocket discount for CDR-2000 radios sold to each account. If account size were the primary driver of pocket price band width, then you would expect the account to align along the diagonal labeled "expected fit"—that is, the larger the account, the larger the pocket discount. But the scatter of accounts—a virtual shotgun blast—shows no correlation between account size and pocket discount level. A number of relatively small accounts, like accounts 96 and 83, were buying at very low pocket price levels. At the same time, several large accounts, like accounts 8 and 17, were buying at relatively high pocket price levels.

Perplexed by this apparent randomness, Soundco managers launched an immediate investigation to understand what really explained the scatter. It was thought that there might be extenuating circumstances to explain some of the smaller accounts' positioning above the "expected fit" line in

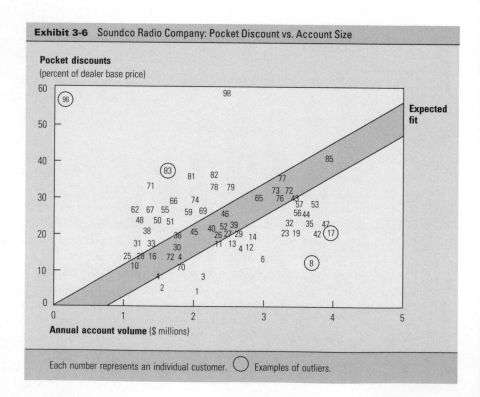

Exhibit 3-6 Soundco Radio Company: Pocket Discount vs. Account Size

Each number represents an individual customer. ◯ Examples of outliers.

Exhibit 3-6, such as a retailer's location in a depressed market or in a region where competitive intensity was extremely high or where Soundco's competitive position was particularly weak. In fact, such extenuating circumstances explained the position of only a few of the small accounts above the expected fit line.

It was discovered that most of the over-discounted smaller accounts had no legitimate reason to be paying such low pocket prices. Most turned out to be experienced and clever accounts. These customers had been dealing with Soundco for 20 years or more and knew just whom to call at Soundco headquarters to get that extra exception discount, that percentage point of extra co-op advertising, that extra 30 or 60 days to pay, the large-order size discount on small orders. They had close relationships with regional Soundco sales managers who regularly gave them preferred treatment on off-invoice promotions and specials. These favorite old accounts were granted extra discounts based on familiarity and relationships rather than on economic justification and performance. These experienced customers understood the Soundco pocket price waterfall better than Soundco and were working it against the company.

CAPTURING THE OPPORTUNITY AT SOUNDCO

Soundco senior management finally realized that its transaction pricing process was out of control, that decision making up and down the waterfall lacked discipline, and that no one was focusing on the sum total of those decisions as reflected in pocket price. The end result had been a transaction pricing reality that did not square with Soundco's intended strategy of rewarding account size with lower prices, and that reality was costing Soundco millions of dollars.

To begin correcting its transaction pricing shortfalls, Soundco mounted a three-part program. First, it took aggressive corrective actions to bring the over-discounted "old favorite" accounts back into line. Marketing and sales managers identified the problem accounts and explained the situation and its overall impact on Soundco profitability to the sales force. Then Soundco gave the sales force nine months to fix or drop those outliers. Fixing meant decreasing the excessive discounting across the waterfall so that outlier accounts' pocket prices were more in line with other accounts of similar size. A specific negotiation plan was devised for each outlier account, focusing on the waterfall elements that were driving pocket price down most. Sales reps who could not negotiate their outlier pocket prices up to an appropriate level (or drive account volume up to a level that aligned with existing discounting) were instructed to find other accounts in their territory to replace them.

Over the next nine months, the sales force was able to correct 90 percent of the outlier accounts. The sales force's newfound realization that every element of the waterfall represented a viable negotiating lever contributed much to this success. And in most cases, salespeople easily found more profitable replacement accounts for the 10 percent that could not be fixed.

Second, Soundco launched a program to stimulate sales volume in larger accounts that had higher-than-average pocket prices compared with accounts of similar size. Management singled out these attractive accounts for special treatment. Sales and marketing personnel researched them carefully and even interviewed some customers to better understand the nonprice benefits to which these accounts were most sensitive. Soundco ultimately increased volume in these accounts, not by lowering price, but by delivering the specific benefits that were most important to each: higher levels of service to some, shortened order lead times for others, more frequent sales calls for still others.

Third and finally, Soundco instituted a crash program to get the transaction pricing process under control. This program included, among other components, clear decision rules and guidelines for each discretionary item in the waterfall. For example, Soundco capped discretionary on-invoice discounts at 5 percent and granted them only after a structured evaluation of volume, margin, and market impact. Soundco's IT department set up new information systems to help guide and monitor transaction pricing decisions, and Soundco established pocket price as the universal measure of price performance in all of these systems. It began tracking and assigning, transaction by transaction, all the significant off-invoice waterfall elements that were previously collected and reported only on a companywide basis. Individual pocket price targets were established for each product line within each account to help prevent the recurrence of the shotgun-blast chart comparing pocket price and account size. Further, pocket price realization against those account-specific targets became a major component of incentive compensation for salespeople, sales managers, and even product managers.

From these three transaction pricing initiatives, Soundco reaped rich and sustained rewards. In the first year of implementation, average pocket price levels increased a full 3 percent, and, while unit sales volume remained flat, operating profits swelled 44 percent. Soundco realized additional pocket price gains in each of the two subsequent years as skill in transaction price management grew across the organization.

As is often the case, Soundco also received some unexpected strategic benefits from its newfound transaction pricing capability. Account-specific pocket price reporting revealed a small but growing distribution channel for radios where Soundco's pocket prices were consistently higher than average. Increasing volume and penetration in this emerging channel became a key strategic initiative for Soundco that generated further incremental earnings. The fresh and more granular business perspective that senior Soundco managers gained for their involvement in transaction pricing became the catalyst for an ongoing stream of similar strategic insights and opportunities.

POCKET MARGIN WATERFALL AND BAND

In the flooring company and Soundco Radio cases, companies were selling standard products and essentially standard services to all accounts. In such situations, pocket price is usually a representative and prescriptive measure of price performance. Generally the higher the pocket price, the higher the attractiveness of the transaction for a particular standard product sold to multiple customers.

But what about product and service offerings that are not standard—products that are tailored to specific customer applications, or standard products where the accompanying service (and the cost of that service) varies widely across customers? It could be argued that in these situations, pocket price may not tell the entire story of pricing and transaction attractiveness. In such situations, the pocket price concept may require an extension to what is called *pocket margin* to be useful. (Appendix 1 also presents a selection of pocket margin waterfalls.) The following case shows how this refinement to the pocket price waterfall works.

ALLEN GLASS COMPANY DIAGNOSIS

The Allen Glass Company makes tempered glass used in the cabs of heavy-duty trucks (both over-the-road and off-road applications) and in earth-movers and other construction and agricultural equipment. While all of its products are tempered glass, no two customers share exactly the same product. For example, the windshield designed for one truck will not fit another manufacturer's truck. Each product must be designed for each specific truck or equipment manufacturer. And products vary not only in size and shape but also in annual volume and customer service requirements. For instance, some higher volume truck manufacturers require windshields and side-glass to be shipped in special containers that are compatible with material handling equipment within the truck manufacturers' assembly plants. Pocket price would clearly not provide a complete and useful measure of transaction attractiveness for Allen.

Extending the pocket price waterfall to the *pocket margin waterfall* makes it relevant to the business situation at Allen. This extension still has pocket price at its foundation. Pocket margin is defined as the pocket price for a transaction minus direct product costs and any account-specific costs-to-serve. Exhibit 3-7 shows the average pocket margin waterfall for Allen.

The starting point is the base target price for each glass product. That target price is established when each individual glass application is specified by the truck manufacturer. It is calculated based on expected standard material and processing costs and expected annual unit volume, and is further fine-tuned based on the market segment of the application. For ease of comparability, we have indexed this base target price to 100 and shown all other waterfall elements as a percentage of that index. So, from that base target price, a negotiated on-invoice discount that averages 10 percent of base is subtracted to yield an average invoice price of 90. Off the invoice, cash discounts and receivables carrying costs average 3.5; a volume bonus averages 5; and standard freight is 4.5 on average. Allen is also required from time to time to pay emergency freight to manufacturers, which averages 2 percent of base price. The resultant pocket price is 75 percent of base.

Exhibit 3-7 Allen Glass Company: Pocket Margin Waterfall (Base Target Price Indexed to 100)

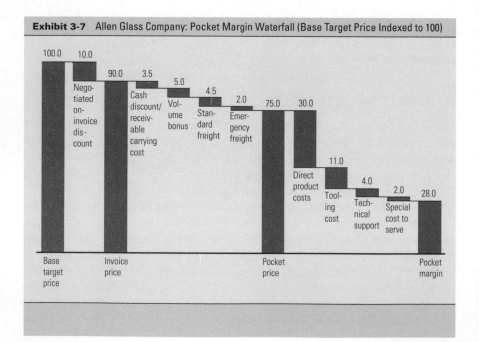

From pocket price, direct product costs of 30 are subtracted first. Allen often has to incur tooling costs for custom glass applications, which are on average 11 percent of base. Technical support varies widely by account and application, but comes in at an average of 4 percent. Miscellaneous special costs-to-serve, such as special packaging or special applications support, average another 2 percent. When these direct, account-specific, and special costs are subtracted from pocket price, the resultant pocket margin is 28 percent of base target price.

With pocket price as its revenue foundation and direct and special costs used on the expense side, pocket margin can be an effective indicator of transaction attractiveness in nonstandard product situations. However, Allen had traditionally focused the majority of its pricing energy on constructing the base target price for a customer product and then negotiating the very visible on-invoice discount with the customer. When calculating customer profitability, Allen paid little attention to off-invoice price items or to costs beyond direct product costs, which were aggregated in general accounts. The result was an incomplete picture of the transaction price and transaction margin.

As is most often the case for pocket price, the elements of pocket margin tend to vary widely across customers and transactions as well. So extending the pocket price band to a *pocket margin band* is a logical next step. Exhibit 3-8 shows Allen's pocket margin band. The horizontal axis is pocket margin as a percent of base target price. The height of the bars corresponds to the percentage of sales dollars at each pocket margin level. According to this graph, Allen had transactions with pocket margin as high as 55 percent and as low as a loss equal to 15 percent of target base price—altogether, a 70 percentage-point pocket margin range. Furthermore, when Allen's fixed costs were applied to its sales volume, a pocket margin of 12 percent was required for operating profit breakeven. The band shows that a major portion of Allen's book of business, more than a quarter of its sales, was below breakeven.

CAPTURING THE OPPORTUNITY AT ALLEN

The same basic routine to uncover opportunity across a pocket price band was executed by Allen to find and capture opportunity across its pocket margin band. Allen sales and marketing managers put transactions at the extremes of the pocket margin band under the microscope to begin to understand the sources of the exceedingly wide variations in pocket margin. Incidentally, given that they tried to apply a consistent and thoughtful discipline when setting base target price and negotiating the on-invoice discount, Allen managers were astonished at just how wide the resultant pocket margin band turned out to be. Remarkably

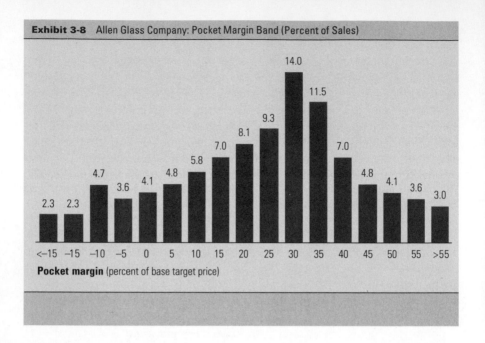

Exhibit 3-8   Allen Glass Company: Pocket Margin Band (Percent of Sales)

Pocket margin (percent of base target price)

clear but previously unperceived patterns of business attractiveness were uncovered as Allen took the hard look at its pocket margin band. Certain customer and product combinations tended always to cluster at the high end of the pocket margin band—for example, specific combinations like medium volume, flat or single-bend door glass sold to certain customers. Different customer and product combinations tended to cluster at the low end, such as high volume, multi-bend windshields sold to another set of manufacturers. It quickly became clear which types of glass applications were inherently more profitable for Allen and which were not.

For the applications that were by pattern unprofitable, Allen found that the transactions consistently underperformed on three elements of the pocket margin waterfall: excessive receivables carrying cost, high freight cost driven by erratic ordering behavior, and excessive per unit tooling costs driven by design complexity and overly optimistic customer estimates of annual purchase volume.

Unambiguous sales and marketing initiatives flowed directly from these very granular insights on pocket margin differences. First, Allen identified and aggressively pursued every glass application in its "sweet spot," those that were inherently more pocket margin rich for Allen.

This focus caused their win rate for these jobs to increase gradually over time. Second, Allen applied extra care and diligence when bidding on glass applications of the type that populated the low end of their pocket margin band. They negotiated such deals much more aggressively and put in place explicit customer penalties for poor receivables performance, erratic order quantities, and unit sales significantly below the annual volume targets specified in the purchase contract. This aggressive stance caused Allen to lose some business that would have generated pocket margin losses anyway, and to win only when conditions were in place to move such business to pocket margin profitability. These very specific customer and market initiatives aimed at the extremes of its pocket margin bands resulted in a 4 percent increase in Allen's average pocket margin and a 60 percent increase in operating profit within one year.

* * *

The transaction level is the most detailed and precise of the three levels of price management. Here the primary issue is how to arrive at the best price for each and every customer transaction. The pocket price waterfall was introduced as a core tool to help understand and manage the full range of pricing elements, both on and off the invoice, that affect pocket price—the amount that you actually put in your pocket. The pocket price band demonstrates the often surprisingly wide degree of variability that occurs in pocket price, even when exactly the same product is offered to different customers.

When products provided are not standard across customers, the pocket price waterfall can be refined and extended to create the pocket margin waterfall, which recognizes important product and service differences across transactions. In such situations, the pocket margin band then becomes the appropriate analytic tool for looking at pocket margin variations across customers and transactions.

Wide pocket price bands and pocket margin bands occur in almost every business. Most companies just let these bands happen. As we have shown, businesses that excel at the transaction level actively and intentionally manage the shape of their pocket price and pocket margin bands. They know the shape and composition of their bands; they know where individual customers and transactions reside on their bands and why; and they take deliberate steps to improve the pocket price and pocket margin of customers who are unjustifiably low on their bands, and to gain volume and share from customers at the high end. They modify or discontinue waterfall elements that are not effectively influencing positive behavior by their customers. They set clear targets (often account by account) for pocket price or pocket margin realization, and they monitor performance against those targets. Furthermore, they build incentives that reward sales and marketing personnel for improvements in pocket price and pocket margin by customer.

Excelling at the transaction level is an absolute prerequisite for any business that aspires to create and sustain the price advantage. Excellence at the other levels of price management is fruitless unless it is ultimately delivered in the form of correct and well-managed transaction prices.

CHAPTER **4**

Product/Market Strategy

The next level of price management, the product/market strategy level, is all about getting your price position right relative to competitors. It is about arriving at prices that position your products correctly against competitors' products on a price/benefit basis for every customer segment you serve. While transaction pricing tends to be tailored to individual customers and transactions, pricing at the product/market strategy level is more general. It focuses on price levels that are usually quite visible to customers and competitors alike and that publicly communicate what you believe your product is worth relative to those of competitors. Decisions here center on setting list prices, base prices, or manufacturer's suggested retail prices (MSRPs) that often serve as the starting point for negotiations at the transaction level.

The goal at this level is to position each product, by customer segment, at exactly the right spot to capture the greatest reward for the benefits delivered without undermining good overall industry pricing conduct. Pricing excellence at the product/market strategy level assures that the investment and work that flow into developing superior products and delivering them effectively to markets generate a just return.

Pricing at the product/market strategy level entails managing the crucial tradeoff between benefits and price. Marketers implicitly address this when they talk about positioning their product vis-à-vis competitors' offerings and setting the right price premium or discount compared to competitors' prices. To approach this level systematically, pricers should consider four aspects of product/market pricing.

First, there is the value map for a market segment, which shows a product's position against competitors' offerings in that segment. In essence, this is a snapshot showing how customers view the tradeoffs between the perceived price and perceived benefits of available products. Next, competitors may raise or lower prices, add or subtract benefits, or some combination, which can change the value map. Markets constantly change, and a move by one competitor can quickly affect how others are perceived and will often trigger competitive reactions. The third aspect is understanding how customers populate the value map. Markets are seldom homogeneous, and different clusters of customers often seek different combinations of benefits and price. And finally, a company must understand the variability in customer price and benefit perceptions. An additional technique, the value profile, shows where customer perceptions do not align with a company's desired positioning. Excelling at the product/market level requires a thorough comprehension of these four topics, which allows a company to diagnose the situation and prescribe key steps toward its most desirable price position in a market.

MAPPING VALUE

Value may be one of the most overused and misapplied terms in marketing and pricing today. *Value pricing* is too often misused as a synonym for low price or bundled pricing.

The real essence of "value" revolves around the tradeoff between the benefits a customer receives from a product and the price paid for it—or, more accurately, the *perceived* benefits received and the *perceived* price paid. It can be expressed with a simple equation: Value equals perceived benefits minus perceived price. Using this equation, it is easy to see that increasing perceived benefits, decreasing perceived price, or doing both will lead to higher value and, as a result, a greater likelihood that customers will buy that product.

That benefits are *perceived* by customers makes the benefits side of value equations particularly difficult for businesses to manage well. Many benefits are by nature subjective and defy measurement. But even when there are clear metrics for benefits, there can be a gap between perception and reality. For years, IT professionals said that a manager was never fired for buying IBM products, even if they cost more. Although many competitors could meet or beat IBM performance on such measurable criteria as speed, durability, and interoperability in specific applications, the perception that the sum of all benefits provided by IBM was greater was quite strong and has lasted for many years.

The perception element of price can be just as tricky to understand and manage. At first blush, a price is a number that should be comprehended easily, but the devil is in the details. In a simple example, grocery shoppers often expect, and therefore assume, that a larger carton of orange juice is cheaper per ounce than a smaller package. Reality can be quite different.

Larger sizes could be more expensive per ounce if, for example, retailers are offering smaller sizes with promotional discounts.

In B2B markets, transactions can be much more complicated; and even though professional buyers are often involved, there can still be important perceptual aspects to price. How price is structured, communicated, and eventually collected can easily shift a customer's perception of price level. (We will look at these topics in detail when we discuss pricing architecture in Chapter 12.)

DRAWING A VALUE MAP

Once a company understands the true meaning of value, a straightforward tool called the value map can provide insight into how to manage the price/benefit tradeoffs that comprise value in real markets. Exhibit 4-1 shows an example of a value map. Each dot in this map represents the product offering of a different company. In this basic example, perceived prices are tracked on the vertical axis and perceived benefits—which, say for a computer system, could be a combination of speed, memory, reliability, and many other factors—form the horizontal axis. Manufacturers with

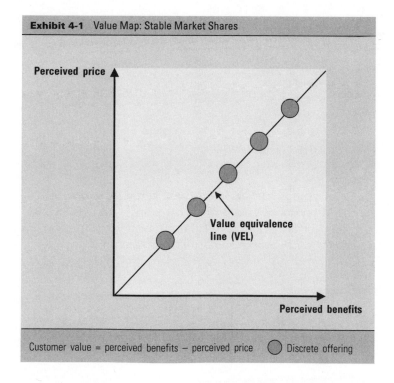

Exhibit 4-1   Value Map: Stable Market Shares

Perceived price

Value equivalence line (VEL)

Perceived benefits

Customer value = perceived benefits – perceived price   ◯ Discrete offering higher-priced, higher-benefit systems are in the upper right, and those with lower-priced, lower-benefit systems are in the lower left.

If a market is stable (market share is not shifting among competitors), and if perceived prices and perceived benefits have been measured accurately, then the competitors will align along a diagonal called the *value equivalence line* (VEL), as shown in Exhibit 4-1. At any desired price or benefit level, there is a clear and logical choice of which computer to buy. In such markets, customers clearly get what they pay for. If customers want more benefits, they will have to pay more; if they want lower prices, they will have to be ready to forfeit some benefits. This clarity of choice virtually defines a stable market. But while the shares are stable (barring some exogenous shift in customer demand), they are not necessarily equal. There could easily be more customers who want a high-priced, high-benefit computer than who want a low-priced, low-benefit one.

If shares are changing across competitors in a market, then a properly constructed value map will look more like Exhibit 4-2, with some companies positioned off the VEL. Company B is below the VEL in a *value-*

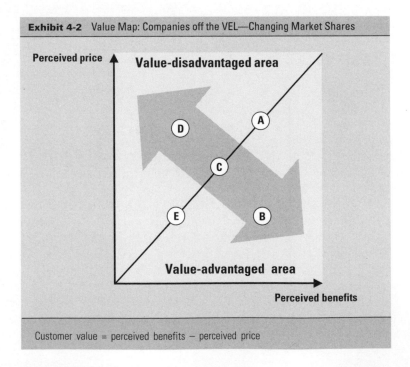

Exhibit 4-2 Value Map: Companies off the VEL—Changing Market Shares

Perceived price

Value-disadvantaged area

D

A

C

E

B

Value-advantaged area

Perceived benefits

Customer value = perceived benefits − perceived price

advantaged position and is gaining share. Looking at the value map, we see that if a customer wants a low-priced system, the choice is clear between companies E and B, since Company B offers a better computer at the same price. At the same time, a customer who wants a high-benefit computer also has a clear choice between companies A and B, since both offer similar benefits, but B is priced much lower.

In contrast, Company D is above the VEL in a *value-disadvantaged position*. In this position, Company E offers equal benefits for a lower price, and Company A offers more benefits for the same price. Not surprisingly, if this value map is accurate, Company D should be losing market share.

BENEFIT PERCEPTIONS

Understanding the basic concepts of value maps, we can turn our attention to the practical application of this tool. There are two primary research methods used to develop value maps. The first is direct questioning, such as deep-structure interviews and focus groups. These open-ended, dialogue-based methods are the best way to identify the full list of buying attributes and to examine more deeply why specific answers were given. The second method is tradeoff-based research, such as conjoint and discrete-choice analysis. These methods, which require that the company already knows the relevant buying attributes, probe the customer's decision-making process by assessing how the full suite of these attributes are considered jointly. (A case study illustrating conjoint analysis is given in Chapter 14.)

Building on our basic computer system example, the experience of Alpha Computers shows how internal misperception can skew value analysis and how an accurate value map can suggest profit-building actions. Alpha supplied advanced computer networking systems and prided itself on its engineering skills and its ability to deliver high technological performance at a reasonable cost. Unfortunately, much to its surprise, Alpha had begun losing market share.

To help diagnose the problem, Alpha built the value map shown in Exhibit 4-3, based on their *internal* understanding of how customers perceived benefits and price in its market. Perceived price was believed to be straightforward since industry prices were scrutinized carefully by outside analysts, published routinely, and highly transparent. Also, the mix of volume discounts, rebates, and payment terms offered by computer makers was on average fairly standard. Alpha was also comfortable with its internal understanding of the benefit attributes that drove customer systems choice: It believed customers chose networking systems based primarily on processor speed and system reliability.

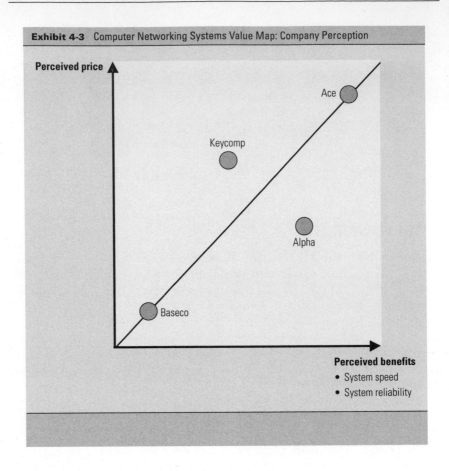

Exhibit 4-3   Computer Networking Systems Value Map: Company Perception

Using its internal views on benefits and price, Alpha plotted itself and its key rivals—Ace Computer, Keycomp, and Baseco—on the value map. Alpha saw itself in a value-advantaged position, meaning it should have been picking up rather than losing market share. Ace was the obvious premium competitor, ranking highest in price as well as in system speed and reliability. But compared to Keycomp, Alpha's computers were not only cheaper but also faster and more reliable. Company managers were stumped to find an explanation for their server's disappointing market performance. Why were they losing share instead of gaining share as their value map would seem to predict they should?

THREE TYPES OF BENEFITS

The benefits that suppliers provide to their customers fall into three categories: functional, process, and relationship.

■ *Functional benefits* relate to the physical nature or performance of the product. These can be, for example, processor speed for a computer, flow rate for a pump, purity of a chemical or metal alloy, or the acceleration of a sports car. Since this category of benefits is the easiest to measure and compare against competitors, it is often the first—and too often the only—category considered.

■ *Process benefits* are those that make transactions between buyers and sellers easier, quicker, more efficient, or even more pleasant. Examples of these include ease of access to product information; automated restocking or re-ordering systems; and online or electronic data interchange (EDI) payment options. In some markets, process benefits can provide more of the net benefits delivered than functional benefits, especially when they are the benefits that differentiate suppliers.

■ *Relationship benefits* are those that accrue to the customer from entering into a mutually beneficial relationship with the seller. They include both softer relationship benefits like a customer's emotional connection to a brand or personalized service, as well as more tangible relationship benefits like differentiated loyalty rewards or exchanges of information that provides benefits to both customer and supplier. In many markets, these relationship benefits are becoming increasingly powerful drivers of actual buying behavior.

Alpha faced a common problem. It understood its products well, but not its customers. Although managers thought technical superiority was important, they never took the time to research carefully what attributes customers considered when choosing network servers. To determine exactly what perceived benefits drove customer choice, Alpha's marketing department stepped back from its assumptions and commissioned a market study. Sixty buyers in Alpha's targeted customer segment were interviewed about their criteria for selecting a network server supplier.

The first steps were to understand clearly which benefits were important to the market and to compare Alpha's relative performance in those areas against the competition. Using conjoint analysis, Alpha identified the key buying factors that were important to the marketplace. The results, shown in Exhibit 4-4, revealed that system speed was indeed very important. The next factors, in order of importance, were professional services (the technical skills of the sales and professional staff), system interoperability (the ability to communicate with other systems), and system reliability.

Further insights arose when Alpha compared its performance against the competition based on these key factors. While system speed was important, as Exhibit 4-5 shows, all of the main players were comparable on this attribute. Alpha's slight system speed advantage over Keycomp was not a critical factor in driving customer decisions because both met minimum requirements. However, there was a distinct gap in other benefits, such the perceived quality of professional services and system reliability. In these areas, which were the key differentiating factors of customer choice, Keycomp performed much better than Alpha.

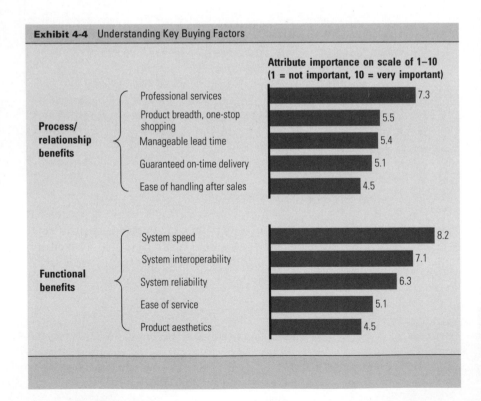

Exhibit 4-4 Understanding Key Buying Factors

Attribute importance on scale of 1–10
(1 = not important, 10 = very important)

Process/relationship benefits
- Professional services — 7.3
- Product breadth, one-stop shopping — 5.5
- Manageable lead time — 5.4
- Guaranteed on-time delivery — 5.1
- Ease of handling after sales — 4.5

Functional benefits
- System speed — 8.2
- System interoperability — 7.1
- System reliability — 6.3
- Ease of service — 5.1
- Product aesthetics — 4.5

Exhibit 4-5 Understanding Relative Performance

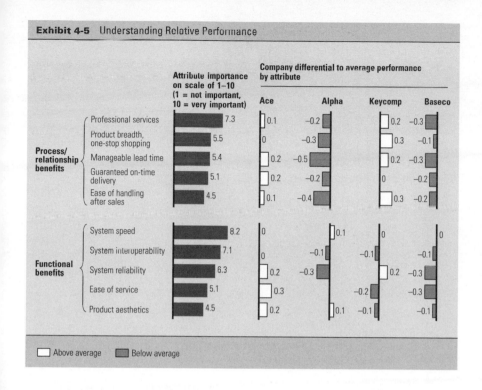

Exhibit 4-6 shows a more accurate value map based on *customer* perception of benefit attributes and the performance of suppliers against those attributes. Since Keycomp scored well on attributes most important to customers, it sits in a value-advantaged position despite its higher price, which explains why that company was gaining market share. Alpha has shifted into a value-disadvantaged position since it performed relatively poorly on the attributes most closely linked to buying decisions. The reasons for Alpha's poor market performance were now clearer.

Armed with these fresh insights, Alpha began a crash program to tackle its problems. Many of its customers faced compatibility problems linked to their enterprise resource-planning (ERP)[1] systems, as well as configuration and energy usage problems. These problems were corrected with a minor rewrite of the software and the introduction of a

---

[1]Enterprise resource-planning systems are massive computer applications that allow a business to manage all of its operations—financial reporting, manufacturing requirements planning, human resources, and order fulfillment—on the basis of a single, integrated set of corporate data.

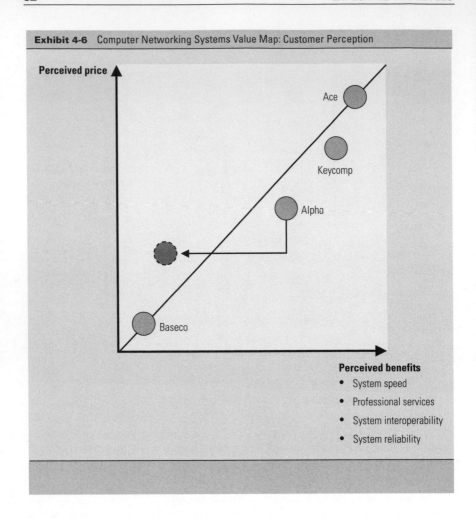

Exhibit 4-6 Computer Networking Systems Value Map: Customer Perception

standardized configuration tool. Reliability problems from an earlier generation continued to taint the market's perception of Alpha's new system, so the company mounted an aggressive marketing campaign to demonstrate the reliability of the latest model. And finally, the sales and professional staff were given new training and improved configuration tools that simplified the sales process and better matched customer integration requirements.

Within six months, Alpha shifted its position on the value map dramatically, as shown in Exhibit 4-7. Customer perception of the benefits of Alpha's new systems improved so much that it was able to increase its price by 8 percent and regain 5 percent of market share. The price and

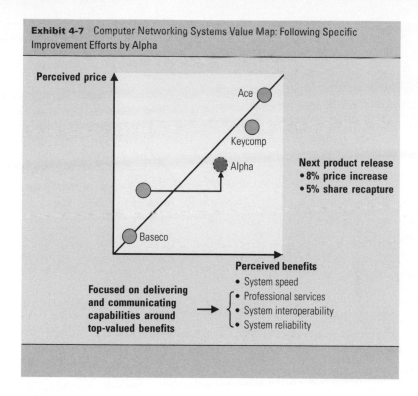

Exhibit 4-7 Computer Networking Systems Value Map: Following Specific Improvement Efforts by Alpha

volume increase more than doubled the company's operating profits in this product line.

What does the Alpha Computer case show us about managing value? First, the key to success is often gaining a clear understanding of the real attributes driving customer choice and their relative importance. Trusting internal perceptions of which attributes drive customer choice, rather than information from the customers themselves, can be a fatal mistake. Also, in many situations, softer, nontechnical attributes like perceived reliability, support quality, and the ease of doing business can match or outrank measurable technical features in the minds of customers, especially when several suppliers can meet most customers' minimal technical requirements.

Channel partners create an added complexity to understanding a company's value position. These intermediaries run the gamut from retailers and distributors, who simply include a company's products on their shelves or in their catalogues, to value-added resellers (VARs), who perform a wide range of services linked to the product, such as design, modifications, installation, and maintenance. Whatever the relationship, the channel partner becomes an integral component in the delivery of benefits and value to the customer and must therefore be carefully managed.

When dealing with channel partners, a company must face an unavoidable conflict: Its partners' economics often are based on getting the best price from their suppliers, suggesting that it would be smart to play down a product's actual benefits when dealing with their suppliers. But a partner must also actively promote the product to its own customers—in other words, emphasize these same benefits. These conflicts and dilemmas make it more difficult for the supplier to get an accurate reading of end-user demand, as well as a true measurement of the benefits being delivered to and through its channel partners. Although the water here is murkier, a company must endeavor to use the same standards for understanding the benefits delivered to and through its channel partners as it does in other situations.

PRICE PERCEPTIONS

Understanding customers' price perceptions can be as difficult as pinpointing benefits perceptions. In B2B and consumer environments alike, price can be a very sensitive subject to research directly with customers. As discussed in Chapter 3, a seller may not realize what its real pocket price is. In the same way, customers faced with multiple levels of discounting and diverse price structures across competitors may find price comparisons inherently difficult. For example, a buyer may think one supplier is higher priced than another based on invoice price, while in reality that supplier might be the less expensive option when off-invoice discounts are fully considered. In other examples, a brand's low-price reputation may cause consumers to perceive its price as lower than it actually is or, conversely, a brand's reputation for high quality may trigger higher price perceptions even as it tries to enter a more cost-conscious market segment.

The key message here is that price levels, just like benefit levels, are perceived, and the perception of price can be influenced in any number of ways, including how you communicate price, how you structure price, and how you time payments. (A more complete discussion of this topic is included in Chapter 12.)

Price perception provides a platform for enhancing the value map framework. The value equivalence *line* that we have drawn on previous value maps might imply that price perception by customers is precise and that any price movement—no matter how small—might change a supplier's value position and affect customer choice.

In fact, there is usually a range of prices—a *zone of indifference*—over which a customer will buy a given product. Depending on a host of factors, the zone of indifference can be very narrow (for instance, less than plus or minus 1 percent) or very wide (plus or minus 5 percent or more). It can vary by customer segment and even by individual supplier. When price elasticity research is conducted, it must be explicitly designed so that the magnitude of the existing zone of indifference can be determined. Increasing list prices or base prices within this zone of indifference can be one of the most risk-free ways of quickly improving price and boosting profits.

TAKING ACCOUNT OF PRICE ELASTICITY

In any analysis of market pricing, especially when changes are being considered, price elasticity becomes relevant. While the concept is straightforward (elasticity shows how volume would change when prices are moved), in practice elasticity is complex and can mean different things in different applications. Rather than offering a primer on how elasticity is calculated,[2] we will outline specific areas where understanding elasticity can help answer common pricing questions.

■ *Calculating the zone of indifference.* Elasticity is a key ingredient for determining the width of this zone. Whether affected by visibility, increased hassles, or real switching costs, there is a range of pricing moves that will not impact purchasing behavior at all.

■ *"Big number" syndrome.* Price elasticity is rarely linear, and as the price gap to alternatives gets progressively bigger, the elasticity will change. Big numbers (and occasionally small numbers) can make buyers far more sensitive to price changes. (In fact, a price can get so high or so low that it breaches the zone of credibility, and buyers will not believe that any set of benefits could be worth *that* price or that anything priced *that* low could have any benefits. In essence, elasticity will have become infinite.)

■ *Variance by segment.* Just as different types of customers will have different needs and benefits perceptions, they will also differ in how sensitive they are to price moves. Companies must take care not to generalize price elasticities blindly across customer segments.

[2]Many books detail the intricacies of calculating price elasticity. One very good book is Kent B. Monroe, *Pricing: Making Profitable Decisions* (New York: McGraw-Hill/Irwin, 2003).

(Continued)

TAKING ACCOUNT OF PRICE ELASTICITY *(Continued)*

■ *Variance over time.* Markets evolve as time passes. Customer needs will change; customers will become more comfortable with existing offerings and, inevitability, will push for new products and more benefits. Companies must continually reevaluate their elasticity numbers to make sure they are up to date.

■ *Variance by price communication method.* How a price is communicated—for instance, as a daily rate, monthly rate, or yearly rate—can have a strong effect on how sensitive customer segments are to the same net change in price.

■ *Variance by waterfall element.* As we saw in Chapter 3, the final pocket price is derived from a series of waterfall elements, each of which can drive different behaviors. Even if the pocket price remains constant, different customers will be more or less sensitive to changes in different waterfall elements.

■ *Creating demand or shifting shares?* A company that cuts its price and gains attractive volume may conclude that its market is elastic and be tempted to cut further. The underlying dynamics could tell a different story. The core market might be inelastic (lowering the price simply gave away money), but the lower prices may have attracted customers from substitute markets—for instance, soft drink consumers switching to a 100 percent juice option. A correct read of the situation would suggest better market segmentation, while an incorrect read may lead to further misguided price moves.

■ *Cross-product elasticity.* There are customer needs that can be met by several distinct products—for instance, cars, buses, trains, and airplanes are all travel options between Berlin and Paris. In these cases, elasticity analysis must not only gauge how a price change will affect an individual product, but also whether it will cause customers to shift to viable alternatives.

MAKING MOVES ON THE VALUE MAP

Understanding the benefit level perceived by customers, determining their price perceptions, and seeing where those benefit and price perceptions position a product relative to the competition on a value map are fundamental components to assessing and setting product/market strategy. But they are just the beginning.

So far, we have looked at value in a stable or static environment. However, the real competitive world is dynamic. Neither competitor positions nor customer perceptions are frozen. On the supply side, new features and benefits are constantly being introduced, cost-cutting and efficiency programs often lead to lower prices, and new players are always watching for opportunities to enter the market. At the same time, shifts in customer needs and desires keep the demand side in flux. For example, a new technology such as high-speed Internet access can increase the demand for related products such as high-performance home computers. In general, there is always pressure to offer more for less.

As a result, value maps are constantly changing in important but often predictable ways. In this environment, it is essential for a company to manage its value position continually and proactively. Top managers must understand exactly how they want the value map to evolve and where they want to position their products in today's dynamic, competitive environment. They need to plan carefully where on the value map to position new products for optimal returns, and be ready to capitalize on economic swings and market cycles. (See Chapter 6 for a fuller discussion of new product pricing.)

THE DYNAMIC VALUE MAP

Any change in product positioning by one competitor—a price cut or feature improvement, for instance—will cause other players to react, either to preempt shifts in market share or to adjust to them. *Dynamic value management* is the discipline of managing price/benefit positioning in light of the likely changes in the value positions of competing products and in the benefits perceptions of customers.

A case involving electric motors shows how misjudging these dynamics can destroy earnings. Sure Motors made motors for heavy-duty industrial uses, such as in machine tools that are often exposed to corrosives or extreme environments. Its products were high quality and very durable, and the company had broad application expertise. Sure Motors and its three primary competitors were each positioned along the VEL in a stable market.

Industry dynamics changed drastically when Sure Motors released a new line of motors that was a little more durable than the previous model and carried a slightly better warranty. Managers at Sure Motors, under pressure from their large customers to deliver increased value in a very competitive market, decided to hold prices steady, especially since manufacturing costs were roughly the same for both models. As shown in Exhibit 4-8, this strategy shifted Sure Motors into a value-advantaged position, and, as customers began recognizing the new value position, it started to pick up volume.

Since the total market for electric motors did not expand with the introduction of Sure Motors' new model, the increased volume came at the expense of its competitors, particularly from Rotation Co., the

Exhibit 4-8 Dynamic Value Management: Sure Motors Adds Features, but Leaves Price Unchanged

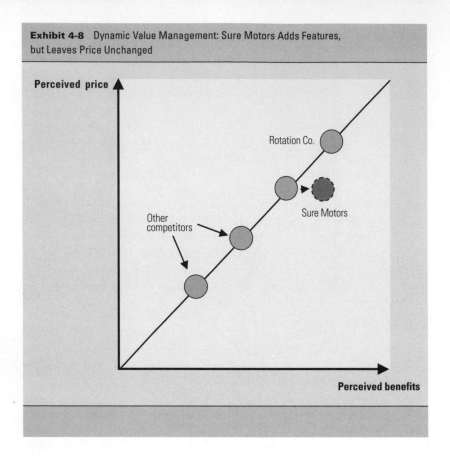

premium player in the market. At first the strategy seemed promising and Sure Motors gained market share, but soon competitors started to react to protect their share positions. Rotation faced the most immediate threat, since the benefit gap between Rotation and Sure Motors had closed, and it responded by improving its own warranty and lowering prices. Other suppliers saw the top players repositioned on the VEL, but did not have the expertise or resources to match the increased benefits. So, faced with falling sales, they reached for the only measure available: lower prices.

As shown in Exhibit 4-9, Sure Motors' strategy triggered a series of moves across the market that pushed the VEL lower. Overall prices are reduced, while each player's market share remains for the most part unchanged. The collective actions of these companies essentially nullified Sure Motors' value-advantaged position. The lowered VEL is good for cus-

Exhibit 4-9 Dynamic Value Management: Competitors Respond by Cutting Prices

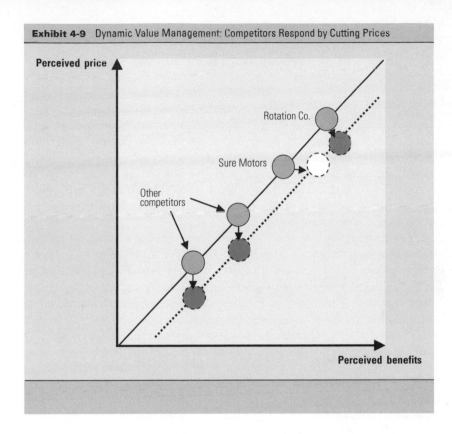

tomers because they get more for their money, but the suppliers get less for their products. The final effect is a wholesale transfer of economic surplus from suppliers to customers.

Could Sure Motors have managed the value dynamics of this situation better? Possibly. If it had raised the prices of its new motors proportionally to the increased benefits being offered (staying on the original VEL), it would probably have held its traditional share, but at the higher price. Since in this scenario competitors would not lose market share, they might not react at all. As a result, industry prices generally would have remained stable, while Sure Motors' profit would have increased significantly.

TWO MOVEMENT OPTIONS

Whether improving customer benefit perception, adjusting price perception, or some combination of these, marketing managers have two basic options: staying on the VEL or moving off it, usually into value-advantaged territory.

These are the choices whether the move is proactive or reactive. It is vital that a company understand the nature of its move (on or off the VEL), because each may lead to a very different outcome—different competitor and customer reactions, as well as different prices, volume, profit, and risk.

As companies begin designing moves on the value map, they should address a central question: How do they want the value map to look in the future? A business that has developed the price advantage will often look years down the road and determine its desired future value map, showing its own preferred position and the preferred positions for each of its competitors. Then, with that value map as a target, the company will plot the best strategy to position itself and influence how competitors are positioned, in order to reach that goal.

For instance, say a new competitor enters a stable market with a stated market share aspiration of 10 percent. The savvy incumbent, instead of aggressively fighting the new competitor across the board, might instead project the value map for five years ahead and determine a position for the new competitor that is best for the incumbent—for example, allowing the new player to take its 10 percent share from the low price/low benefit territory, and, in the process, preventing a wholesale drop in the industry VEL. This would prescribe a whole set of customer-targeting and benefit-creation initiatives for the incumbent designed to corner the new entrant into the low price/low benefit value position.

Repositioning along the VEL.   Repositioning a product along the VEL requires corresponding changes in price and benefits. It is usually a less aggressive move and carries a smaller risk of strong competitive response than moving off the VEL. Moves along the VEL are generally focused on increasing profits, rather than market share, although they can also lead to changes in market share depending on where customer clusters and competitors are located. To appreciate how the value map will change with any given move, a company must fully understand the prevailing layout of the value map, including its own position.

In moving along the VEL, a company can remain within the price/benefit boundaries set by the current competitive positioning or it can move to a position beyond the two extremes (represented by the high- and low-end players). Staying within the current landscape can succeed if the new location represents a more attractive customer cluster and the company's product can stand out from its competitors. A movement within the prevailing value/benefit boundaries is unlikely to expand the overall market, so as market shares shift, competitors faced with declining sales will probably react. If that reaction is likely to be a price cut, which is often the case, a company should consider its strategy carefully to avoid touching off a downward price spiral.

On the other hand, a new position outside the prevailing boundaries could expand the market by tapping into latent consumer demand, either at the high end or the low end of the market. Since the company is laying claim to new territory, other players are less threatened and less likely to retaliate immediately. (However, if the move is successful, others might try to follow suit.) Success can bring significant returns, but to succeed a company must accurately identify and quantify a pocket of unmet demand. This can be difficult because consumers may not know what they want or how much they would pay for it until the product and its price tag are in front of them. (New product pricing is discussed further in Chapter 6.)

Whichever repositioning is taken, a company must understand the risks and opportunities it faces when moving a product along the VEL. When a product moves, it will undoubtedly lose some customers who preferred the old positioning and gain customers who prefer the new positioning. Obviously, the goal is to gain more customers than are lost, but by misunderstanding this tradeoff a company could lose an attractive block of customers in exchange for a less attractive cluster or one where there are more competitors.

If a company wants to stay on the VEL, it must accompany any change in benefits with a corresponding change in price (or, on rare occasions, vice versa). As seen in the Sure Motors case, not increasing the price enough to complement added benefits will often force competitors to react, generally by cutting prices. In contrast, raising the price higher than justified by the benefits improvement will lead to a loss in sales volume. The market research tools noted earlier in this chapter can help companies find the appropriate price for a change in benefits.

Companies moving up or down along the VEL should also be aware of hidden traps that go beyond unilaterally adjusting prices and benefits. A company moving up the VEL into a higher-end market may find that customers in the new region expect a different range of benefits than the company is willing or able to offer. Though a company can charge higher prices, the costs to serve these customers could also be higher. For example, moving into a completely natural or organic category in the grocery market will allow a company to charge premium prices, but the move would also bring increased costs for storage and packaging.

Similarly, moving down market can also cause unexpected problems. All too often, a supplier is unable or unwilling to reduce service levels on lower-priced products. For example, a company's brand might be tarnished if it provides lower service levels even for a lower-priced product. If it does reduce the service levels, a down-market option may hurt the relationship benefits associated with the brand. On the other hand, if the down-market offer is good enough, the company risks cannibalizing its higher-end business. In addition, companies moving down the VEL often cannot create a competitive cost position for the low-end market, partly because it could be difficult to change a development and production model designed for higher-end products. As a result, margins will be tight and the return on investment (ROI) may not be enough to justify the move.

Moving off the VEL.   A move off the VEL into value-advantaged territory might seem attractive on the surface, but, as many companies have discovered, such a move requires a much better understanding of the dynamics, risks, and opportunities than does a move along the VEL. While repositioning along the VEL is likely to threaten only one or two of the nearest competitors on the line, a move below can often define a new and lower VEL, forcing every industry player to reconsider its own position.

Moving the VEL upward is more difficult and less common. To do so requires that customers accept an across-the-board lower level of value, and that most suppliers move in the same direction. Typically, the VEL will shift upward when pushed by structural changes in an industry, such as dramatic increases in raw material or production costs or new regulations that increase costs. In addition, when conditions are right, price leadership can also shift the VEL upward. (Chapter 5 discusses price leadership and followership, and the conditions and initiatives required for success.)

Two basic questions—how and how far—must be answered when a company moves off the VEL. It can move off the line by changing benefits, price, or both, but a company must be clear on which attributes and what price levels actually influence customer behavior. The answer to how far off the VEL to move depends on balancing several factors, including how aggressively a company wants to hunt additional market share, how much it wants to risk competitor retaliation, how long it can hold the new position while awaiting results, and how sensitive the market is to changes in levels of value.

When a product is repositioned below the VEL, its "horizon" of potential customers grows, as shown in Exhibit 4-10. The new positioning in this case continues to appeal to old customers, who are now being offered higher benefits at a lower price (unless the new benefits go beyond the needs of some clusters). At the same time, it would attract two new customer groups: those who were paying more for a set of benefits similar to

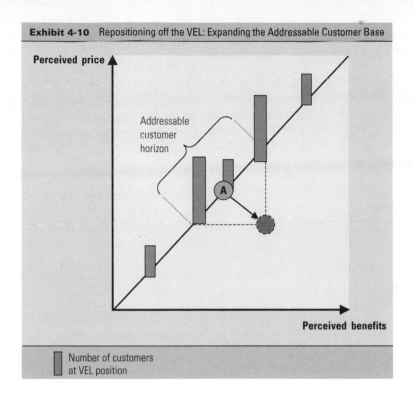

Exhibit 4-10   Repositioning off the VEL: Expanding the Addressable Customer Base

Perceived price

Addressable customer horizon

A

Perceived benefits

Number of customers at VEL position

the product's new positioning, and those who were getting less benefit at the same new price.

But moving off the VEL to expand the horizon of customers does not guarantee success. First, market research must establish that the expanded horizon includes new concentrations of customers and not just empty space. Exhibit 4-11 shows how, for example, a premium supplier might try to cut its price in order to increase its market share. Unfortunately, the new price is not low enough to pull in a new group of customers. The next addressable cluster of customers is satisfied with the benefits it is receiving and has no desire to pay more, even for an increase in benefits. As a result, the premium supplier does not gain market share, but faces a substantial loss of profit under the new prices. The same effect can happen anywhere along the VEL.

Companies must also be sure that their move off the VEL is large enough for customers to notice. Marginal moves often backfire. Consumers may not see enough difference in the new position to make them

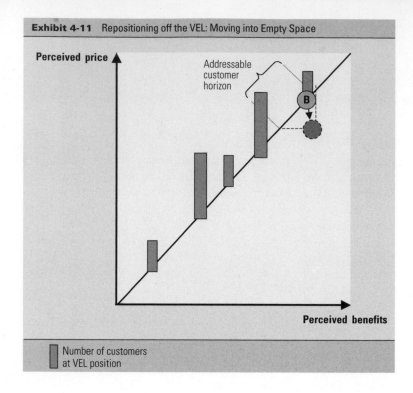

Exhibit 4-11　Repositioning off the VEL: Moving into Empty Space

switch suppliers (in essence, the move keeps prices within the zone of indif-ference). But competitors follow such moves very closely, and if they decide to copy it, the VEL can drop while market shares remain stable. In the heating and air conditioning equipment installation market, one company cut its labor fees by 5 percent, and its main rival reacted with a similar cut. But architects and contractors consider bids based on total installed costs, and a 5 percent cut in labor costs amounted to a reduction in total costs of less than 1 percent, which was not enough to influence any decision. In the end, the installers simply gave the money away.

Just as fundamental as understanding customer preferences and behav-ior, a company contemplating a move off the VEL must also have a solid appreciation of its competitors' positions and strategies. Rivals will rarely stand by and watch volume or market share drop. Faced with these market changes, they usually improve the attributes of their own products, cut their prices, or both. Careful consideration should therefore be given to how competitors are most likely to respond.

Often competitors will try to match the change that triggered the shift

ESTIMATING COMPETITOR RESPONSE

Over time, businesses usually respond rationally to events in the marketplace. Past behavior and recent strategic steps can offer valid clues to a company's likely response to a price move. Several factors to watch are these:

- *Strategic intent.* A company with a product that is a strong profit generator or that has made a public announcement to target a specific area is more likely to fight for its market than one that is looking for a way out of the market. Companies can make what appear to be irrational decisions from a profit perspective when core products are threatened.
- *Recent investments.* Companies that have recently invested in capacity expansion or an expensive marketing campaign, for instance, are also unlikely to give up without a fight, even if their products are based on older technology or are otherwise inferior.
- *Range of options.* Competitors may not have the ability to match the new features or other benefits delivered by a product. On the other hand, their cost structure might preclude a defensive price cut.
- *Level of threat.* Not all competitors will react in the same way or with the same intensity. The strongest reaction, whether a move on benefits or price, is likely to come from competitors closest to the product on the value map. Competitors who feel insulated from the product may not react at all.
- *Market position.* Players already in a value-advantaged position may not respond as aggressively as those that are already disadvantaged.
- *Financial health.* Robust income statements and balance sheets can give the luxury of patience, buying more time to gauge the true effect of a rival's move on the value map.
- *Maturity.* Companies that have survived multiple business cycles and learned the risks of reacting too quickly or too strongly are likely to weigh their response to a rival's price move more carefully.
- *Industry tradition.* Past patterns, such as matching innovation with innovation or avoiding price wars, or, conversely, aggressively defending share, could likely be repeated.

in market share. If a company cuts price, its rivals are likely to follow suit; if it increases services, its rivals will probably try to add the same types of services, if possible. With this in mind, the less damaging move off the VEL is often a repositioning along the benefits axis, rather than the price axis, since it often takes longer for competitors to mount an equivalent response. It is also easier to retract benefits that are rejected by the market or cannot be provided economically, than to try to raise prices after a round of reductions. As we have seen, however, a shift in benefits does not always prevent a wave of price cuts. If others in the industry cannot match the improved attributes, they are likely to reach for the only lever at hand—lower prices.

If pricing behavior moves the VEL downward, customer clusters will probably also shift. As the line moves downward through different combinations of price and benefits, volume distribution along the VEL could break up into smaller clusters, as illustrated in Exhibit 4-12. Some cus-

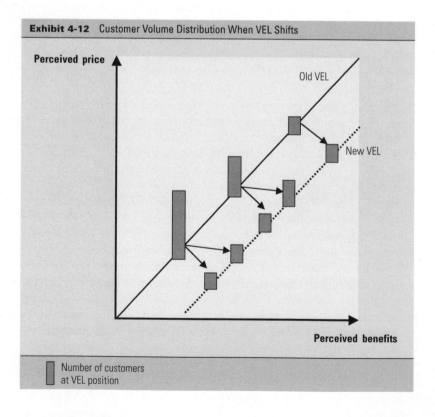

Exhibit 4-12 Customer Volume Distribution When VEL Shifts

Perceived price

Old VEL

New VEL

Perceived benefits

Number of customers
at VEL position

tomers might not want additional benefits, while others might use the changes to rethink their price/benefit tradeoffs. New offers could also stimulate latent demand.

A move into the value-advantaged region of the value map will not necessarily spark increased sales. Among other reasons, there may be no untapped demand at the new position or customers may simply be price insensitive. In consumer dental hygiene products, for example, a private label attacker tried to grab market share in a particular line with an aggressive, low-priced move against a dominant incumbent. The incumbent's immediate reaction was to consider a defensive price cut, but before making a move it took the time to probe the market. It found that only a small portion of the market was price sensitive and likely to switch. In addition, the research showed the incumbent had very high customer satisfaction ratings. Using the market discontinuity as an opportunity to adjust its offerings, the incumbent released several new varieties of the product and raised prices across the board. Volume loss was much less than originally feared, and the higher prices drastically increased the profitability of the category.

A move off the VEL can bring increased profits if it taps into a valuable customer cluster and can be sustained amid aggressive competitive reactions. In many cases, however, the move is made blindly with little notion of what customers really want, how competitors will react, and how demand patterns might change in the new landscape. Such short-sightedness can kill profitability, as well as the high hopes that were behind the decisions.

PUTTING CUSTOMERS ON THE VALUE MAP

As touched on in the previous section, positions along the VEL are not created equal. Even on a value map describing a well-defined customer segment, customers are not spread evenly along the line. Instead, customers are typically clustered at various points on the VEL, with some positions commanding higher volume than others.

One reason clusters form is that many customers can be *benefit-bracketed*. They will not accept any products with benefits below some minimum level nor even consider any product with benefits exceeding some maximum level. Market research shows that break points exist for some products and services at which a small increase in the benefits offered will lead to a large increase in the value a customer perceives.

The bottom of a benefit bracket represents the minimum requirements of a buyer. For example, some automotive component buyers will not accept delivery reliability below a certain level no matter how advantageous the price. On the other hand, benefit ceilings usually show the maximum level of benefits for which a customer is willing to pay. Some computer buyers, for instance, know how much memory would satisfy their needs, and additional memory would not offer them additional benefits. At times, additional benefits, even at the same price, can even alienate customers. A corporate purchaser, for instance, might choose a bland ballpoint pen over an elegantly styled alternative at the same price, simply to avoid the impression of extravagance.

Clusters also form because many customers are *price-capped*. They are unwilling to spend more than a fixed amount for a particular product. For many, the caps are formed by budgetary constraints, but there can also be psychological aspects. For example, the price of the average home personal computer (PC) in the United States held at about $1,000 for several years around the late 1990s even though performance improved sharply during the period. This suggests there were price-capped customers at around this level who were unwilling to spend more, even if they could get additional features.

Just as there are customers who fall into both categories, there are others who fall into neither. These buyers are willing to consider the full range of tradeoffs along the VEL. In corporate environments, as long as the ROI is positive and better than a lower-priced alternative, price is only one of many factors considered, and the entire range of offerings is on the table. Even in certain consumer markets, in areas ranging from treats (coffee or ice cream) to luxuries (perfume or designer clothes) to necessities (life-saving medical procedures), price can be no object.

Nuances of benefit perceptions can also lead to clusters. For example, order of entry can play a major role, particularly in sectors like telecommunications and utilities. Even if a new player meets or exceeds an incumbent's value proposition in terms of "hard" benefits such as product quality or service offerings, it could face an insurmountable challenge as it tries to grab market share. This is because "soft" benefits—those linked to lower risk and increased comfort—are often tied to historic relationships and are almost impossible to replicate. Distorted impressions of how much it would cost to switch to a new supplier, whether in terms of actual expense or hassle, can also contribute to customer inertia, even if the added value of a new supplier is obvious.

Understanding volume distribution along the VEL is crucial to making an intelligent decision about product position. In many cases, however, volume distribution is poorly understood, which leads to bad decisions. Companies tend to make two typical mistakes:

1. *Blank space.* An otherwise competitive product could be positioned amid blank space on the VEL where there is no customer volume. A

maker of metal-coating machinery positioned a new product technically halfway between two competing products, hoping to pull in customers not entirely satisfied by either. Unfortunately, it did not realize there was no significant volume between the two positions; no customers were willing to buy at that intermediate price/benefit point. Each offered a specific speed required by customers, and there was no demand for an intermittent speed. Even though the new coating machinery was competitive based on technical specifications and price, the manufacturer could not attract the sales volume it expected. Failing to understand volume distribution along the VEL forced it to take a multimillion-dollar write-off.

2. *Cutting off customers.* Pushing beyond the extremes of the VEL can inadvertently exclude a large portion of price-capped or benefit-bracketed customers. A quality and price leader, for example, might strive for continuous improvements and unknowingly move into blank space at the top of the VEL. Alternatively, a low-cost producer could bring prices so low that customers find any benefit proposition incredible. A cheap car might be marketable, but a model could become so cheap that buyers doubt its safety.

VALUE PROFILING

While the basic value maps can be very useful in diagnosing problems and uncovering opportunities in the market, an additional level of insight can be achieved with a technique we call *value profiling*. Price and benefit perceptions can vary significantly, and making a detailed profile of how the market sees a product's value can uncover misalignments between a company's desired value positioning and its actual positioning. With this information as a starting point, a company can pinpoint the problem—for instance, ineffective benefits communications, inappropriate discretionary discounting, or benefits delivery problems—and design a solution.

Thorough analysis of perceived benefits, perceived pricing, and the zone of indifference allows a company to change the shape of a product's positioning on the value map from a point to an ellipse, as shown in Exhibit 4-13. The height of the ellipse from its center point is determined by the standard deviation of price responses from the research, while the width is set by the standard deviation of the benefits responses. As with earlier value maps, the ellipse can fall within the zone of indifference or in the value-advantaged or -disadvantaged areas, as shown in Exhibit 4-14.

The complete picture formed by value profiling can be the basis for

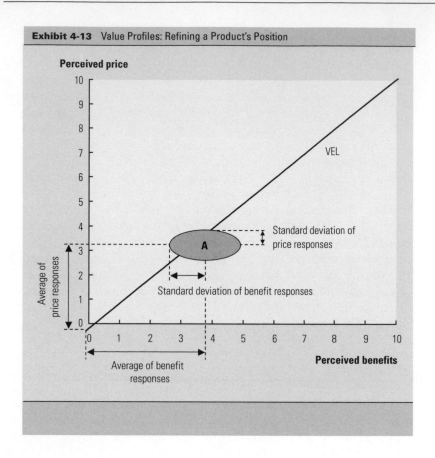

Exhibit 4-13   Value Profiles: Refining a Product's Position

sound pricing decisions. We have already discussed the implications of being above or below the VEL, but the shape of the ellipse can bring additional insight, especially when the variance of price or benefit perception is larger than expected. Typically, misshapen ellipses suggest that the market is not clear on a product's price or benefit position—or perhaps both. Exhibit 4-15 shows three typical problems. In the first value map, product A's benefits perception varies widely; in the second, its price perception is the problem; and in the third, both price and benefit perceptions show significant variation. Failure to understand what forces are shaping these ellipses can lead to erroneous pricing decisions.

One common explanation of misalignment is that a company has inadvertently combined multiple market segments into the same pool. Consequently, for an identical offer that is communicated in the same way, some

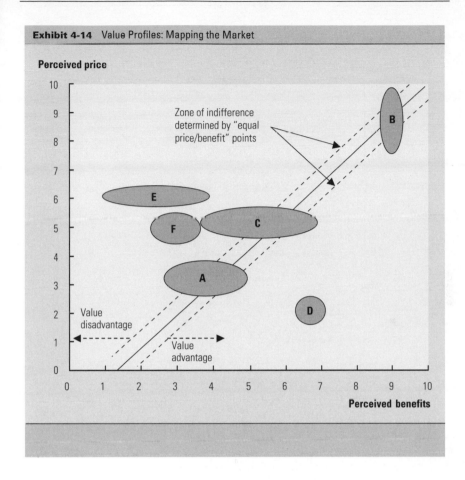

Exhibit 4-14 Value Profiles: Mapping the Market

customers may view it as too expensive, others as a great deal, and similarly some could view it as rich in benefits, while others will view it as insufficient. The challenge here is either to develop different communication or go-to-market approaches by segment, or, in more severe cases, to develop differentiated offerings that better align with the specific needs of the corresponding segments.

The problem of segment pooling could also explain differences in either price or benefit perception in isolation. Assuming that the value profiles accurately reflect the views of a discrete market segment, let us look at other opportunity areas as shown in Exhibit 4-15.

In the first case, the market has a precise view of a company's price

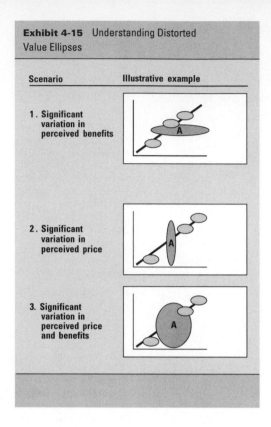

Exhibit 4-15 Understanding Distorted Value Ellipses

Scenario	Illustrative example
1. Significant variation in perceived benefits	
2. Significant variation in perceived price	
3. Significant variation in perceived price and benefits	

positioning in the market, but individual customers perceive a broad spectrum of benefits delivered. Two explanations present themselves. First, the physical delivery of the value proposition may vary significantly by customer—for instance, because of a product changeover, quality problems, or differences in local support capabilities. Second, there may be inconsistencies in the company's ability to communicate the benefits. This could, for instance, be due to the complexity of the offering, inadequate marketing support, or inconsistent sales skills, and it may suggest that a more effective marketing and sales communication strategy is needed.

In the second situation, the market perceives a common benefits level, but perception of price varies widely. Lack of pricing discipline is a frequent explanation. As the range of pocket prices is allowed to spread outside of acceptable limits, different customers may begin to see huge price variances for essentially the same offer.

In the third situation, the offering's perceived value position is simply unclear. In essence, this is a combination of the two previous situations. This case requires careful consideration because the problem could be driven by some combination of benefits miscommunication, lack of pricing discipline, or failure to recognize multiple segments.

*   *   *

The product/market strategy level of price management is centered entirely on customer value. The primary issue here is how to determine and manage price/benefit positioning relative to competitors—to come up with list prices or base prices that reflect, for each market segment, the best value position for a company's products over time. The value map was introduced as the core tool to help understand how the critical price/benefit tradeoff works and drives customers' selection of suppliers.

Businesses that excel at the product/market strategy level are obsessive about understanding customers. They regularly invest in research to comprehend in detail the benefit attributes that influence customers' buying behavior and choice of supplier. They understand the current and changing importance of each attribute and their own performance against those attributes, as well as the performance of key competitors. They sustain an equally well-informed perspective on customers' perception of their own and their competitors' price levels. For their most important segments, they maintain current value maps—showing the value positions of their own offerings and those of competitors—that are updated whenever significant market events occur.

These businesses use these value maps to guide strategy by segment—for instance to adjust proactively list prices and benefit offerings, to react to competitive repositioning of price and benefits, or to determine the price positioning of new products. Beyond static management of value position, they use these current value maps to understand market dynamics—to anticipate competitor reactions to their own and others' value moves. They look into the future, create target value maps of desired competitive value positions, and then take the necessary actions over time to move themselves and to influence their competitors' movements toward those target positions.

Without this level of rich understanding of customers and competitors and this level of thoughtful price and market strategy based on that understanding, no company can truly claim the price advantage as its own.

CHAPTER 5

Industry Strategy

The industry strategy level is the broadest and most general level of price management. The critical issue here is industrywide price levels—knowing them, predicting them better, and, if possible, influencing them in a positive direction. Failure at this level can, at worst, lead to destructive price wars or, at the very least, create unnecessary downward pressure on industry prices. Success here can result in constructive industrywide pricing conduct. This is not measured by prices that outstrip the benefits delivered to customers—such a situation is never sustainable. Rather, it is measured by bringing prices to a level justified by the benefits delivered to customers and the work behind the products. Managers who overlook this level risk having all of their hard-fought pricing gains at the transactional and product/market levels wiped out by falling industry prices.

Companies that excel at this level have a better understanding of the supply, demand, cost, and other trends that affect overall industry price levels, and of the factors that drive these trends. They independently and unilaterally become proactive in facing and encouraging the trends that benefit the industry, rather than passively accepting the market's invisible hand. Using their superior understanding of the industry's microeconomics, they can adjust their tactics ahead of the market, for instance, by avoiding long-term, fixed-price deals just before an expected upturn, or by adding new capacity in a way that matches expected increases in overall demand.

This chapter discusses industry strategies on pricing. In most jurisdictions, collective actions by industry participants are legally sensitive. The approaches outlined here are not intended to recommend actions that would be contrary to any applicable laws. While reasonable efforts have been made to ensure that the actions are legally permissible, given the legal sensitivity of the issues, company executives should always seek appropriate legal counsel before taking action.

But positive changes in industry microeconomics do not automatically cause prices to rise. While a clear understanding of industry microeconomics may suggest when and how much prices might change, price leadership and followership are often required to trigger such a price move. Price leadership is taking the initiative to lead prices upward when conditions are appropriate and supporting competitors' independent decisions to follow. It is a legitimate strategy to promote, within the letter and spirit of the law, good industry pricing conduct. This means, among other aspects, shunning actions that could fuel destructive price wars, being transparent in its pricing actions and motives, promoting a longer-term view of industry profitability, and recognizing when the conditions are right to try to lead industry prices higher. Price leaders and rational followers can independently and unilaterally influence industry economics and shepherd prices to their appropriate levels.

Companies miss opportunities at the industry strategy level for many reasons. First, few have anyone assigned to maintain an overview of industry pricing by, for example, systematically looking for patterns of competitive behavior that might suggest a price leadership or followership opportunity. Second, the unrelenting focus on immediate shareholder value has increased competitive rivalry and turned the focus to near-term volume and market share, at the expense of longer-term price and profit improvement. Third, small- and medium-size companies may underestimate how much influence they can exert on industry prices—for instance, by adding marginal capacity or positioning themselves as the market's low-price alternative. And finally, many companies underestimate the range of tools available to forecast industry trends, their own ability to influence those trends, and the legal degrees of freedom.

These factors regularly cause companies to miss the intricate yet promising opportunities industry strategy can offer. But companies also miss low-hanging fruit simply because they are not looking. For example, one specialty chemicals company failed to spot two price increases announced by a competitor over a period of five years. Since no one followed its lead, the competitor rolled back prices each time, and everyone missed opportunities to turn around declining industry profits. Because the company had not watched for such price moves, it never even had the internal discussion about whether to follow the competitor's move. We have seen numerous cases in which companies have missed opportunities to lead or follow price increases because they overlooked favorable conditions that should have been easily recognized.

PROFIT FROM BETTER PRICE PREDICTIONS

Companies that are better at predicting industry price changes can capture substantial rewards from this knowledge. This is particularly true for cyclical products, such as commodities, and those with short life cycles, such as high tech. For example, at one consumer electronics company, a two-week delay in dropping prices at the end of a product's life cycle could have increased its annual profit by as much as 17 percent.

At the root of better price prediction is a more complete understanding of the industry factors at play. These factors are felt by and affect pricing decisions at every company in an industry. A complete discussion about how to model industry supply and demand, cost curves, and other essential tools is available from several sources,[1] and we will not belabor those points here. But generally, three areas need to be constantly watched for indications of a shift in industry price levels:

- *Cost changes*, which, for instance, may be triggered by an abundance or shortage of key raw materials, new manufacturing or distribution approaches, or improved technology.
- *Supply changes*, which may be triggered by events such as new capacity coming online, patents expiring, or plant closures.
- *Demand changes*, which, for example, may be triggered by market shifts for supplemental or complementary products, changes in consumer tastes, new benefits that uncover latent demand, or new regulations.

While high-level analysis is needed, it is also essential to take the pulse of the market by gathering information from the frontline sales force. However, care must be taken to assess anecdotes from the field correctly and seek collaborating information. For example, a report that a competitor is experiencing supply problems could be a false rumor, outdated information, or simply incomplete.

Anticipating these microeconomic changes requires not only an in-depth awareness of events within a company's own industry, but also familiarity with the events in its suppliers' and customers' markets. For example, labor problems may trigger a disruption in suppliers' operations, leading to higher costs throughout your industry; or regulatory changes that affect your customers' operations may impact their purchases from your industry.

Understanding what drives industry prices can give managers additional confidence, assist in communicating with customers, and cut the time spent investigating recent price movements. But the greatest value from improved industry price forecasting comes from two fronts: proactively preparing for an expected price change and fine-tuning production levels.

---

[1]One excellent book is Kent B. Monroe, *Pricing: Making Profitable Decisions* (New York: McGraw-Hill/Irwin, 2003).

PLANNING FOR AN EXPECTED PRICE CHANGE

A company that anticipates a price change can prepare for the shift and respond more quickly once it takes place. For example, in the U.S. styrene industry, as in many other markets, prices soar when demand pushes production capacity to its limits. As Exhibit 5-1 shows, the fly-up in spot prices and the accompanying margins can be significant. But the price shift usually lags the move toward full capacity because customers pressure their suppliers to keep the old prices as long as possible. (There is no similar lag when prices drop.)

If a major producer carefully tracks industry utilization and realizes that the spot price increases portend a longer-term structural increase in industry prices, rather than a temporary aberration, it can use this knowledge to drive and justify earlier and higher increases in contract prices. In addition, it might build inventory beyond current demand, which it could then sell once prices rise. Such an approach could allow a company to gain an extra 5 to 7 cents a pound for styrene over three months during a fly-up year. For a typical company producing about 2 billion pounds a year, this would bring $2 million to $3 million in additional operating profit.

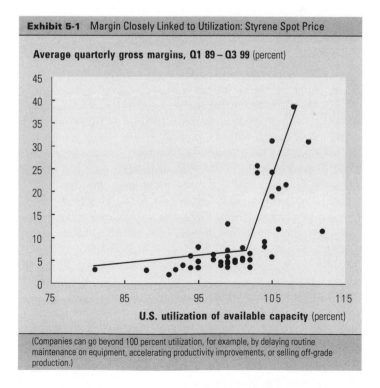

Exhibit 5-1   Margin Closely Linked to Utilization: Styrene Spot Price

Average quarterly gross margins, Q1 89 – Q3 99 (percent)

U.S. utilization of available capacity (percent)

(Companies can go beyond 100 percent utilization, for example, by delaying routine maintenance on equipment, accelerating productivity improvements, or selling off-grade production.)

Responding quickly to unanticipated supply changes can also bring a substantial payoff. One electronics supplier added an estimated $25 million in annual profit by reacting more quickly than others when earthquakes in Taiwan in 1999 caused temporary market shortages for a key component.

In addition to moving more quickly on price, companies can use other tactics to benefit from superior industry price predictions. For example, ahead of an upward price trend, a company can shorten the term of new contracts to avoid being locked into the lower price well after industry prices have moved upward. Also, if the price increase will be driven by increased input costs, a supplier might push hard to insert a clause into the contract that allows it to pass these increases on to its customer if they occur.

And if industry prices are expected to drop? A company could profit by taking the opposite tack, such as pushing for longer-term contracts or eliminating the input-cost clauses. For example, some pharmaceutical companies have offered discounts to their customers if they sign longer-term purchase commitments just as a patent is due to expire. While these discounts might hurt short-term profits, in the longer term the supplier maintains relatively stable earnings in the face of increased competition and keeps the medication's presence in the market.

MAINTAINING OPTIMAL PRODUCTION

In industries where prices are very sensitive to changes in supply—for instance, those with steep cost curves at the current price levels—companies should be particularly careful that their capacity decisions do not spark unnecessary price declines. Usually, producers with low or moderate relative costs will run at full capacity to maximize profits. But if microeconomic analysis shows that the industry is near a break point, where a small increase in supply could push prices much lower, these companies may want to avoid production levels that risk breaching this point. This can be the case, for instance, when the marginal producer—the supplier with the highest costs that is still in the market—has costs that are significantly higher than its closest competitor and demand is just enough to keep it in the market profitably.

Some companies have taken on creative strategies to help maintain prices at an attractive point along the supply curve—for instance, by taking actions that have the effect of discouraging large additions of new capacity. In the mid-1990s, Shell Chemical began auctioning capacity shares in "virtual ethylene plants." Shell, a low-cost producer, had ethylene production capacity it did not need for its own derivatives manufacturing operations. Other players, who did not always have the ethylene production capacity to meet their own needs, would often go to Shell in a pinch. To discourage these companies or others from adding ethylene capacity in an effort to become totally self-sufficient, Shell offered these virtual shares. The buyers benefited from both Shell's low-cost position, which they probably could not replicate, and an assured ethylene supply; and Shell's efforts helped the industry maintain relatively high utilization and stable margins during the latter half of the decade.

PRICE LEADERSHIP

A profound understanding of the microeconomics of an industry can lead to quick wins, such as taking supply/demand–driven price increases sooner or fine-tuning contract terms to take advantage of expected industry price movement. Beyond the microeconomic opportunities is another related but largely overlooked industry strategy opportunity—the pursuit of constructive price leadership or followership. Through effectively inspiring good pricing conduct throughout an industry—avoiding price wars, maintaining regular price increases, and capturing the full value of innovation—and knowing when the time is right and how best to move prices higher, a company can unilaterally contribute to a rise in the level of the sea and contribute to increased industry profitability.

Price leadership, at a high level, means designing a sound pricing strategy that does not overestimate customer price sensitivity and that takes into account the potential that competitors may follow a price move, rather than undercut it. It also means being clear and consistent in communicating pricing strategy, its rationale and value. Price leaders also use specific approaches to try to discourage other players (resellers, customers, and competitors) from undermining their pricing strategy. In markets where clear price leadership has evolved, industry ROS has risen by 2 to 7 percentage points.

For many companies, the price leadership opportunity is shrouded by several misconceptions. The first is that it is illegal. Indeed, a price leadership strategy requires careful attention to laws that prohibit collusive action among competitors. But there are important and substantial distinctions between price leadership and unlawful activities. (For a fuller survey of legal considerations, see Chapter 11.)

- Price leadership is about being aware of competitive pricing intentions; it is not about reaching any type of agreement with competitors.
- It is about communicating pricing and pricing information to a wide range of stakeholders for justifiable purposes; it is not about using price statements to signal competitors unlawfully.

■ It is about maintaining vigilance against destructive pricing; it is not about using price and market power to push competitors out of business.
■ It is about unilateral resale price policies; it is not about agreements with resellers or coercion to get them to set a certain price.

Many managers also mistakenly think only an industry's low-cost or market-share leader can effectively lead prices or that leadership can only be exercised when a new product is released. They also worry that seemingly irrational behavior by a competitor would preclude the possibility of leadership. And finally, managers feel their hands are tied: Like the weather, there is not much that can be done about industry prices. All of these beliefs are generally misguided. Any company that recognizes the opportunity has a chance at price leadership, either by taking the initiative to be the leader or by encouraging competitors to lead by being a visibly faithful follower.

So what underpins successful price leadership? We have found three basic requirements. First, there must be *visibility* of pricing across the industry. It is hard for a company to move upward comfortably if prices are hidden and it does not know how other players are acting. Second, there must be *common motivation* centered on growing profits through better pricing rather than on aggressive volume gains. That is, the major competitors have to be independently playing a similar game. Third, competitors need the internal *resolve* to pursue price leadership persistently. Becoming a price leader requires tough choices, be it walking away from an account that could add incremental volume, instituting greater controls over frontline price decisions, or taking a visible position with customers regarding bringing prices up.

INFLUENCING THE ELEMENTS OF PRICE LEADERSHIP

Structural industry conditions can set the stage for effective price leadership and followership, but alone they will not bring about higher prices. Successful price leaders understand that they can influence and use the three essential elements—visibility, common motivation, and resolve—to encourage good pricing conduct throughout the industry. For each element, there are several practical tools readily at hand to move toward this goal.

VISIBILITY

Companies that aspire to price leadership take pains to assure that their own pricing actions are visible and not misinterpreted by the market or competitors. Generally, good leaders strive for transparency in two areas:

price and rationale. While these two are often interwoven in execution—a single announcement may feature a new price list and the reasoning behind it—they address very different issues.

Transparent Prices. In many industries, there is no accurate barometer for prices. Deals are negotiated individually, and the only information about competitors' prices may be hearsay. Even if the information is accurate, it could easily be outdated. In these conditions, gauging industry price trends can be excruciatingly difficult.

In such industries, leaders can increase price transparency by encouraging an independent source, often a trade magazine or association, to develop and publish a standardized price index. Price indices are created to help buyers peg prices to the industry, ensuring that they are not paying more than their competitors for a key manufacturing input. For suppliers, this can provide needed visibility for overall price trends in a market. To be successful, major players would have to cooperate with the index producer and take steps to ensure that its specific price levels are not disclosed to third parties. But the approach has worked, for example, in many sectors of the chemicals industry.

There are other ways, some quite creative, to increase price transparency. For example, prices in the elevator industry had historically been opaque. Each order was as unique as the building it would occupy, and the price depended on a combination of various features: the number of floors serviced, elevator size, desired speed, and interior features, to name a few. Each feature had numerous options, opening the door for an infinite number of configurations and prices for any given elevator. In addition, closed bids were the market norm, creating an environment where it was very difficult for competitors to discern general price trends. In the early 1990s, one company decided to change this. It created a "building designers' elevator guide" that detailed three "standard elevators"—hypothetical models that would never be built—and published a price for each. This guide gave designers, for planning purposes, a rough estimate of approximate elevator costs for a new building. Actual prices for an elevator installation would be built up from these standard prices based on the customized features needed for each project. These hypothetical units became an effective tool to bring visibility to price trends in the market. Whenever the company thought the time was right to take prices up by, say, 2 percent, it would simply republish its guide, with the prices for the hypothetical standard models increased by 2 percent.

But it is not enough for a company to improve its own price transparency. It must also actively look for and understand moves made by others in the industry. Even the clearest pricing action can be missed if no one is watching. A distilled spirits company had a policy of maintaining a routine price premium over a specific competitor in selected markets. Despite this policy, close analysis of resale prices revealed that the specific competitor had brought its prices up over the course of two years, at one point reaching parity with the brand that had traditionally been premium priced. The spirits company had failed to track competitive pricing at the local market level and missed an opportunity to increase prices. In contrast, successful price leaders and followers systematically monitor competitive pricing, generally and for specific markets, and closely track public announcements by others in the market to keep abreast of any changes in the industry landscape.

Transparent Rationale.   In addition to price transparency, a company must also be sure that the rationale behind a price move is clearly stated to avoid misinterpretation by customers and other stakeholders. A clear rationale can help competitors develop a rational response, particularly in the wake of a price decrease. Without an explanation, a rival is likely to interpret a price cut as an aggressive move to gain market share, while the true motivation could be much more benign, such as the need to clear obsolete inventory. In the case of an increase in prices, a clear rationale can help customers, investors, and other stakeholders evaluate and develop their responses better.

Beyond the words, the method of communicating a price increase to customers can also indicate the motive and commitment behind a price move; and here, too, companies must be careful to avoid misinterpretation. Every pricing move sends a message. The way it is done, when it is done, how it is announced, who announces it . . . the list goes on and on. Each component can increase or decrease the impact of the message. For example, a company can follow precedent and put a price change into effect on a specific date, such as January 1, or it can send a stronger message by picking an effective date that breaks precedent. The announcement can be either buried in a press release or a key point in a speech by the CEO. Many companies try to minimize communication around price increases, believing that sneaking an increase through will minimize resistance. But price leaders (and good followers) understand how to communicate that message clearly and carefully to customers to maximize the outcome of their price increase initiative. As Exhibit 5-2 outlines, managers have many options for using their price increase approach for delivering a high-impact message of price leadership.

COMMON MOTIVATION

Behind every act of business, there is motivation. Companies excelling in price leadership realize that to have price increases stick, the most important competitors must have a common general motive. And further, the

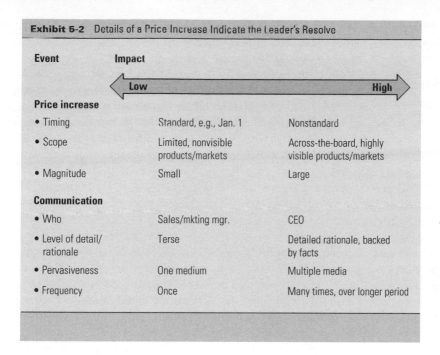

Exhibit 5-2 Details of a Price Increase Indicate the Leader's Resolve

Event	Impact	
	Low	High
Price increase		
• Timing	Standard, e.g., Jan. 1	Nonstandard
• Scope	Limited, nonvisible products/markets	Across-the-board, highly visible products/markets
• Magnitude	Small	Large
Communication		
• Who	Sales/mkting mgr.	CEO
• Level of detail/ rationale	Terse	Detailed rationale, backed by facts
• Pervasiveness	One medium	Multiple media
• Frequency	Once	Many times, over longer period

common motivation should be profit growth. If there is a significant player intent on share growth, it will be much more difficult for prices to move up. In such cases, price leadership efforts must first focus primarily on convincing industry participants on the benefits of profit growth as a motive. Successful price leaders find ways to encourage the industry away from a fixation on share and toward a focus on profit and price increases.

Legal forms of market communication, of course, are necessary tools in aligning industry motivation. By announcing its own motives, a company is telling the market that it has analyzed the situation and concluded that its actions are the most reasonable way to attain a specific goal. Competitors who have reached different conclusions will often independently reexamine their own situation.

In many situations, actions can indeed speak louder than words. In one industrial products category where prices had been stagnant over three years, one of the major companies used targeted price increases to trigger a shift in motivation. It raised prices on product lines that competed with its main rival's core products, but left the prices of its own core product untouched. The strategy was clear: We are not after market share, but we are also not willing to risk losing market share in our core business. The competitor responded rationally. It matched the price increases that had already been announced, and it also raised prices on products that competed with the first company's core products. In the end, prices in the industry were up almost across the board.

Another aspect of motivation is to recognize that competitors *do* act rationally and they are likely to be driven by the same profit motive (rather than an obsession with market share). Quite often, when companies forecast the possible results of a price increase, they fail to consider that competitors might match the increase. When potential followership is factored into the analysis, bolder price moves become more attractive, and managers are assured that they are weighing the full range of potential outcomes.

Successful price leaders are also willing to challenge assumptions about customers' price sensitivity. Internal estimates of price elasticity can be less than rigorous and reflect a conservative approach to change. A major tire manufacturer under constant pressure by retailers to keep prices low decided to research demand elasticity for its products and cross-elasticity with competitors' products to understand its true risks, as well as the risks faced by its retailers. The project revealed that the company and its retailers had erred in their high elasticity estimates. Customers were much less sensitive to price than the companies had thought, and the likely effect of a price increase would be greater profit, rather than a significant loss in volume. Armed with that information, the company gained a clearer picture of the potential advantages of price leadership: Even if competitors did not follow, they would make a lot more money with little share loss. Unfortunately, too many companies fail to invest the time to get a true handle on the risks and rewards of price leadership.

RESOLVE

Organizational resolve is vital for price leadership because the full rewards for success are rarely immediate. While price increases may succeed in the near term, successful price leadership is a long-term strategy and must be backed by internal resolve to see it through over time, as well as by an industrywide belief that success will bring long-term benefits for all players. This resolve must be behind every move, because competitors will judge you by your worst pricing behavior. Ninety-nine out of a hundred contracts may be consistent with a price leadership strategy, but the hundredth, which gave away lower prices, will be the one competitors remember and talk about. Invariably, such a lapse will be misread as an indication of your true pricing intentions.

Companies create resolve in four important ways: strong internal controls, continual and consistent communication, active monitoring of competitive action (and appropriate responses when necessary), and specific tools to influence resellers to support their pricing strategy.

Internal Controls. Resolve, both internal and industrywide, is founded on a belief that success is attainable and worthwhile. The goals of price leadership must be supported throughout an organization, using many of the same tools we discussed in relation to transaction pricing in Chapter 3: sales incentives focused on profitability, strong management controls, and organizational alignment around the strategy. In one case, as a company was trying to maintain a price increase, its top sales rep was using large discounts as an incentive to close a major deal with a highly visible customer. Had a manager not caught the incongruity, the prices and discounts being offered would have undermined the company's extensive efforts to support the price increase. (Top managers must also exercise self-control, because field reps will take their cues from executives before risking their careers by holding tough during a critical negotiation.)

Communication. If price leadership is seen as nothing more than a one-time tactic, resolve will be weakened. Messages must be repeated to each important stakeholder and reinforced to build credibility and understanding. One consumer durables company that launched a major price leadership effort published internally a detailed "price leadership communication plan" on how to explain its strategy, including a price increase, to customers, shareholders, market analysts, employees, trade press, and retailers. As Exhibit 5-3 outlines, the company did not launch all of these efforts at once. In an effort to be clear in its resolve, it designed the plan to make sure that stakeholders would receive many mutually reinforcing messages during the launch phase.

Monitoring. As an industry moves toward improved pricing conduct, leaders must continually monitor the situation and be ready to act appropriately to reinforce the benefits of resolve. Occasionally, this may also mean taking steps to counter disruptive behavior. In 1998 price leadership seemed to be working in the U.S. beer industry, with two of the larger breweries taking prices up in most markets. But when one player saw that the other was attacking one of its strongholds by offering discounts, it responded with its own aggressive price promotion in that market. The detractor relented, and prices turned back upward. Other moves that reinforce pricing resolve include writing contract stipulations such as meet-the-competition clauses, in which a company agrees to match lower prices offered by competitors to the customer; and most-favored-customer clauses, in which a company agrees to match lower prices offered by it to other customers.

Resellers. In multitiered distribution environments, a successful price leadership strategy is heavily dependent on resellers supporting the effort

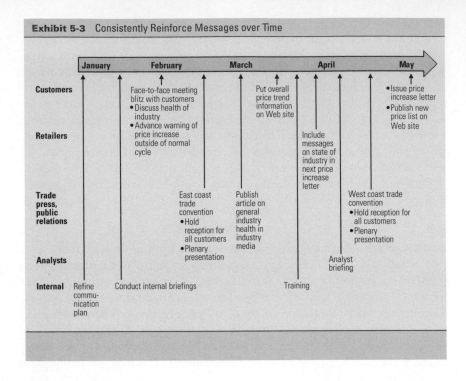

Exhibit 5-3 Consistently Reinforce Messages over Time

or, at least, not derailing it. But retailers, who may not have the same market perspective or information, may have agendas that conflict with those of price-leading suppliers. And, as mentioned earlier, market concentration is making retailers increasingly powerful.

Rather than raising their hands in surrender, suppliers can use a range of tools to influence their resale channels. These include promotional allowances for advertising a product at a certain price level, or end-of-year rebates tied to meeting specific average retail price targets. But market knowledge is often the most powerful tool, as one home appliance maker found.

Catering to the low-end market, this supplier had once commanded very healthy margins on its appliances. But the market changed when a low-priced competitor that could match its performance standards entered. For seven years, the appliance supplier did not raise its prices once. Meanwhile, as raw materials costs rose, the appliance maker began losing money.

To combat this trend, the company took a closer look at its market. Consumer pricing research revealed two attention-grabbing insights. First, even though the two low-cost brands were technically similar, its products had quite strong brand equity—enough to raise prices 10 to 15 percent before its customers began switching. Just as interesting, the research showed that if retailers rebelled against a price hike and dropped the brand, most of their customers would trade up to more expensive models that were less profitable for the retailers. The supplier shared this information with its retail outlets and announced a 10 percent price increase. It also suggested to its retailers that they could raise their prices by 12 to 15 percent without risking volume. The choice was simple: Go along and make more money, or drop the brand and lose money. No retailer opted to drop the brand.

A WORD ON FOLLOWERSHIP

In almost all of the successful cases of price leadership we have seen, one of the top three players in a market was the primary price leader. However, in each case, a key to success was that other companies, large and small, were good followers. These companies played key supporting roles that were essential to achieving overall good pricing conduct. In one case, we saw a company match the leader's price increase within days with an announcement of a price increase that explained its rationale in similar detail. In other cases, followers were the first to rein in the discounting discretion available to the sales force or change the company's objectives from trying aggressively to take share from the leader to increasing profits.

Not everybody can be a leader, but everybody can follow a good leader. This is particularly true at the industry strategy level of pricing. A story from the electronics components industry shows how important faithful followers are to a leader. In a sector plagued by low profitability for several years, one supplier took a brave step in the late 1990s and announced a bold 4 percent price increase. Then it waited. And waited. For two weeks it waited for a key competitor to follow, but nothing happened. So it decided the move was too risky and rescinded the price increase.

Unfortunately, the reason there was no reaction was that the competitor's president, who had the final word on raising prices, was on vacation and so no decision could be made. The president returned and was about to authorize a price increase when word arrived that the first company had taken back its own price hike. Eventually industry prices were brought higher, but the companies lost about six months' worth of increased revenue and higher profits because of the miscue.

Obviously, faithful price followers can support a leader by acting in its own economic self-interest and matching the leader's pricing moves. But as Exhibit 5-4 shows, there are many ways to follow a leader, and some have more impact than others. For example, a company that

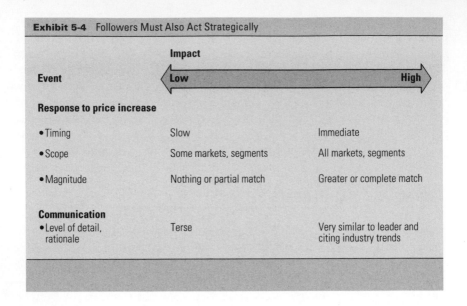

Exhibit 5-4 Followers Must Also Act Strategically

Event	Impact Low ⟷ High	
Response to price increase		
• Timing	Slow	Immediate
• Scope	Some markets, segments	All markets, segments
• Magnitude	Nothing or partial match	Greater or complete match
Communication		
• Level of detail, rationale	Terse	Very similar to leader and citing industry trends

follows slowly or hesitantly can stymie the leader's motivation and commitment. In addition to following the price move itself, followers can support the pricing initiatives internally by maintaining transactional discipline and making sure that sales reps are not attempting to poach accounts aggressively when a competitor may be most vulnerable.

*   *   *

The focus of the industry strategy level is on industrywide price levels and trends. The central issues at this level are predicting industry price trends more accurately; responding to them effectively; and, where possible, influencing them positively. A number of well-documented microeconomic frameworks like industry cost curves and demand analysis can help companies predict price shifts related to structural changes in an industry. Companies that are distinctive at the industry strategy level deliberately invest in gaining deep understanding of the underlying drivers of industry price trends—supply, demand, regulations, costs, and competitors, among others. As a result they predict price shifts better, react to them to their greater advantage, and influence them where possible.

However, the price advantage at this level is more than just mastery of industry structure dynamics. It also entails, as we have shown, being clear on when to lead or follow price moves in the industry. Excellence here requires the creation and support of legally permissible price visibility, common motivation across competitors, and organizational resolve. It re-quires a degree of orchestration throughout the entire organization to as-sure that its actions are consistent and thus the market sees it as an unambiguous price leader or a rational price follower.

Excellence at the industry strategy level forms the foundation of the price advantage. Alone, it can yield multiple percentage points of price in-creases. Furthermore, it decreases the risk of destructive competitive pric-ing actions and creates an environment where the pricing gains generated at the transaction and product/market strategy levels can be sustained.

Special Topics

New Product Pricing

Why do companies habitually undercharge for their hard work? When releasing a new product, they often cede far too much of the value to the market by setting a price that is much lower than the product's enhanced benefits warrant. Indeed, getting the price right for a new product is complex. With revolutionary products, for instance, there is no convenient market reference for guidance, and companies tend toward an overly cautious approach that seems more likely to assure volume targets for the launch are met. For others, production costs might be lower than for the product being replaced, and again the tendency is to be cautious, perhaps using traditional profit margins as a yardstick for setting the new price. And there is often an internal strategic conflict, either visible or below the surface, between rapid share growth or margin maximization.

At the same time, other factors bring additional pressure. Customers, whether businesses or private consumers, expect new products to offer more for less. For example, PC prices have been pushed downward despite increased processor speed, more memory, and other additional features. Throughout consumer electronics and in other high-tech industries the same pattern is evident.

Of course, charging too much for a new offering can also cause problems, but this is relatively rare and more easily corrected by bringing the price to a level the market can accept. As companies have found time and again, once a price hits the market, it is difficult to raise it. In our experience, when a new product pricing error is made, 80 to 90 percent of the time the release price is too low.

Companies have more room to maneuver than they commonly believe, but exploring the space is not easy. Discovering the full breadth of potential price options requires a concerted effort that brings together knowledge drawn from all three levels of price management. Also, new product pricing demands even more intense cross-functional cooperation, bringing together teams from R&D, sales and marketing, finance, and sundry other disciplines.

To begin the discussion, we will look at the pitfalls encountered when pricing a new offering. Next, we will detail a new approach that can help companies avoid these traps and be confident that the release price best reflects the new benefits being offered by the product.

THE NEED FOR A NEW APPROACH

New products are highly visible. Investors, managers, and employees are eager to see signs of success. Unfortunately, the most immediate measurement of success is often sales volume and market share figures, which can lead managers to use a low introductory price. By and large, businesses take a conservative approach to pricing a new product, fearing that too high a price could jeopardize the new product's future. Companies worry that if the price is too high, business may not be won (or indeed may be lost), they may not be able to justify the premium sufficiently, or share growth or market penetration might take too long.

The result is a relatively straightforward, incremental approach that puts the price within a seemingly safe percentage difference to what is already in the market. For B2B products this percentage is often based on differences in costs of production or a narrowly defined view of the added benefits the product offers customers. In consumer markets, companies often focus on a price that is a bit above or below their main competitor's price. Even for truly revolutionary products, there is usually some market reference product that the company uses as a starting point. For example, when laser eye surgery debuted, its price may have been assessed against the lifetime replacement costs of eyeglasses or contact lenses.

Such incremental approaches may underestimate the benefits delivered to customers. For example, one of the first makers of portable bar code readers, devices used in inventory tracking and management, based its release price on the economic improvement resulting from the faster assembly speeds that its product offered manufacturers. The improvements were brought largely by quicker data entry and improved component tracking. Faced by anxious investors, the company also wanted to ensure that it penetrated the market quickly. Using improved assembly times as the yardstick, the company set the price of the portable reader proportionately above that charged for the older, stationary readers.

But the added benefits offered by the portable reader went well beyond incremental improvements in assembly times. It ushered in entirely new business processes by allowing real-time inventory control and improved logistics planning. For many companies, portable bar code readers reduced the need to hold large inventories. They were also a key enabler for such innovations as just-in-time delivery. Buyers quickly recognized these substantial benefits and flocked to the low-priced product, outstripping the company's production capacity. Not only did the company fail to capture the full profit potential of its reader, it also set the enduring customer price expectations for the product at a very low level. With a single bad decision, the company not only reduced its own profitability, but erased more than $1 billion in potential industry profit over the life of the product.

Even with their advanced market research, consumer markets are not immune to the pitfalls. Japanese car maker Mazda introduced its Miata sports car to U.S. markets in 1990. With its retro look, the little roadster captured the imagination of aging baby boomers nostalgic for the classic British MGs and Triumphs of the 1960s and 1970s. As much fun as its British predecessors, but better built and more reliable, the Miata was an instant hit in the United States.

But Mazda grossly underestimated the appeal of the simple, unique Miata. The car maker set the manufacturer's suggested retail price at $13,800, which was disproportionately low for its perceived benefits, as shown in Exhibit 6-1. Mazda dealers were quick to recognize this imbalance, and

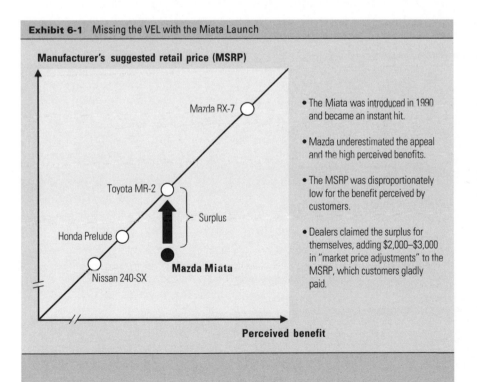

Exhibit 6-1 Missing the VEL with the Miata Launch

Manufacturer's suggested retail price (MSRP)

Mazda RX-7
Toyota MR-2
Surplus
Honda Prelude
Nissan 240-SX
Mazda Miata

Perceived benefit

- The Miata was introduced in 1990 and became an instant hit.
- Mazda underestimated the appeal and the high perceived benefits.
- The MSRP was disproportionately low for the benefit perceived by customers.
- Dealers claimed the surplus for themselves, adding $2,000–$3,000 in "market price adjustments" to the MSRP, which customers gladly paid.

added an extra \$2,000 to \$3,000 to the MSRP in the form of "market price adjustments." Customers willingly paid the higher price, and the dealers eagerly pocketed the surplus for themselves.

In addition, companies often fail to have a clear understanding of the market position their new product will hold. Products entering the market can range from revolutionary to me-too offerings, and each requires a different emphasis and nuanced approach to setting the release price.

LAUNCH POSITION

A critical step—quite often the first stumble—in releasing a new product is to understand the true level of its innovation. Whatever its price category, a product hits the market in one of three positions, as shown in Exhibit 6-2:

1. *Revolutionary.* Products so new that they create their own markets pose the challenge of quantifying the benefits delivered to customers in the absence of anything similar for comparison. Often customers themselves have trouble envisioning the benefits. For the supplier, explaining the product's benefits to an untested market takes skill. A price that is lower than optimal leaves little room for maneuvering and can severely limit an industry's potential profitability. Recent revolutionary products include mobile telephones and personal digital assistants (PDAs).
2. *Evolutionary.* These products include next versions, upgrades, and enhancements to existing products. If the new product provides too many new benefits at too low a price, a price war can ensue, so a firm grasp of potential competitor reactions is essential. It is also critical to make sure that there is a large enough customer base at this new level of benefits. CDs and digital video discs (DVDs) are examples.
3. *Me-too.* These are products that bring a company in line with the rest of the market, without enhancing the customer benefits that are generally available. Careful cost analysis is needed to avoid catastrophe. Finding a profitable niche in an established market and setting a price that does not conflict with brand positioning can also be difficult.

LAUNCH POSITION *(Continued)*

Too often, companies overplay the benefits of a new product, touting it as revolutionary when, at best, it is evolutionary, and rarely acknowledging when they are playing catch-up. But it is critical for a company to make an honest internal assessment of its product's position since each has different priorities in defining an appropriate pricing strategy. As we look at the key elements needed to price a new product, we will highlight areas where launch position can play a decisive role.

Exhibit 6-2 Three New Product Pricing Situations

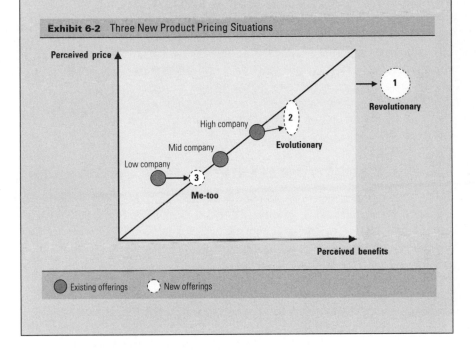

Once the launch position is understood, the company should follow a systematic approach. There are six essential elements that take a company through the process of determining the pricing boundaries, zeroing in on a release price, and executing pricing policy effectively: A company should

■ Assess and quantify benefits.
■ Gauge the market size.
■ Determine the price floor.

- Target a release price.
- Predict competitor response.
- Go to market.

Some elements may carry greater priority, depending on the situation, and some may be addressed simultaneously or in a different order. But whatever the situation, crafting and launching that new product price will require thoughtful preparation, and each element should be considered for maximum impact.

THE SIX ELEMENTS OF NEW PRODUCT PRICING

The six elements of new product pricing can release a company from an incremental mindset that needlessly confines it to a relatively narrow range of price options. They ensure that *every* appropriate price is up for consideration and that prices that are inappropriately low are quickly identified. They also help a company to zero in on the right price, based on its own strategic goals and likely competitor responses, as well as to execute its pricing plan.

ASSESSING AND QUANTIFYING BENEFITS

When launching a new product, a company should clearly assess and quantify the benefits being delivered, as shown in Exhibit 6-3. As discussed in Chapter 4, these benefits can be functional (microprocessor speed for a computer or the flow rate for a pump), process-related (on-line purchase options or a continuously manned call center for technical services), or relationship-based (emotional relevance of the brand or customer loyalty programs). The key is to gather information from the market rather than merely accept internal beliefs. By assessing and quantifying the benefits delivered to customers, a company creates an effective price ceiling, either virtually from scratch with a revolutionary product or in relation to other products already available. This theoretical maximum price may ultimately be unattainable—there may be no market at that price level, it may leave too much room for competitors to enter, or customers may be strong enough to demand a greater share of the value the product creates—but knowing where this ceiling lies opens the discussion to all pricing options.

Of the many standard market research tools available, conjoint or tradeoff analyses are especially useful for judging relative benefits, since both are helpful in making comparisons of similar products. Such assessments can quantify the improvements a product adds for upscale con-

Exhibit 6-3 Pricing a New Product: Understanding the Benefits

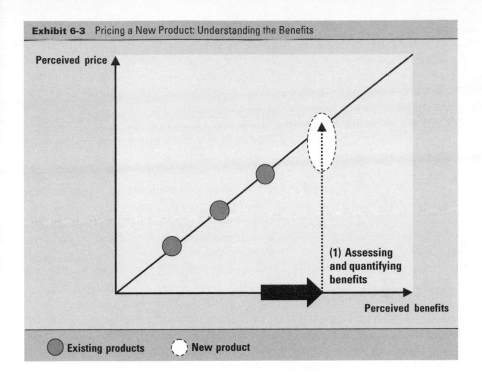

sumers, bargain hunters, or any other market segment relative to what is already being offered. Trade-off analysis can be especially helpful in moving beyond a focus on functional benefits to include process-related and relationship-based benefits, such as how customers feel about using a specific brand. As a new product becomes more revolutionary, providing attributes not yet experienced by the market, conjoint insights are typically less precise.

When exploring attributes that are not familiar to the market, better information can be gathered through a more open-ended approach to market research. Such an approach allows customers the freedom to express their views of a product's benefits, rather than simply responding to the supplier's assumptions. For example, a controls manufacturer developed a high-pressure steam valve for nuclear power plants that was not comparable to anything on the market. When the company first researched the market, it described the benefits and asked customers how much more they would pay for the new valve than their current valves, which were used in low-pressure environments. Most felt a 20 to 25 percent premium was justified.

The company later redid the research, this time asking more open-ended questions to establish how much benefit the new valve would deliver to the business systems of its customers. Instead of first asking them to compare the new valve with an existing one, the company now sought to evaluate the cost of planned maintenance shutdowns, for example, and the role the new valve could play in reducing the number of shutdowns. With a fuller picture of the new benefits—a picture based on the customers' economics—the company again asked how much customers would be willing to pay for them. This time, the customers gave a figure that was several times the price of the existing valve. The supplier had a more accurate picture of its pricing options.

Another technique to gauge the relative benefits of a revolutionary product is to let a trusted customer test it free of charge. This pilot user would then frankly assess and quantify the benefits of the product, giving the supplier candid feedback. Test markets and focus groups can also be helpful.

GAUGING THE MARKET SIZE

The next aspect of defining the boundaries for a new product is sizing up the potential market at the product's level of benefits, as seen in Exhibit 6-4. An accurate assessment of the potential market is not only necessary to determine a product's viability but is also an essential element in analyzing its costs.

While a benefit analysis will tell a company that certain customer segments place a higher value on the benefits offered by the new product, market analysis shows the size of each of these segments. In essence, it asks the question: How big is the potential market at various price points at and below the ceiling?

Not only can segment analysis give a clearer picture of the attractiveness of various pricing levels, it can also warn a company if a product is heading for a dead zone in the market. One computer storage maker decided to develop a lower-priced version of its data network by stripping some of the features from its successful high-end product. When released, however, sales were paltry. The market was polarized between high- and low-end purchasers, and there were very few customers who wanted that mid-range combination of price and benefits. Eventually, it took a closer look at the market segments and developed a much smaller, bare-bones offering at a much lower price (and cost) point that could compete effectively for the low-end market.

As we have seen with the portable bar code reader discussed earlier in the chapter, underestimating a market is also a costly error. When Ford released its first high-end sports utility vehicle (SUV), the Explorer, in 1990,

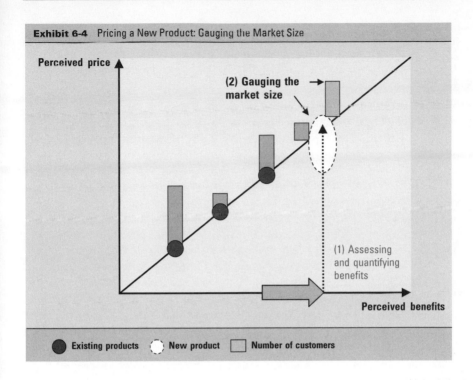

Exhibit 6-4   Pricing a New Product: Gauging the Market Size

the car maker greatly underestimated the benefits of the Explorer's more rugged image and its combination of trucklike characteristics (four-wheel drive, a high driver and passenger compartment) with standard passenger car features (interior space, greater comfort), compared with the SUVs already on the market. When the Explorer hit the market, demand turned out to be more than double the company's original expectations. Ford was caught flat-footed by the success. It had built production capacity based on lower sales forecasts and could not supply the market fast enough. While exposing significant latent demand, misjudging the market gave competitors a chance to scramble to fill customer needs before Ford could take full advantage of its success.

If properly defined, each market segment will be characterized by a distinctive view of a product's benefits and a different price it is willing to pay for those benefits. In addition, market segment analysis can signal whether certain price levels accelerate cannibalization of a company's other products.

PRODUCT CANNIBALIZATION

Cannibalization occurs when one product takes customers away from another product made by the same company. It can be expected in some form with almost any new product. Managers must be clear on how they want to address cannibalization. Here are three typical situations:

1. *Cleaning out the pipeline.* Often when a new product is launched to replace an older version of the product, there is pressure in the system to clean out the inventory pipeline ahead of the launch. From last year's car model to computers that lack the latest processor chip, it is not uncommon to see big price cuts to clear out soon-to-be-obsolete inventories. Two major pitfalls need to be addressed when using this tactic. First, customers will learn to anticipate the price cuts and delay their purchases until end-of-life discounting begins. Second (and much more damaging), big discounts on a new product's previous generation could pull down the VEL and thus the acceptable price for the new model. If a 2003 model has a 10 percent price cut simply to move inventory, the market might expect the 2004 model to debut at a similar level.

2. *Forced phase-out.* In industrial and high-tech environments where multiple generations of systems or versions may exist at the same time, companies may often want to promote the use of the new system and phase out the old one. This could be particularly important to reduce the supplier's maintenance and support costs. There are two common ways to drive this behavior. First, the supplier can simply raise the price of the old version or of servicing the old version. This can be coupled with special buyback or upgrade bonuses to make the transition more palatable. Second, the supplier can impose a time limit for supporting the older version, either in general announcements or as specific contract clauses. Once this limit has passed, the manufacturer would no longer provide customer support or replacement parts.

3. *Coexistence.* Keeping more than one viable version of a product on the market at the same time is the most difficult scenario to manage and runs the greatest risk of unplanned cannibalization. It is also the most common since many companies must have a

PRODUCT CANNIBALIZATION *(Continued)*

steady pipeline of evolutionary products and some overlap is inevitable. Here, segmentation must be used carefully to identify and target unique segments for each version and to minimize the overlap as much as possible. For example, a company may want to put a clear distance between benefit levels of the two products (for instance, offering on-site service for the new version but not the old) or maintain an unmistakable price difference.

Estimating the size of the market at various price points gives direction to the right range of price levels available when releasing a new product. It also promotes better estimates of profitability along the spectrum, as well as more accurate cost estimates.

DETERMINING THE PRICE FLOOR

In addition, a company should determine the absolute price floor, as shown in Exhibit 6-5. A company can fail to analyze correctly which price level is needed to make any money at all from its new product. To build the appropriate floor, a diligent cost-based analysis is necessary. (There is also a price floor that is determined by the market and is revealed through accurate value mapping. Based on the value map, a company would not want to assign a price below a level that would put undue downward pressure on the VEL or breach the zone of credibility. See Chapter 4 for a fuller discussion of these topics.)

Cost-plus pricing is an undernourishing strategy, and when it is used as the only or primary tool for setting a price it is inadequate. Leaning on the cost-plus model can cause a company to overlook entirely the mid and upper limits of its pricing options. But an accurate analysis of costs per unit plus a margin that represents a minimum acceptable ROI shows the company the lowest economically viable price level. If the market cannot bear this price, the company must rethink the product's viability.

Even though the model is well-known, companies often trip up in any of three areas when analyzing costs. First, they do not account for all the costs that should be allocated to a product. For example, R&D expenses associated with a product category, including incomplete and failed projects, and goodwill linked to acquisitions that led directly to the new product are usually overlooked. Such expenses are legitimate items to bring into the cost calculation since they are necessary parts of any

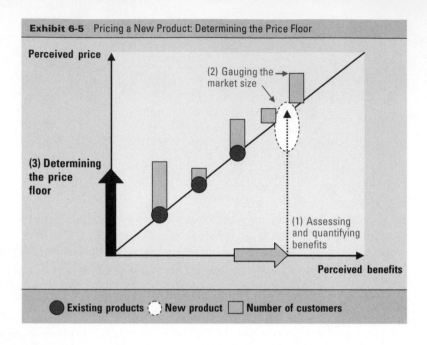

Exhibit 6-5 Pricing a New Product: Determining the Price Floor

development program. Omitting them hides a product's true costs, while accounting for them may influence a company's decision of whether to launch the product at all.

Next, overly optimistic market projections can lead to false cost estimates. One medical products company routinely assumed 70 percent market penetration when analyzing the business case for a new product, even though historically it had held about a 40 percent share for more than a decade, with the exception of short-term market shifts. With each new product, the company believed it would finally secure a dominant position, which often seemed likely at the time of the launch. But once the competition matched the new offering, market shares quickly reverted back to traditional levels. Such rosy assumptions distort fixed-cost allocations in the cost calculations. In a simple illustration, if annual fixed costs were $10 million, costs per unit would be $5 if 2 million units were sold a year, but $10 if only 1 million were sold.

And finally, in contrast to allocating too little of the actual costs, a company may load too much cost onto a new product, making its profitability outlook worse. Common mistakes include burdening a new product with the full weight of the company's overhead costs or, more rarely, allocating too much of the company's R&D expenses. Occasionally, legacy manufacturing inefficiencies can also place a greater cost burden on a new product than appropriate, especially if the new product itself will bring greater production efficiencies.

TARGETING A RELEASE PRICE

With the pricing boundaries established, a company can begin targeting a specific release price, as illustrated in Exhibit 6-6. What exactly is a release price? Simply described, the release price (also know as a launch or target price) for a new product is the price you want the market to associate with that product. In essence, it is the desired perceived price, particularly as compared against the competition. For off-the-shelf products, this would often be a list price, MSRP, or some other bellwether price. For configured systems or products, it could be the perception of the total cost that can be expected for a particular level of functionality. More than any press release, sales pitch, or catalog description, the release price tells the market what a company really thinks a new product is worth.

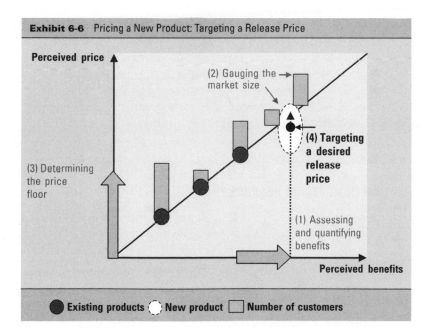

Exhibit 6-6 Pricing a New Product: Targeting a Release Price

One software company learned this lesson when it offered a new data-management system that it said could save large customers hundreds of millions of dollars annually. But to penetrate the market quickly, it released the software with an enterprise-wide license fee of less than $100,000.[1] At this price, the company had breached the zone of credibility and potential customers did not take the claims seriously. If the claims were true, they reasoned, the software package would have been priced in the same range as other ERP packages, which cost $1 million or more.

In creating a release price, a company should try to capture as much of the benefits created by a new product as possible. This price, however, may not be at the top of the range identified when exploring pricing boundaries. In releasing a new product, a company must make an internal assessment about how to divide the value created between itself and its customers. There is no correct formula, and in various situations a supplier may be able to capture as much as 90 percent of the value or as little as 10 percent.

A company must also balance the release price against other objectives, including expected sales and speed of penetration, as well as the market's elasticity to maximize the product's long-term potential. The impact of the new product's price on the company's other products or its brand reputation are also necessary considerations. Even at the lower end of the market, a company with a premium image would probably want to price its products higher than the competition.

And particularly for evolutionary products, the release price should help communicate a company's general market strategy in releasing a new product. A price that is seen by rivals as too low compared to the benefits offered, or value-advantaged, may imply that the company is hoping to steal market share, and thus may trigger a price war. A higher release price, closer to the existing VEL, would suggest a company is targeting profit rather than market share, and could lead to little if any immediate competitor reaction.

PREDICTING COMPETITOR RESPONSE

For evolutionary and me-too products, a clear evaluation of likely competitor response is necessary to prevent a new product's price from destroying value for the company and for the entire industry. A release price that is

---

[1]The company considered this an "at-cost" price, but it actually underestimated its true costs.

PENETRATION PRICING

With every new product, companies feel tempted to build volume quickly through aggressively low prices—a tactic known as penetration pricing. But a fixation on volume usually sacrifices profitability and may ignite a price war. As a result, it is generally better to keep upward pressure on prices and to promote good industry pricing behavior. But on rare occasions, the price lever may be the right tool to undercut the competition.

High Customer Benefits, Elasticity

The first such occasion occurs in new or underdeveloped markets in which there is a mix of high customer benefits perception and high elasticity. If a supplier can build a footprint in such a market quickly, ahead of competition, it can disproportionately tap into latent demand, grow its share, and establish itself as the market leader. Price can be the best mechanism for this strategy. This play works especially well in a market that does not have established product standards and where switching costs are high once entrenched.

This strategy can be risky, however. If consumer choice is driven primarily by benefits rather than price, penetration pricing will only be destructive. Many examples exist in the consumer luxuries, media, high-tech, and pharmaceutical industries where a supplier has priced a new offering aggressively to build share, then lost this share when a competitor released a newer, slightly better product. If a market is focused on content, technical efficacy, or brand appeal, a supplier can needlessly push price expectations lower and forfeit profit by pursuing penetration pricing.

Cost-to-Serve Advances

The next situation occurs when a supplier's cost-to-serve declines sharply and rapidly with volume growth, often because of economies of scale or a learning-curve effect. As volume increases, fixed and variable costs per unit drop, pushing margins higher over time.

But often, as market share grows, competitors quickly react, using low prices to enter the market or minimize their own market share loss. Shared learning from the leading player allows them to reduce their

(Continued)

PENETRATION PRICING *(Continued)*

own cost structure quickly. This can bring continuous downward pressure on prices. Also, as we have already seen, extreme care must be taken if the core driver of acceptance is benefits rather than price.

Limited capacity is another pitfall that can trap a company chasing low costs-to-serve. If penetration pricing ignites demand that cannot be met, the supplier is injured twice. First, margin was lost needlessly because available supplies could have been sold at a higher price. Also, delivery delays or failures could torpedo customer satisfaction, one factor in overall benefit perceptions.

Weak Competition

Penetration pricing could also be appropriate if competitors are structurally unable to match a price because they have higher cost structures or are locked into channel agreements that limit their pricing freedom. In the basic materials industry, Asian and Eastern European suppliers were frequently able to capture market share through penetration pricing once their purity and logistics reached minimal standards, because their low labor and other input costs could not be matched by producers in developed countries.

too low will likely spark a destructive price war. Competitors can rarely react immediately by matching the added benefits offered by a new product, so their sole option to defend their market is often a price cut, as shown in Exhibit 6-7. (Ways to gauge probable competitive response to a price move are discussed in Chapter 4.)

Particularly for evolutionary products, setting a low release price relative to the new benefits position is likely to be viewed as an aggressive move to capture market share and will usually trigger strong competitive reactions. A price that stays within the zone of indifference along the VEL, resulting in a percentage point or two shift in market share, is much less likely to be seen as a threat. If the zone of indifference is large, this can offer a new product a broad range of pricing options before it even shows up on the market's radar screen.

Companies releasing revolutionary products (and to a lesser extent evolutionary products) must gauge how quickly others might enter the market,

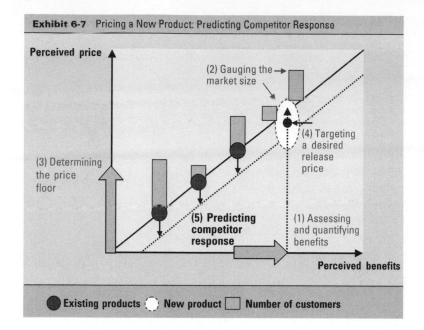

Exhibit 6-7 Pricing a New Product: Predicting Competitor Response

Perceived price

(2) Gauging the market size

(3) Determining the price floor

(4) Targeting a desired release price

(5) Predicting competitor response

(1) Assessing and quantifying benefits

Perceived benefits

● Existing products ◌ New product ☐ Number of customers

and whether their pricing strategy leaves too much room for attackers. For example, a high-tech product might have a substantial early-adapter segment that is willing to pay a premium to be the first with a product, and a company might set a high release price with gradual, planned reductions to attract latecomers ahead of new market entrants. But if, after careful analysis, a company believes an attacker can follow into the market too quickly with similar costs, a better strategy may be to focus immediately on the latecomer segment, leaving less room for the attacker.

GOING TO MARKET

At the launch, presenting the price to the market requires astute communications and patience, as shown in Exhibit 6-8. Especially with revolutionary products, companies must carefully articulate the benefits of the new item to a market that is often quite skeptical. But whatever position a new product faces, a company must be careful not to let its value message be undermined by faulty execution of its pricing strategy.

The first six to twelve months that a new product is on the market are critical to establishing its value position. During this period especially, companies must keep firm control of their pricing operations, all the way

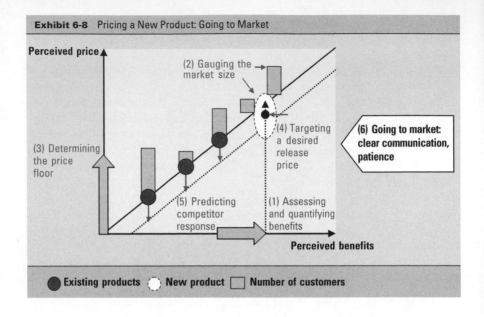

Exhibit 6-8   Pricing a New Product: Going to Market

down to individual transactions. Discounting or special price promotions, for example, which could be routine on existing product lines, could undermine the release price of a new product.

But if managers see the need to push a product into the market faster, there are ways that do not sacrifice the release price or the market's value perception. Three of the more common are to give it to a small group of customers who have a high profile or significant market influence, to offer free samples, and to offer a free trial period. Each of these speed market penetration without establishing a lower release price. Standard discounts or rebates are usually a mistake, since they effectively lower the release price and raise doubts about the benefits claimed by the product.

Other marketing methods—from piloting the product in isolated test markets to partnered product development with a key customer—can also give managers added confidence in their benefits analysis and price decisions.

*   *   *

Companies must be patient and resolute when bringing a new product to market. Some internal and external observers will be pushing for faster penetration and criticizing a product's seemingly high price as an obstacle to a fast ROI improvement. At the same time, customers will be pressuring for lower prices, and competitors may be making threatening noises. But by systematically defining and understanding the market boundaries, by targeting an appropriate release price based on benefits delivered, by anticipating competitor reaction, and by charting an optimal rollout plan, managers can be secure in their decisions. Such fact-based confidence can allow them to ride out the initial turbulence and use their price advantage to claim the true value of the product they created.

CHAPTER 7

Solutions, Bundles, and Other Packaged Offerings

In the modern marketplace, you do not have to look far before bumping into a *solution*. Increasingly popular, solutions are being touted in almost every business. There are IT solutions and transportation solutions, logistics solutions and energy solutions, and even home-dining solutions. The term seems to pop up in any venue where a supplier offers anything to a customer.

What is the allure? First, of course, there is the marketing message that says: We offer more than just a product or service; we offer something the others don't; we offer a *solution*. Appealing to a customer's desire to have a problem solved—whether the problem centers on data storage or what to eat tonight—can be very effective. Behind the marketing message, however, there is an underlying belief that if a supplier can actually deliver a solution, it will form a closer business relationship with its customers that will result in increased sales and higher margins.

What does success look like? IBM started a revolution in 1991 when it launched its Global Services business. Beginning with a set of specific, integrated business offerings targeted to well-defined market segments—for instance, a customer-relationship-management (CRM) system for a retail bank—IBM did something new: It took complete responsibility for an operational system, from design to installation through ongoing support. This included responsibility for all of the hardware, software, and service elements of that system, whether they came from IBM or its partners. The packages were unique, and IBM used technical professionals who understood the business implications in detail to sell them.

In delivering the solutions, the company also avoided two common traps. First, it did not try to provide everything to everybody, which would have left it distinctive at nothing. And second, it did not try to slip inferior products or services into the bigger package.

For IBM, the key to unlocking the additional value came through effective pricing. First, it defined, quantified, and communicated the economic value created by its solutions—customer by customer. Then it developed a pricing approach that equitably shared this value over the life of the solution. As a result, by 2000 the solutions business was the primary driver behind more than 70 percent of IBM's growth, had added about $9 billion in gross profit to the bottom line, and helped IBM stock outperform the Dow Jones Industrial Average by a factor of three.

It is rare to find a company that delivers a true solution. Rarer still is the solutions provider that is making money off its efforts. The missing link is often an appropriate pricing strategy. The price must accurately reflect the benefits delivered by the package, which requires that a company understand that not all offers combining more than one product or service are solutions. Other roles—bundlers and integrators—can also be profitable, but the key is to be honest about the role you are playing and then to tie your pricing strategy to your assessment of the perceived benefits being delivered.

WHAT IS A SOLUTION?

In our view, a company provides a solution when it has taken responsibility for a specific business need that is unique to a customer, by providing an integrated, customized package of discrete components, such as hardware, software, and services, that have been engineered or tailored to work better together than separately. The litmus test for a true solution should be that it creates at least 50 percent more economic benefits than the next-best alternative.

To put this view of a solution into context, contrast it with the three other potential roles a supplier can play, as illustrated in Exhibit 7-1. A company that sells discrete products or services, even when customized to fit a particular customer need, is a component specialist. One that aggregates a set of discrete components and sells them as a package is a bundler. And finally, a company that sells integration or customization services, even to the point of designing and installing a functional system, but does not take on full responsibility for the package, is an integrator.

No role is better or worse than another, and there are profitable companies in each. Underlying each role is a different business model that will profitably meet the needs of a specific group of customers when delivered well.

Exhibit 7-1   The Four Supplier Roles

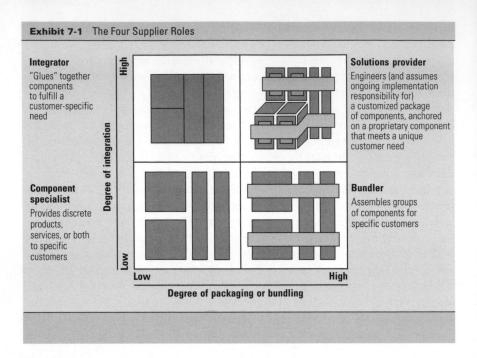

Integrator
"Glues" together components to fulfill a customer-specific need

Solutions provider
Engineers (and assumes ongoing implementation responsibility for) a customized package of components, anchored on a proprietary component that meets a unique customer need

Component specialist
Provides discrete products, services, or both to specific customers

Bundler
Assembles groups of components for specific customers

Degree of integration — High / Low

Degree of packaging or bundling — Low / High

Our experience shows that companies that offer true solutions can command margins 20 percent higher[1] than their competitors or more. However, the risks are also significant, either of offering a solution and failing to deliver on the promise or of failing to capture the true value of the solution. In either case, mistakes are rarely minor. We have seen that more than 75 percent of the companies that try to offer solutions fail to recover even their initial investments.

A successful example of building a solutions business comes from a leading player in the automotive coatings sector, which includes paints, laminates, and other spray-on applications. This company developed a process with which it could manage the coating operation and optimize the application of different colors at varying thicknesses, even in build-to-order systems, by vertically integrating into the original car manufacturers' plants. As car makers began turning to it to run their coatings operations, the coatings company was able to charge by the car, rather than by the

---

[1]Although we believe the benefits delivered by a true solutions provider should be at least 50 percent above the nearest competitor, companies would rarely be able to extract the full value of these additional benefits from their customers through similar premiums.

liters of paint used. Working at a number of plants over several years, the company was able to reduce the coating consumption per car by more than 20 percent in some cases. The key to the solution's profitability was crafting a pricing strategy that allowed it to keep a fair share of these savings for itself. As the business model evolved, it eventually captured much more than 60 percent of the global market share for this class of coatings solutions business.

Another company, this one a global lubricants producer, took a different tack. Faced with tough competition for its traditional lubricants and additives businesses, the company tried to expand its value proposition by selling solutions. To do this, it acquired a series of businesses—primarily service businesses specializing in areas like environmental auditing and technical testing—to complement its robust product line. After spending more than $100 million on the acquisitions, the company went to its largest customers with its new solution offer: a full suite of services that covered lubrication needs from application to disposal.

Unfortunately, the offer was not a truly integrated solution and was easily unbundled. Faced with the possibility of losing high-volume customers, the company acquiesced. Rather than pricing to capture the value of the package provided, the company agreed to throw in its newly acquired services for free. The value destruction was enormous. From a core business with an ROS of about 5 percent, it had added acquisitions with ROS's of about 15 percent, but in the end the company's ROS fell to even less than the original 5 percent. The company may have been better off keeping the service businesses separate but part of an integrated offering, rather than trying to bundle them into a solution. To succeed with a solution offer, the company may have wanted to make a bolder move—for instance, taking over an entire process from its customers—and then to stand firm under pressure to unbundle the offer. A key question, though, is whether its largest customers wanted such a solution.

As these cases help illustrate, a true solution can only be successful if the supplier clearly understands how the new offer creates benefits and how that affects its role in the value chain. Also, once a company is clear on its new role, it must price appropriately, and with conviction, in order to capture the value of its solution.

SEVERAL RELATIONSHIP OPTIONS

As we saw earlier, a true solution is one of a quartet of relationships a supplier can have with its customers. The type of relationship that is appropriate (and carries the highest potential) depends primarily on how much packaging or bundling the customer wants and on the amount of product and service integration that is necessary.

The matrix shown in Exhibit 7-1 highlights four distinct roles for the supplier: component specialist, bundler, integrator, and solutions provider. While these terms are used often in business circles, there is rarely a common understanding of their meanings, even within the same company. A common definition is important because each role prescribes a unique pricing approach. A company that offers true solutions but charges like a components specialist is giving away an extraordinary amount of value. On the other hand, a bundler that presents its offering as a premium-priced solution risks delivering benefits below its promises, alienating customers, and destroying value.

COMPONENT SPECIALIST

A component specialist is the most basic type of relationship between buyer and seller. For the most part, a component supplier offers stand-alone products or services that are sold to the customer directly or through a channel partner. A customer ordering widgets gets widgets. They may be off-the-shelf or customized to match a specific need, but the customer still pays for and gets widgets. A customer wanting standard maintenance service gets that service. The benefits delivered by these components, whether products or services, rest on the discrete functional features and other attributes of that component. Although extras such as shipping or financing may be part of individual transactions, these additions are tangential to the core business of a component specialist.

BUNDLER

A bundler also offers components but, unlike a components specialist, it offers additional benefits as a single-source provider across a wide range of components and by offering lower prices through its own volume discounts and other cost advantages to the customer. This offering is standard for all customers whether the bundle comprises products and services, such as a pizza shop that offers home delivery within 30 minutes, or a package of products, such as a distributor offering a range of garden supplies.

Components offered by bundlers may be produced by the bundlers themselves or by other companies. Along with distributors and pizza-delivery shops, grocery stores, wholesalers, and multi-product manufacturers are common examples of bundlers.

INTEGRATOR

Integrators provide the knowledge to make a group of components work together. The components could be collected by their customers, built by the integrator itself, purchased by the integrator from third parties, or some combination. The key value they add is the ability to put the pieces together and make them work for specific customers.

An example of an integrator would be a wedding planner, who brings all the pieces together—the caterers, the florists, the photographers, and others—and coordinates and manages the whole event. A B2B example is a software integrator, who puts together various components to create a functional system that matches a customer's needs.

SOLUTIONS PROVIDER

Solutions providers work collaboratively with their customers to solve a specific business need. There are three characteristics necessary to constitute a true solution:

- A proprietary component that is a core driver of the value creation.
- The ability to engineer the components to work together seamlessly.
- The assumption of ongoing implementation responsibility.

Bringing these three characteristics to the table, a solutions provider offers truly differentiated benefits compared with the next-best alternative. Simply put, if a business turns to a solutions provider to meet a specific need, the accountability for making the solution work is clear. If all goes well, the benefits added by the solutions provider can be discretely quantified and apportioned between the two parties as agreed. If the solution does not work, the solutions provider is accountable. Because of this, a solutions provider is held to a higher standard. The benefits offered by a solution must be clearly identifiable and measurable, and the price must reflect how that value is shared between customer and supplier.

FALSE SOLUTIONS PROVIDERS

At this point, it may be useful to look at why, despite legitimate aspirations, bundlers and integrators are not true solutions providers. In fact, businesses could destroy value rapidly if they try to market themselves inappropriately as solutions providers and charge a solutions premium. A pizza delivery service does not provide a home-dining solution. Although bundling the pizza and the delivery adds benefits for the customer, it does not offer a holistic, customized approach to fulfilling a customer's need for a meal. A true home-dining solutions provider would understand a customer's tastes, provide a menu that matches those tastes, and handle the entire process from setting the table to putting away the clean dishes. Rather than catering to individual needs, bundlers are customer segmenters, offering a standard set of components that, when combined, offers distinct benefits to a specific group of customers, such as young, price-sensitive diners wanting to stay home.

Integrators, since they do add the intellectual glue that brings components together, are even more prone to think of themselves as holistic solutions providers. While an integrator might work closely with a customer to, for example, install a software system, it focuses on a narrower slice of a project than a solutions provider would and usually does not take full responsibility for the completed system. A software integrator that installs an optional network security program during the course of a project may want to be seen as a solutions provider, but merely adding a component to an integrative service does not create a solution.

Beyond the risk of not meeting the promise of providing a solution, an integrator marketing itself as a solutions provider also risks losing much of the value of its knowledge. If a business bundles its knowledge with a few readily available components, it will likely find it difficult to articulate the benefits of that knowledge to customers. By separating the two parts of the value proposition—much as a mechanic charging for labor and parts individually—a business can discuss more clearly the benefits of its knowledge.

PRICING BY SUPPLIER ROLE

While a company can be quite successful in any relationship with its customers, the core business drivers of each role are fundamentally different, which leads to unique implications for pricing. Exhibit 7-2 lists some of the more common pricing mechanisms for each of the four supplier roles.

COMPONENT SPECIALIST

Being an effective components specialist means managing the value map against other component providers. A supplier that produces components that are perceived as value-advantaged over its competitors and pursues operational excellence to maintain its margins could successfully sustain this model for the natural life cycle of its products.

The pricing implications for component specialists are also straightfor-

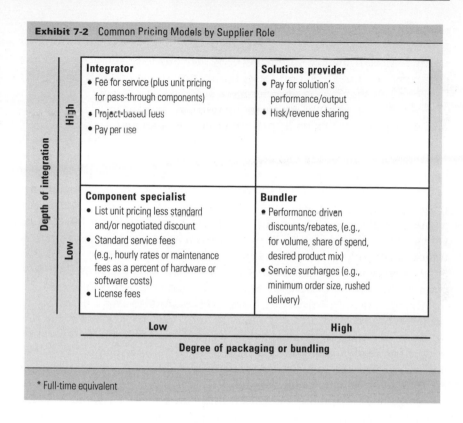

Exhibit 7-2   Common Pricing Models by Supplier Role

	Low	High
High	**Integrator** • Fee for service (plus unit pricing for pass-through components) • Project-based fees • Pay per use	**Solutions provider** • Pay for solution's performance/output • Risk/revenue sharing
Low	**Component specialist** • List unit pricing less standard and/or negotiated discount • Standard service fees (e.g., hourly rates or maintenance fees as a percent of hardware or software costs) • License fees	**Bundler** • Performance driven discounts/rebates, (e.g., for volume, share of spend, desired product mix) • Service surcharges (e.g., minimum order size, rushed delivery)

Depth of integration

Degree of packaging or bundling

* Full-time equivalent

ward. Price levels and price models are geared to capture a discrete return from the benefits delivered to each customer, often in direct relation to a competitor's offer or a next-best alternative. Usually, if the component is a product, this means there is some form of standard or list price, often with the possibility of a discount (or in rare instances a surcharge) based on the perceived benefits of competing offers. If the discrete component is a service, there is typically a standard rate, such as a rate based on time worked or, for system maintenance service, a percentage of the list price of the hardware and software being maintained. Discounts off this standard rate are also commonplace for services.

BUNDLER

A supplier in the lower right corner of our relationship matrix adds more and more products or services to the portfolio offered to customers. As customers spend more on purchases from this supplier, they will want relatively lower unit prices. From the supplier's perspective, success is driven by reducing net costs more than the price cuts demanded by its customers, while at the same time driving volume higher. These cost reductions are spurred by many factors—among others, the volume-driven price cuts it is getting from its own suppliers and the reduced costs-to-serve because of larger order volumes from its customers.

As long as a supplier appreciates that in bundling the goal is to use volume increases to cut its own costs, the role can be quite lucrative. Too often, however, bundlers make one of two mistakes. First, in their eagerness to capture a greater share of a customer's wallet, they assume that they can keep the same price levels, or even get higher prices, because they offer one-stop convenience to their customers. But bundlers can rarely hold the line on prices, because their customers understand that their own power increases in tandem with their order volume. Also, added convenience is a soft argument that is difficult to quantify with hard cost savings to the customer, and therefore difficult to sell.

In a more insidious trap, many bundlers inadvertently allow their own costs to rise because of new needs associated with delivering a bundled offering. For example, acquisitions and R&D efforts may be necessary to complete the bundled offering. Or, if the offering includes more complex products, there could be additional costs associated with administration and logistics or training staff to handle and sell the new lines. In this case, volumes may go up, but costs are rising while unit prices are falling—altogether a questionable business model.

One bundler handling industrial parts watched as a seemingly sound strategy to promote increased volume was torpedoed by additional costs. The supplier offered its largest customers increased rebates if they agreed to bigger volume commitments. Many customers took the offer eagerly. Unfortunately, the offer was driven by total volume, with no stipulations regarding order size or complexity. Volume increased by more than 10 percent, but individual orders became smaller and more complex. Overall, costs-to-serve almost doubled, and the bundler began losing money on some of its largest customers. To stop the hemorrhaging, the company instituted a surcharge on small orders. Customers either began ordering in bigger lot sizes, such as full truckloads, which reduced the cost to serve, or paid a premium for ordering smaller lots. When the new policy was rolled out, the customer defection rate did not increase.

The appropriate choice of pricing architecture is critical for a bundler as it works to lower its own costs and increase volume. Four objectives stand out. The bundler must create an architecture that promotes increased volume, encourages purchases of higher-margin items, and leads to cost-effective ordering behavior. As a final objective, the bundler must also make sure that it collects the premium due for the benefit-advantaged components being sold. (For a detailed description of pricing architecture see Chapter 12.)

INTEGRATOR

For an integrator, the challenge is to price the glue that makes a series of components at the core of a distinctive benefit delivery work together. These components can come from a range of suppliers or even from the customer itself. An integrator maintains the flexibility to choose from a host of qualified component providers, and the costs of these components are typically passed through directly to the customer, occasionally with a markup. Ultimate responsibility for component performance remains with the component vendors, and ongoing responsibility for the complete package remains with the customer. Therefore, an integrator cannot lay claim to a portion of the ongoing benefits created.

A good example of excellent integrator pricing is shown by a global automotive supplier that makes engine and power train components. Over time, the company developed such distinctive expertise in the design and fine-tuning of engine and power train systems that it created a separate division to provide those services to car manufacturers. With no credible competition, even from the car makers' own product development groups, the supplier was able to charge a substantial fee for this service. From the outset, the automotive supplier chose not to link this service business to its component businesses, for instance by offering a "total engine solution," because it feared its high-volume customers would pressure it into giving away the value-added service in order to maintain their large component orders.

An integrator's pricing model should link pricing to the benefits delivered by the service, rather than to the people who are delivering the service. Instead of the time-based rates charged by general service providers, an integrator should typically quote prices on a per-project or per-usage basis. If a project is priced based on the people involved, the integrator opens the door to aggressive price negotiation by customers who could scrutinize each individual on the integrator's team. The integrator would find it difficult to hold fast on its aggregate fee structure as a customer pushes for a smaller team, a team with a larger share of junior (and less expensive) employees, or to substitute its own employees for some team members. Not only would the integrator's price suffer in this situation, but, since the optimal team is being redesigned as a result of these negotiations, the project could take longer to complete and the quality of the final product could be lower.

SOLUTIONS PROVIDER

The unique role of a solutions provider allows it to discuss and push pricing in a way fundamentally different from other supplier roles. Component specialists, bundlers, and integrators price relative to alternatives. However, a true solutions provider can set price to capture its due share of customer-specific economic value created.

The benefits delivered in solutions are much greater than the sum of the component parts and will vary greatly from one customer to the next. A solutions provider must also gain an intimate understanding of its customers' economics and the benefits delivered on an ongoing basis, which may be a new and unfamiliar skill for traditional suppliers.

For example, one storage network provider offered customer-specific solutions that combined core and periphery hardware, operating and application software, and professional design services. Leveraging proprietary components, including servers and software, and distinctive engineering capability, the supplier could demonstrate that the benefits of the total solution were at least twice as great as the nearest competitor's, allowing the supplier to stand firm on a combined system price that was 30 to 50 percent higher.[2]

As we have seen, a solution's price cannot be calculated simply by summing the pieces. In the same vein, communications with customers regarding the price cannot be linked to individual components. Since solutions tend to be expensive and attract attention from top management within the customer's organization, suppliers must carefully develop a clear message that continuously focuses on total benefits being delivered and discourages component-to-component benefit discussions.

Because solutions are tailored to individual customers, the benefits being delivered and hence the price charged can also vary widely. For the storage network provider described earlier, much of the core platform of its offering to customers was the same, but the benefits of a fully functional storage network are much greater for one customer than another. For instance, an online retailer or a bank handling real-time automated teller machine (ATM) or credit card transactions has a critical need for reliable, real-time data storage, while the need is less pressing, for instance, for a hospital or a government agency that must process large volumes of data but can do it during off-peak hours. Pursuing identical pricing strategies in such different worlds of benefit delivery would probably leave significant money on the table.[3]

---

[2]Often total benefits delivered is a starting point for price negotiations. In the end, the additional value is usually shared between the buyer and seller.

[3]While we have focused on the pricing issues faced by solutions providers, fuller discussions of how to create a solutions business are available in two articles: Daniel G. Doster and Eric V. Roegner, "Setting the Pace with Solutions," *Marketing Management*, Vol. 9, No. 1 (Spring 2000), 51–54; and Juliet E. Johansson, Chandru Krishnamurthy, and Henry E. Schlissberg, "Solving the Solutions Problem," *The McKinsey Quarterly*, 2003, No. 3, 117–125.

There are three additional pricing challenges that a solutions provider faces. First, it should appropriately configure the price of the solutions offering. All too often, solutions providers err when configuring their price by simply forgetting portions of the offering or miscalculating the business risk they assume when taking on implementation responsibility.

Second, it should carefully handle the increased complexity of the pocket price waterfall. Because of the complexity of a solution, the pocket price waterfall must take into account multiple pricing elements that will vary over time—for instance, updated software, replacements, expansions, or maintenance services. When crafting the pocket price waterfall, companies should take care not to compromise future revenue streams. Similarly, since solutions are commonly delivered and implemented over longer periods of time, it is critical that companies shape the evolution of ongoing revenue following the sale.

And finally, a solutions provider must also manage the profitability of the solution following the sale. As the pocket margin waterfall in Exhibit 7-3 shows, there will be many customer-specific costs that can quickly escalate out of control if not actively managed, resulting in a pocket margin much lower than originally anticipated. For example, a pricing model must

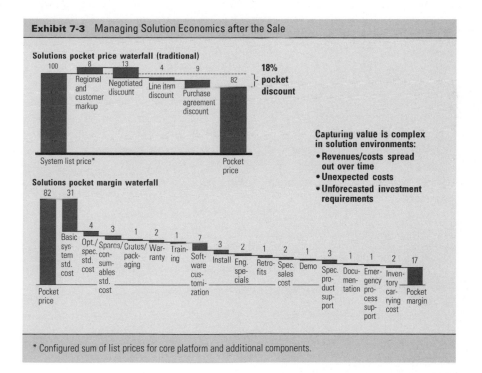

Exhibit 7-3   Managing Solution Economics after the Sale

Solutions pocket price waterfall (traditional)

18% } pocket discount

Capturing value is complex in solution environments:
• Revenues/costs spread out over time
• Unexpected costs
• Unforecasted investment requirements

Solutions pocket margin waterfall

* Configured sum of list prices for core platform and additional components.

allow payments for customer-requested moves, adds, or changes (MACs) that would otherwise simply be absorbed by the supplier.

There are several imperatives a solutions provider must keep in mind when constructing its price strategy:

- Quantify and communicate the solution's economic value to your customers' key decision makers.
- Price the offering to capture your rightful share of the solution's economic value.
- Do not disaggregate the price since the value delivered is greater than the sum of the parts.
- Make the price specific to each customer.
- Actively manage delivery economics following the sale.

*   *   *

The task of pricing a solution or other integrated package can be one of the most challenging and rewarding in the pricing arena. From honestly assessing the supplier role played and pricing accordingly, to assembling a deep understanding of each customer's business needs, the effort requires careful planning, thoughtful analysis, and rigorous execution. But painstaking, proactive management can mean the difference between pricers who come home heroes or villains.

Four

Unique Events

CHAPTER 8

Postmerger Pricing

Most large and mid-size companies will eventually face a merger or acquisition. Whether the goal is to move into other geographic markets; to acquire technology, product lines, or capabilities; or to find operational synergies and lower costs, mergers and acquisitions (M&A) hold great potential for improving profitability, but unfortunately many fail to meet these expectations.[1] Although there are many reasons M&A activities fail, one persistent problem is a disconcertingly lax approach to pricing. Despite the enormous potential to use pricing to drive value, many otherwise rigorous postmerger integration efforts do not put pricing high on the agenda.

Pricing opportunities can contribute as much as 30 percent of postmerger synergies, but they rarely attract the same attention as other potential synergies from the armies of investment bankers, senior managers, accountants, and consultants that swarm over each M&A. Why not? First, these teams are focused on the more traditional synergies brought by M&A, such as reorganization and overall cost-cutting. But also, as we have stressed throughout this book, pricing is generally misunderstood. M&A teams may avoid pricing issues because they incorrectly think pricing opportunities are limited to across-the-board price increases that make headline news, raise regulatory concerns, and alienate customers. In the end, many simply expect market forces to equilibrate prices automatically.

Postmerger pricing involves delving into the details of the pricing policies of the two merged companies to assure that new policies reflect any

---

[1]A recent McKinsey study found that 58 percent of mergers in the United States actually shrink shareholders' interests in the acquiring company and 33 percent ultimately destroy value in the combined entity.

change in the company's value proposition to customers, reconcile different discount approaches, and support a new price architecture that may result from changes in operations and distribution. The goal of postmerger pricing is not to use the merger to obscure price increases, but rather to ensure that the very synergies targeted by the merger are revealed and realized, which benefits not only stockholders and employees but also customers, who should receive greater value from the merged company. Postmerger pricing gains are not automatic, but managers who proactively seek pricing opportunities after a merger are often richly rewarded.

A TEMPORARY WINDOW OF OPPORTUNITY

All aspects of postmerger integration must be tailored to creating a winning company and not simply to getting the merger done quickly. Setting aspirations, identifying value drivers, creating organizational effectiveness, and even designing the integration approach itself require rigorous execution. But along with putting these difficult tasks on the agenda, a merger opens a window of opportunity for change. The period after a merger is a rare moment to review pricing without the usual internal and external resistance. It is a time during which customers, employees, and competitors expect change and are likely to accept any move as just one of the many adjustments triggered by a merger. But the window can close quickly, and the moment is lost.

CUSTOMERS

During a normal business period, customers are generally skeptical of pricing changes. After a merger, however, customers expect changes in many aspects of the new company including staff, structure, value proposition, product line, and pricing. This expectation provides an opportunity to devise and implement the most advantageous pricing approach, focusing on moving prices up to the highest appropriate price rather than down to the lowest.

For example, a company's published schedule of terms, conditions, and discounts could represent a rich opportunity, particularly if sales are through intermediaries such as retailers, wholesalers, and distributors, since these schedules tend to be very complex. When two industrial equipment companies merged recently, they compared their schedules and discovered great differences in the terms and conditions that each offered their distributors. In particular, they charged different interest rates for financing dealer inventories, they had different volume discount hurdles, and they offered different rebates for cooperative advertising.

In normal circumstances, the two companies would have had difficulties convincing their distributors that changes in the terms and conditions were needed, but because of the merger, customers understood that the companies had to rectify policy discrepancies. In addition, the newly merged company made the changes more palatable by announcing them in a comprehensive communications package that outlined all the benefits distributors would gain from the company's new pricing strategy. The company explained that for distributors the changes in terms and conditions would be more than offset by changes in the distribution structure. Overlapping territories would be eliminated, and the distributors that remained would benefit from greater volume. These modifications to terms and conditions resulted in ROS rising almost two percentage points, while overall volume remained stable.

However, the opportunity is fleeting. Once customers and distributors start to buy the combined product line from the new company, usually within six to twelve months after the merger closes, they begin to accept whatever terms, conditions, and discounts are offered as the new pricing model. Once the opportunity passes, a company will face much more resistance to change. Companies needing more time to consolidate pricing structures can keep the window open a little longer by delaying the publication of the new schedules, but even then the opportunity will not last indefinitely.

EMPLOYEES

Like most customers, employees whose jobs are linked directly to pricing policies—product managers, sales reps, controllers, and many others—are sometimes resistant to price changes. Altering the price structure raises a host of sensitive issues. Who has the authority to grant discounts? Who collects and analyzes account information? These decisions can affect a product manager trying to grow a brand, a sales rep trying to make a commission, and a general manager trying to secure profit for the shareholders. Not only do prices have a direct bearing on the corporate success of these employees, but these employees are key to implementing any policy change. It is their cumulative behavior, guided by high-level policies, that results in a company's net realized prices.

Although employees are generally nervous following a merger, particularly if job cuts are on the table, there is also a sense of anticipation that can be used as a catalyst for change. After a merger, employees expect some change in pricing, and resolving conflicting price policies can be one of the first tangible examples of the merging companies working together. Unless the two companies' operations remain separate, some change in pricing practice is inevitable. Either the practices and policies from one of the companies will be adopted, a hybrid model will be implemented, or a completely new model will be created.

In an effort similar to what should be occurring in other policy areas, the newly merged company must analyze each company's pricing methods, procedures, and information to create the optimal structure. Exhibit 8-1 shows the pocket price waterfalls for two pulp and paper companies. Comparing similar products that were viewed as commodities, one company was netting a pocket price that was almost 5 percent more than the other. This insight gave the new company the impetus to evaluate critically its entire pricing architecture to ensure that the merged company would achieve the highest possible pocket prices.

Following a merger or acquisition, the companies involved should move quickly to understand each other's pricing process, to identify gaps and inconsistencies, and to create a unified policy. Not only will employees soon accept whatever policies are in place as the status quo, regardless of whether they were deliberately chosen, but during the period of uncertainty both companies could lose some of their sales momentum if sales reps must wait too long for their new marching orders.

Exhibit 8-1   Postmerger Insight on Pricing Differences

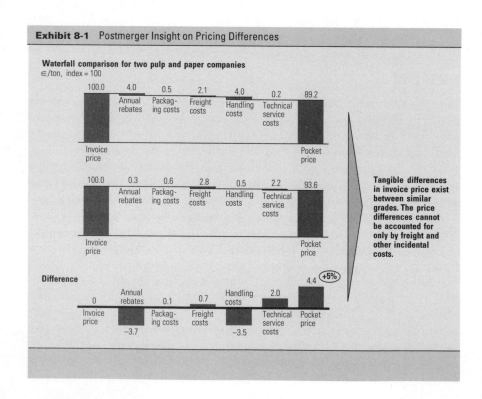

COMPETITORS

Mergers also open a promising opportunity to influence industry pricing conduct. Supply and demand will generally dictate price floors and ceilings within an industry, but the individual conduct of competitors within the industry plays a significant role in determining where prices fall within that range. For a short time after a merger, competitors are particularly attentive to the merged company's actions. They watch carefully for clues to how the combined company's behavior in the marketplace will change—and changes in marketing strategy and pricing can alter the intensity of price competition for the whole industry.

While the postmerger environment offers an opportune time to reestablish good pricing conduct in the market, both through across-the-board and account-specific actions, this window also closes quickly. Competitors will quickly perceive the new company's actions as the norm for future behavior and will start setting their own policies accordingly. Once competitors return to business as usual, it could be harder to demonstrate that the merged company has made a fundamental change in its market policy.

During the postmerger period, any action that shapes customer, employee, or competitor perceptions and illustrates how the merger may affect pricing policies can prove invaluable. For example, press releases, internal newsletters, bulletins, and client meetings can keep the window of opportunity open longer and create a more accepting climate for any moves that prove necessary.

OPPORTUNITIES AT EACH PRICING LEVEL

Postmerger pricing opportunities exist at each of the three levels of pricing, as shown in Exhibit 8-2. In rare cases, a company's new market and competitive position may justify a price increase for all its customers. There may also be opportunities to consolidate smartly or bundle overlapping products and services. In other cases, a complicated or undermanaged discounting approach may indicate transaction-level price opportunities.

INDUSTRY STRATEGY

Industries can be reshaped by mergers. Two midfield players can combine to become an industry leader. The merged company may significantly increase, reduce, or redistribute its supply of products to the market. It may force the industry into a destructive price war or choose to focus its competitive

Exhibit 8-2   Common Sources of Postmerger Pricing Improvement

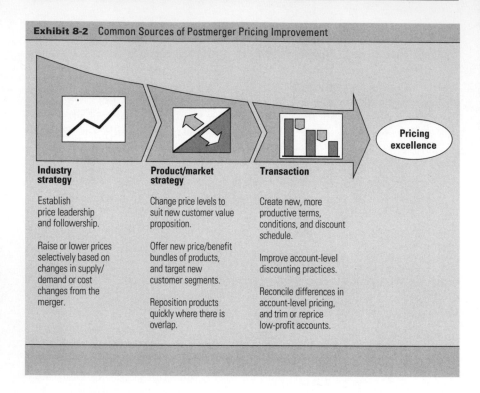

Industry strategy	Product/market strategy	Transaction
Establish price leadership and followership.	Change price levels to suit new customer value proposition.	Create new, more productive terms, conditions, and discount schedule.
Raise or lower prices selectively based on changes in supply/demand or cost changes from the merger.	Offer new price/benefit bundles of products, and target new customer segments.	Improve account-level discounting practices.
	Reposition products quickly where there is overlap.	Reconcile differences in account-level pricing, and trim or reprice low-profit accounts.

efforts on product benefits. A company that understands this potential can independently and unilaterally take action to improve pricing conduct for its own benefit and for the industry's in general.

Newly merged companies often have an opportunity to influence industry pricing conduct through decisions such as whether to focus on market share or profit. Also, since the combined company is larger than its predecessors, it likely has more ability to invest to achieve these goals. And finally, industry conduct is influenced by the perceptions of competitors, who are also reassessing the merged company's intentions and abilities.

An example from the consumer packaged goods (CPG) industry shows how this can work. The two market leaders, Simmons and Jeffrey, traditionally fought furiously for market share, often engaging in destructive price wars. They poached each other's prime accounts and angled, largely in vain, for exclusive arrangements with retailers.

Then Caesar, a company that sold unrelated consumer products, bought Simmons, and soon after the acquisition it became obvious that the competitive landscape had changed. Caesar fired the Simmons vice president for sales, who had a reputation for emphasizing volume. Meanwhile, Jeffrey's president ordered an analysis of the merger's likely impact on the company's strategy.

Managers reported that Caesar focused on profits and rarely competed on price. Based on this information, Jeffrey announced that it would no longer seek exclusive relationships with retailers and would increase price on a number of its products by 2.5 percent. Breaking from tradition, Simmons matched the price hike quickly. Also, soon after the takeover, both companies stopped spending all their time targeting accounts held by the other. Instead, they shifted to investments in product and package innovation to drive consumption. Both Jeffrey and Simmons benefited from the new pricing behavior, with profits increasing by 25 and 17 percent, respectively.

Another way to influence industry conduct is by taking initiatives following a merger that allow unilateral price increases for selected products. This could, for example, include renegotiating a labor agreement to allow for plant closures and lower supply or, if the newly merged company has access to greater resources, spending more on marketing, which could stimulate demand. Each may allow for higher industry prices.

PRODUCT/MARKET STRATEGY

Mergers often change the customer value proposition. The synergies derived from a merger can improve product quality, add product attributes and services, or improve the terms and conditions of ownership. The goal of any strategy is to set prices that take into account the additional benefits gained by customers as a result of a merger. That means price should change commensurate with the change in benefits, moving the products higher along the VEL discussed in Chapter 4.

The U.S. banking industry offers an example of changing prices to capture the increased benefits offered to customers after a merger. In the mid-1990s, a large national bank aggressively expanded its network by acquiring many local and regional banks. After each acquisition, the bank assimilated the acquired branches into its established marketing umbrella. The integration gave customers who stayed with the bank a number of benefits. These included access to the company's ATM network, which became one of the largest in the country, and access to a larger suite of leading-edge products and services, such as a credit card with an expansive loyalty program and one of the first Internet banking systems. In addition, many customers felt more comfortable banking with the larger, better-capitalized organization.

As the mergers were completed, there was a clear opportunity to reposition prices to reflect these service improvements. After each acquisition, the newly acquired branches adopted the pricing program of the national bank, which meant some higher fees and restructured fee schedules. The move invariably resulted in improved profitability per customer at the acquired banks with very little customer attrition.

As the bank example shows, merging companies should seek to understand intimately whether the additional benefits brought by the merger are truly valued by customers. Market research techniques such as conjoint and discrete-choice analysis can help decipher the likely customer reaction when faced with a new combination of price and benefit levels from the new company. Care should be taken as well on the timing and communication of such changes to ensure that customers recognize the increased benefits they are being offered and do not misperceive the pricing move as an attempt to take advantage of greater market power, which could easily trigger high attrition.

Another way to pursue the price advantage following a merger is to use price skillfully to consolidate product lines during the integration. When two North American auto parts suppliers with similar pricing structures merged, they saw a fertile opportunity to increase profits by consolidating their product lines. Together, they had hundreds of stock-keeping units (SKUs), some identical and many that were quite similar.

To find out how many products could be consolidated, the company formed a six-person pricing team that comprised representatives from both companies' marketing and sales, product development, and engineering departments. The team matched products across the two organizations, looking for opportunities to merge lines or phase out products. In particular, they looked at whether each product was making money, was increasing or losing market share, or was a brand leader. They also looked at minimum efficient production levels to determine at what point a low-volume product should be dropped.

The analysis revealed that the potential for savings was even greater than expected. Along with clearing overlaps in the product line, the newly merged company used the opportunity to drop some undesirable SKUs, such as unpopular or inefficient package sizes. As a first step, the company terminated about a third of its products immediately. In other cases where, for instance, profit margins were small, the company increased prices by an average of 20 to 25 percent to wean customers from those products and shift them to another product in its line. Through this program, the company cut about 60 percent of its overlapping SKUs, increased prices on some of its remaining products by 5 percent, and increased overall ROS by 1.5 percentage points.

Following a merger, a company may also find that synergies between its product lines can be used to fuel demand. This can be done through a new pricing structure that, for example, links customer incentives to broader use of the merged company's expanded product line. In a recent integration, two large mattress makers took advantage of their combined marketing and merchandising insight to do just that.

The companies that merged came from two ends of the market spectrum: One manufactured high-end mattresses, and the other catered to the mid-tier and low-price segments. Following the merger, retailers carrying the products gained several advantages. The merged company now offered a one-stop shop for the complete range of mattresses and, because of its larger size, marketing and merchandising support increased. But nothing in the old price structure prevented retailers from taking advantage of these increased benefits without returning anything to the merged company. For example, many of the retailers used the company's high-end mattresses to get customers in the door, then directed consumers to lower-end mattresses from another maker that were more profitable for the retailer. Since the added benefits accrued to the intermediaries rather than to the end customers, a price increase on the products to complement the improved benefits, as illustrated in the banking example, would not have helped the situation.

After carefully analyzing the various options for its discount structure, the merged company adopted a performance-based "Dealer Partnership" program that encouraged dealers to stock the full breadth of the company's expanded product line. The program rewarded dealers that purchased multiple brands from the merged company and did a large percentage of their business with the merged company. Smaller competitors with narrower product lines could not match these incentives. The merged company gained greater exposure at retail stores, while the retailers got a clear assortment of mattresses for their high-, mid-, and low-tier customers, as well as increased efficiency.

A new pricing structure could be beneficial to a merged company if the merger changes how the new company wants its distributors to act. If the new company wants its distributors to alter how they order, how much they order, what product mix they order, or which customers they target, it is likely that the historical price structure will be inadequate.

TRANSACTION PRICING

Transaction pricing is another area that holds great opportunity for a newly merged company. As we have seen in Chapter 3, a company's price model is more than its list prices. It includes a range of discounts, allowances, and bonuses, each of which take away from the revenue that the seller eventually receives, leaving the pocket price. When companies with different price models merge, the leaders of the merged company need to understand the historical pocket prices being realized at both companies, recognize leakages that could occur if both structures remain in force, and decide how best to capture the value of transaction price excellence.

A coincidence of events in the commercial printing industry in the late 1990s illustrates clearly the value of scrutinizing transaction policies following a merger. Two large printers, X-Act Copy and FastPress, each acquired companies of roughly the same size in the same year. By the end of the year, X-Act Copy posted a 1.5 percentage point increase in ROS, while FastPress marked an impressive 12 percentage point increase. At the end of the year, a top executive at X-Act Copy said its cost-cutting efforts were on track, but it was far behind in resolving pricing questions. FastPress, on the other hand, had tackled these pricing issues immediately.

Soon after acquiring Line-by-Line Printers, FastPress's managers examined both companies' pocket price waterfall. They had believed that Line-by-Line was an aggressive low-pricer and expected the waterfall tiers to be just as generous. In fact, some of the discounts FastPress offered had been an attempt to match Line-by-Line prices for key customers.

Instead, as shown in Exhibit 8-3, they found that Line-by-Line gave up much less between the list price and the pocket price. Despite Line-by-Line's lower list prices, many FastPress customers were getting much lower pocket prices from FastPress because of the waterfall differences. On average, FastPress's pocket price was about 18 percent below list, while the discounts and other incentives offered by Line-by-Line reduced

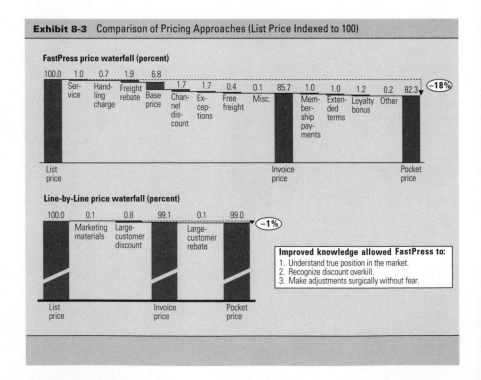

Exhibit 8-3 Comparison of Pricing Approaches (List Price Indexed to 100)

its list price by just 1 percent. In addition, FastPress discovered that its pocket price band was much wider than Line-by-Line's band, as shown in Exhibit 8-4.

FastPress worked quickly to correct the situation. Not only did it rationalize the tiers of its waterfall to reflect the knowledge gained from Line-by-Line's experiences, but it also targeted its own customers that were receiving particularly deep discounts. In many cases, it was able to trim the price waterfall for these accounts, narrowing its pocket price band and increasing profitability.

Reaping benefits at the transaction level following a merger demands meticulous attention to detail. But as the printing example shows, careful consideration of all the waterfall elements offered by the companies involved in the merger or acquisition, as well as a review of how each customer or customer segment is treated, can be very fruitful.

COMMON POSTMERGER TRAPS

Just as astute pricing policy integration can create enormous value, there are also several traps in the postmerger terrain awaiting the unsuspecting

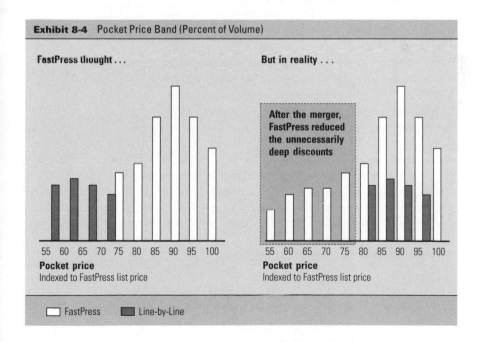

Exhibit 8-4 Pocket Price Band (Percent of Volume)

FastPress thought . . .

But in reality . . .

After the merger, FastPress reduced the unnecessarily deep discounts

55 60 65 70 75 80 85 90 95 100
Pocket price
Indexed to FastPress list price

55 60 65 70 75 80 85 90 95 100
Pocket price
Indexed to FastPress list price

☐ FastPress   ■ Line-by-Line

manager. Failure to take postmerger pricing actions proactively often results in lost synergies and can destroy much of the value created by the merger. Unfortunately, managers that do try to take pricing firmly in hand can make other mistakes that destroy value. We have seen many companies fall into three such common traps.

THE GENEROSITY TRAP

Sometimes, when one company acquires or merges with another that sells products or services of lesser quality, the higher-quality company decides to be generous. Managers of the acquiring company will apply superior practices to its acquisition's operations, improving quality, reliability, or service. If the company does not raise prices in tandem with these added benefits, it can inadvertently cause a price war in the low-price segment of the industry or cannibalize its own more profitable products.

When International Compressors acquired State Compressor in the early 1990s, State's products were similar but less expensive and with fewer design features. State also had a weak field service network and a less comprehensive warranty. To reduce the cost of servicing and administering the two product lines, International equipped its field service team to support State's products and equalized the warranty terms and coverage of the two lines. Despite the improved benefits, it left the prices of State's compressors unchanged. Although International's managers thought design limitations and higher maintenance costs limited the customer value of State's compressors, sales of the lower-priced products skyrocketed soon after the service and warranty changes were made. What the managers did not understand was that the availability of International's superior field service and more extensive warranty had removed the drawbacks and made State's products a great value at the old price.

The new price/benefit position of State's products did not just erode International's market share. It also hurt competitors Micro-Comp and European. Both reacted by cutting prices, and International soon felt compelled to follow suit to maintain its share. As shown in Exhibit 8-5, industry price levels fell by 7 percent within a year, and the profits at the merged company dropped to roughly half what the two companies were recording before the merger. Industry prices eventually recovered after International cut the benefits on State's products, but the generosity trap was very costly for everyone.

THE DISCOUNT ACCUMULATION TRAP

Companies can fall into the discount accumulation trap when they do not properly reevaluate their terms, conditions, and discount schedules after a

Exhibit 8-5 Destroying Value: Easy as 1, 2, 3

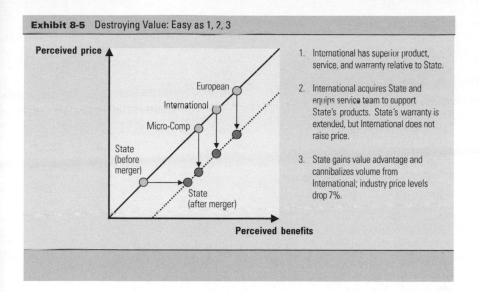

Perceived price

European
International
Micro-Comp
State (before merger)
State (after merger)
Perceived benefits

1. International has superior product, service, and warranty relative to State.

2. International acquires State and equips service team to support State's products. State's warranty is extended, but International does not raise price.

3. State gains value advantage and cannibalizes volume from International; industry price levels drop 7%.

merger. In the worst-case scenario, a company allows both programs to continue, effectively combining the programs and giving unintentionally higher discounts to its customers. Even if a company chooses one discount structure over the other, a lot of revenue can be lost if trigger points are not adjusted properly.

Take two hypothetical companies, Superior Inc. and Elite Co., that sell to the same retailer. Both offer a 2 percent volume bonus on annual purchases of $250,000 to $1 million, and a 4 percent bonus if yearly purchases exceed $1 million. Before the merger, one retailer bought $950,000 worth of goods from Superior each year and $250,000 worth from Elite, earning a 2 percent discount from each for a total benefit of $24,000. If Superior merges with Elite and keeps the old volume bonus structure, the retailer would be entitled to a 4 percent discount on its $1.2 million purchase from the merged company, or $48,000. Without changing a thing, the retailer reaps a $24,000 windfall.

Multiply this effect across a customer base, and it is easy to see that by ignoring the accumulated effects of discount schedules, a merged company would inadvertently destroy significant value. Avoiding the discount accumulation trap requires a careful comparison of the customer base of the two companies being merged. If there is significant overlap, thresholds to qualify for discounts will probably have to be adjusted, but if there is very little overlap there could be less pressure to shift these trigger points.

THE PARENT TRAP

The parent trap can snare any company that arbitrarily believes its approach to the market is superior to that of its acquisition. If incorrect, the acquirer can decrease the value of the merger by imposing its own inferior practices throughout the group and by failing to adopt superior practices brought in by an acquisition. The parent trap can occur around almost any aspect of postmerger integration, but since pricing policy generally receives less attention than other areas, it can be particularly susceptible.

An example of the parent trap comes from the consumer durables industry, where one company acquired a much smaller company with complementary product lines. The takeover target had superior processes and tools to manage account-level pricing. These included the ability to measure account profitability, strict control processes for discretionary discounts, and feedback mechanisms to identify continuously account-level pricing opportunities. But during the integration, the acquirer simply assimilated the new company into its more arcane and loosely controlled system. Without the sophisticated controls previously in place, sales reps of the acquired company began offering customers increased discounts as they tried to maintain or improve volume during the transition period. Not only did the change needlessly destroy a significant portion of the value of the acquired organization, but the parent company also missed the chance to reap what could have been enormous revenue gains, because it failed to adopt the acquired company's excellent transaction management processes throughout the organization.

ANTITRUST LAWS

Many companies are reluctant to use perfectly acceptable and legal opportunities to create value through pricing after a merger. The mere thought of legal repercussions causes them to put pricing considerations on the back burner and accept the status quo, before and after a deal is completed. As a result, by the time many managers feel ready to tackle pricing issues, it may be too late to make a difference.

Antitrust laws rightly protect consumers by barring some activities during M&A processes. But even with these restrictions, there are ways for companies to analyze prices safely and legally and be ready, once a deal is closed, to meet pricing challenges aggressively. In Chapter 11, we provide a more complete survey of antitrust legislation and other regulations that touch upon pricing policies, but here we will focus on areas that affect postmerger integration. As always, legal counsel should be called in if there are any questions.

The U.S. Hart-Scott Rodino Act and the EU European Community Merger Regulation police pre-merger planning in the two markets. In essence, competing companies are prohibited from sharing sensitive information, which is generally defined as anything not publicly available, on prices, contract details, or customer lists because if the deal falls through, such sharing may constitute illegal collusion. Additionally, it is important to note that any analysis of pricing opportunities before closing, whether or not it comes from shared proprietary information, may have to be turned over to antitrust regulators as part of the approval process, or later if the merger becomes a subject of litigation. Regulators will closely scrutinize documents that detail potential postmerger changes in prices and discount structures to gauge if the companies involved will wield too much market power after a merger.

However, with this understanding, there are ways to structure early pricing analysis that do not violate antitrust laws. For example, companies in both markets can use *clean teams*, composed of independent third parties, to work on issues that require competitive information to be shared. Postmerger pricing initiatives have the greatest chance of success if they are begun early in the merger process, and a clean team can ensure that the work begins as soon as possible, while protecting the confidentiality of each company's shared data. This allows the merged company to bring the value of pricing synergies to the bottom line immediately after close, a time when management is typically under very high pressure to deliver results.

Until the merger or acquisition is finalized, a clean team would not be able to share competitively sensitive data, such as product-specific price and cost details, with the companies involved in the deal. But even before the deal closes, the conclusions of the analysis and recommendations could be available to both sides, as long as the information could not be viewed as collusive. Then, if appropriate, these recommendations could be implemented shortly after closure. If the deal falls through, the details gathered by the clean team during its analysis cannot be used by either company. Work conducted by such clean teams may also be subject to disclosure to regulators as they scrutinize a proposed merger.

Two other options can also help companies get a head start on pricing decisions during a merger or acquisition. Each company involved can form its own pricing team to begin the often time-intensive process of gathering its own data and analyzing its own internal issues. The companies involved can also create a joint pricing team that focuses its work before the deal closes on issues that do not require the sharing of sensitive pricing information. This team could then become the core of the merged company's pricing team once the deal is completed.

*   *   *

The first year or so following a merger or acquisition provides a unique opportunity for a company to strengthen its price advantage. Top managers should seize the postmerger pricing opportunities with the same rigor and discipline they apply to operational synergies. There are rich opportunities that are available at no other time, and the pricing window can close quite quickly. After a merger, CEOs and senior managers are typically swamped with proposals for hundreds of integration projects, and pricing is often on the bottom of the list, pushed down by more visible issues. But if the pricing opportunities are not addressed early in the integration process, the window will close and the potential will evaporate. Companies with the price advantage think about mergers differently, resolutely pursuing the significant but fleeting opportunity the postmerger environment presents.

CHAPTER 9

Price Wars

From airlines to personal computers to chemicals to telecommunications to electronic components to automobile tires to fast food, the list of industries racked by price wars in recent years is a long and growing one. These price wars rarely have any real winners—and few healthy survivors. The destruction such battles cause can be so severe and linger so long that the only reliable way to come out ahead is to avoid them altogether.

The price war threat is real—and universal. No company, however well run, is immune. Even companies with superior overall strategies and otherwise exceptional execution can destroy themselves by not managing this make-or-break issue effectively. As we will discuss, all too many price wars start by accident, often through misreads of competitor actions or misjudgments of market conditions. The price war that is initiated as a deliberate competitive tactic is somewhat rare—and rarer still is the one that achieves a positive outcome for either the industry at large or a specific supplier within the warring industry.

Navigating a course away from a price war takes effort and genuine helmsmanship. First, you must understand why prices wars rarely succeed and most often lead to value destruction across an industry, as well as why price wars have been proliferating in recent years. By understanding the environment, you can find ways to stay out of price wars or, if all else has failed, to get out of one with minimal damage. Under rare conditions, a price war might actually be the correct course. In this chapter, we will explore all these areas.

WHY PRICE WARS SHOULD BE AVOIDED

If you have ever imagined that reducing prices to gain share and increase profits might be a sound strategy for your business, think again. Unless you have a dominant cost advantage—by this we mean costs that are at least 30 percent below the competition—reducing prices all too often triggers a suicidal price war. Price cuts are almost always followed quickly by competitors; no one wants to lose customers, volume, or share. The best-run companies go to almost any lengths to avoid price wars, for a host of compelling reasons.

PROFIT SENSITIVITY

Profits are extremely sensitive to even slight declines in average price levels. As we saw in Chapter 1, price is the most sensitive economic lever in business. Any decrease drops straight off the bottom line. If price for the typical Global 1200 company falls by a single percentage point and costs and volume remain unchanged, then operating profit drops by 11 percent.

But can you make up the profit shortfall from lower prices with an increase in volume? Suppose that a price war causes a relatively modest 5 percent decline in price. As also shown in Chapter 1, that means that volume would have to increase by more than 17.5 percent for a company just to break even in operating profit. For this to happen, price elasticity would have to be $-3.5:1$. That is, every percentage point price cut would have to result in a 3.5 percent increase in volume. Price elasticities in the real world seldom exceed even $-2:1$.

So it is highly unlikely that demand will increase nearly enough to offset the drops in price that occur in a typical price war. When you do battle on the basis of price alone, your odds of winning from a profit standpoint are very long. Moreover, if you do have success in attracting additional customers and volume with your price cut, your competitors will most likely cut their own prices to meet or beat yours. After all, slashing prices is just about the easiest strategy to emulate. Anyone can do it.

ADVANTAGES FADE QUICKLY

Price advantages over competitors are usually short-lived. Attempts to boost market share by dropping prices normally lead to traditional shares being retained, but at lower price levels. In a recent skirmish in the PDA market, for example, a 50 percent price cut by Palm was matched in a matter of days by major competitor Handspring. Similarly, it took Compaq less than a week to match an 18 percent price cut by Dell in the business PC market, despite Dell's cost advantage.

PRICE EXPECTATIONS DISTORTED

Amid a price war, customers have their price expectations and price reference points distorted, and these price perceptions remain damaged long after a price war ends. A $199 New York–to–Los Angeles round-trip fare was widely offered during a summer airfare battle a few years ago. Tens of thousands of travelers had it etched in their minds that $199 is the correct and acceptable price for that trip, and when the war was over many still refused to take that trip again unless fares returned to that level. Weak vacation flight demand during the subsequent summer confirmed that travelers' reference points had been moved lower by the previous year's fare war.

These developments are consistent with research on price psychology and price recall. Consumer research has shown that the lowest price someone pays for a product is remembered longest, and remains a reference point for a very long time—often for life. Maybe that is why so many grandfathers remember what they paid for their first Model T Ford. The point, of course, is that the low prices accompanying price wars influence a customer's perception of what is a reasonable price long after the war ends.

CUSTOMER SENSITIVITY SHIFTS

Also during a price war, customers become more sensitive to price and less sensitive to benefits. If you provide a product that is superior, you probably tend to charge a higher price than competitors. Customers buy your product because they perceive that its benefit advantage more than outweighs the price premium they must pay. And as long as customers focus on the benefits side of the equation, superior suppliers can sustain the price premium, as discussed in Chapter 4.

Price wars, however, often upset this crucial price/benefit balance. As price wars play out, suppliers place increasing emphasis on price, bombarding their customers with price rather than benefit messages. The inevitable result is that customers become more and more price-sensitive—and less and less benefit-sensitive. This has happened in the PC industry. Despite a steady stream of quantum performance improvements, there is evidence that an ever-increasing portion of PC buying decisions is made strictly on a lowest-price basis. Even when a price war ends, the price/benefit seesaw does not automatically tip back the way it was before. Price wars change customers—usually adversely, often forever.

INDUSTRY SHAKEOUTS ARE RARE

Price war combatants often hope that the battle will bring an industry shakeout, but this rarely happens. While managers often justify taking part in a price war by claiming it will knock out weak competitors and rationalize the industry, there are at least two problems with this approach:

- ■ Regulators or the courts may construe such a strategy as illegal preda-tory pricing—that is, pricing with the intent of forcing a competitor out of business. (Chapter 11 offers a fuller discussion of the legal issues surrounding pricing.)
- ■ Emotions kick in during price wars, leading companies to stay in a business years after it stops making economic sense for them to re-main. In a segment of the electrical controls industry, for instance, companies engaged in a price war for five years, each enduring huge annual losses, yet not a single competitor exited the business.

Even when a weak competitor does call it quits, its capacity often stays. Take a key subset of the fractional horsepower electric motor in-dustry: brutally competitive, chronically price-embattled, 20 to 30 per-cent excess capacity, and most competitors not even earning their cost of capital over the past decade. Not a pretty picture; not an industry that you would expect entrepreneurs to be lining up to enter. But that is ex-actly what is happening. Every time a competitor decides to leave this industry, new players snatch up that player's assets for 25 cents on the dollar. Then the capacity reemerges and operates on a lower cost basis than before.

As these examples suggest, preventing and avoiding price wars should be high on every company's list of strategic priorities. Price wars destroy huge chunks of company and industry profits, and rarely provide a busi-ness with a sustainable advantage. They often cause irreversible damage to the customer base and seldom alleviate an industry's structural or ca-pacity problems.

WHAT REALLY CAUSES PRICE WARS

Given all of these compelling reasons for avoiding price wars, why is it that so many companies find themselves fighting them so often?

On rare occasions, a company will intentionally embark on a price war as part of a sound overall strategy. It might, for instance, invest in a new technology that slashes costs and then lower its prices to gain share and block competitors from acquiring that technology. But few price wars are started so deliberately or thoughtfully. Far more often, companies acci-dentally stumble into price wars—victims of misreads of competitor ac-tions and market changes, or misjudgments of how competitors will react to their own pricing maneuvers.

COMPETITIVE AND MARKET MISREADS

Managers usually hear about competitors' prices when someone in the field tells them, "Enemy Co. is selling at a lower price. We need to match it to survive in this market." But important collateral information about the price—for instance, that the lower price applies for no more than two days, exclusively to qualified distributors, and then only to truckload quantities—may never be picked up or communicated back to decision makers. As a result, the company matches the lower price across the board, without qualification or limitation. Enemy Co. then sees the lower price offered by its rival to a wide market, compelling it, in turn, to offer the low price to more customers for longer than was ever intended.

This is one common way for price wars to begin and escalate. A company misreading the market will swear that Enemy Co. started the war, while Enemy Co. will see things in exactly the opposite fashion.

One tire company sold a product to retailers at an invoice price of $35. An end-of-year volume bonus of $2 and a marketing allowance of $1.50 brought the pocket price down to $31.50. The company then heard from the field that a competitor was selling a similar tire to retailers at an invoice price of $32. So, fearing loss of business, it lowered its own invoice price from $35 to $32. Only later did it learn that its competitor was not paying a volume bonus or marketing allowance on its $32 invoice price, as shown in Exhibit 9-1. Unable to judge true price comparability, the tire company had lowered its price by $3 to meet a competitor's price that was actually 50 cents higher on a pocket price basis. Unfortunately, this realization came too late to prevent a costly and protracted price war.

Exhibit 9-1 Price Comparisons

	Old price	Competitor's price	New price
Invoice price	$35.00	$32.00	$32.00
Volume bonus	−2.00	0	−2.00
Marketing allowance	−1.50	0	−1.50
Pocket price	$31.50	$32.00	$28.50

Accidents happen. Some years back, an industry association journal erred when it reported total market volume for industrial equipment at 15 percent more than it actually was. Reading the inflated number, the four major competitors in that market all feared they had suffered a serious loss of market share, and immediately dropped their prices in an attempt to recover it, although, of course, it had never really been lost. A correction of the error was published three months later, much too late to prevent a destructive price war that eventually ravaged the industry for more than a year.

Consider still another example: A CPG supplier observed a competitor making an unexpected 10 percent price cut. The supplier assumed that the competitor was strategically repositioning its product line and so matched the price cut. In reality, however, the supplier had misread not the fact that prices were cut, but the reason behind the move. Earlier that year, the serving size stipulated by the U.S. Food and Drug Administration (FDA) for reporting nutritional information about packaged foods had been reset to 6 ounces. The competitor had decided to replace all its $6^1/_2$-ounce packages with a 6-ounce size to align with the new regulations. Rather than repositioning its product line, the competitor was discounting prices only to get its obsolete $6^1/_2$-ounce packages out of the supply pipeline before introducing the new, smaller size. If the first supplier had not reacted with its own deep cuts, prices would have returned to normal in a month or so, once the competitor's obsolete inventory had sold out. Instead, a severe price war erupted that destroyed all industry profits for the year.

MISJUDGMENTS

Managers often assume that only the lowest-priced supplier in a market can ignite a price war. They are mistaken. The culprit can easily be the highest-priced supplier.

As discussed in Chapter 4, customers do not buy simply on price. They buy on value, which is the difference between the perceived benefits that a product provides and the perceived price. The value map is an excellent tool to explore the way that this price/benefit tradeoff works in markets. In the case that follows, the value map clearly demonstrates how the high-priced player in an industry can inadvertently ignite a price war.

The industry here is high-volume blood diagnostic machines used in blood banks and large hospital labs to type and test blood samples. As shown in Exhibit 9-2, MTE was the leading supplier in this industry. Its diagnostic machines were perceived as the highest performing (that is, with the highest test accuracy and fastest test cycle times, among other attributes), and it commanded a justified price premium in this market.

Exhibit 9-2 Positioning of a New Product

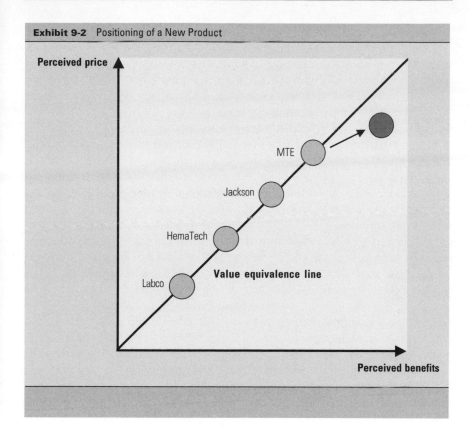

Competitors included Jackson, HemaTech, and Labco, whose machines did not perform as well and thus sold at a discount to MTE. As Exhibit 9-2 shows, the competitors had traditionally aligned along the value equivalence line, with MTE occupying the premium high-benefit, high-price position and Labco occupying the economy low-benefit, low-price position. Jackson and HemaTech sat in between. As would be predicted, this positioning resulted in a traditionally stable market with very little change in market share.

This market stability changed when MTE introduced an innovative new blood diagnostic machine with even higher test accuracy, lower false positive indications, and faster test cycle times. In field test trials, MTE quickly realized that its new innovative design would deliver even higher perceived benefits than its old design, and MTE faced the decision of how to price its great new product. Market analysis determined that MTE had the option to raise prices by 10 percent and still stay on the existing market VEL. Given that the manufacturing cost of their new product was no greater than the one it was replacing, some managers at MTE argued that MTE should price the new product at the same level as the old and pick up market share from a hugely value-advantaged position. MTE ultimately compromised. It raised the price of the new product about 4 percent above the product it was replacing, but not the 10 percent that the new product's benefits justified. So, even with the 4 percent price increase, MTE was clearly occupying a value-advantaged position and expected to gain market share.

When MTE's new blood diagnostic machine was launched, the market recognized its value and MTE's market share rose significantly within three months. Marketers, sellers, and product developers soon began celebrating the success of the great new product. The celebration, however, may have been premature.

MTE had grown market share at the expense of traditional rivals Jackson, HemaTech, and Labco. These competitors did not have the resources or expertise to match MTE's product innovations, so they defended their market shares the only way they knew: They aggressively lowered their list prices. Within six months, each of these competitors had simply cut their price levels to become value equivalent with MTE. As Exhibit 9-3 illustrates, the VEL shifted downward more than 5 percent and MTE's market share slipped back to its earlier level. This turned out to be only the first of several rounds of price skirmishes in this market.

MTE managers were perplexed by the price war that followed their new product launch. They said, "MTE is not to blame for this price war. We *raised* our price 4 percent. Our irrational competitors are to blame." In fact, if MTE had raised its price by 10 percent, as justified by the new benefits, it would likely have held its traditional market share but at a price that would have been 6 percent higher. Because MTE failed to seek a fair premium for their innovative new diagnostic machine, a destructive price war was triggered.

Any player along the VEL—high-, medium-, or low-priced—can make similar mistakes by misjudging competitor response when there is a shift in the price/benefit tradeoff. Ultimately, anyone can instigate a damaging price war.

STAYING OUT OF PRICE WARS

We have shown that price wars usually do huge and often irreparable damage to entire industries and the perceptions of customers they serve, and that they should be avoided at all cost. We have also shown that price wars are all too often stumbled into by combatants—victims of market and competitor misreads and misjudgments. So how can they best be avoided?

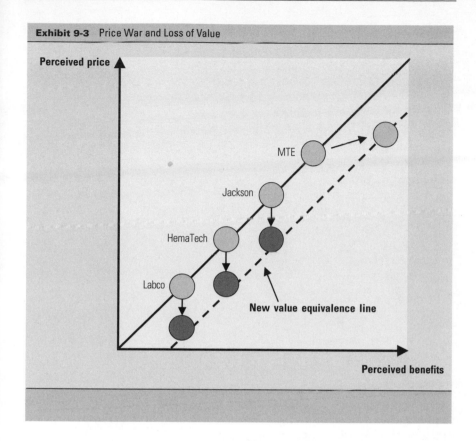

Exhibit 9-3　Price War and Loss of Value

When we look at ways of avoiding price wars, it is worth remembering that some industries run an inherently higher risk than others. As Exhibit 9-4 shows, if a product is an undifferentiated commodity, price is likely to be a more important buying factor, which increases the likelihood of competition on price and, hence, of price wars. Shorter product life cycles tend to spawn more price wars as competitors fight for market position with each cycle of innovation. So do low capacity utilization and declining market size, which ratchet up competitors' volume desperation. And so does customer concentration: When an industry has only a few large customers, they tend to exert strong price pressure on all competitors.

In addition, the more competitors there are in a market, the higher the likelihood that one competitor will choose to price aggressively, and the greater the price war risk. Similarly, risk mounts when barriers to switching suppliers are low, when price sensitivity is high, and when costs are unstable or declining. Finally, industries where the ratio of fixed costs to

Exhibit 9-4 Inherent Industry Price War Risks

Industry Characteristics	Lower Risk	Higher Risk
Product type	Differentiated	Undifferentiated commodity
Industry capacity utilization	High	Low
Market trend	Growing	Stable/declining
Customer concentration	Widely dispersed	Highly concentrated (small number of large customers)
Number of competitors	Few	Many
Price visibility to competition	Low	High
Barriers to switching suppliers	High	Low
Overall customer price sensitivity	Low	High
Cost trend	Stable	Volatile/declining

variable costs is high are usually more susceptible to price wars because companies are lured into price competition by high contribution margins (price minus variable costs) and the desire to utilize their high fixed-cost base fully.

Given these different levels of risk, and the kinds of misreads and misjudgments that, as we have seen, usually start price wars, how can managers build an effective firewall to keep their companies safe? Below, we suggest seven steps that managers can take to build such a wall. They all target the unintentional misperceptions that regularly put tinder to flame.

1. AVOID STRATEGIES THAT FORCE COMPETITORS TO RESPOND WITH LOWER PRICES

Encourage constructive rather than destructive competition by steering clear of actions that shift the competitive playing field from benefits to price. Keep customers focused on differences in benefits, do not overemphasize price in your advertising, and pass up initiatives designed to steal market share rapidly from one or two main competitors. If you want to gain share, do so gradually. Rapid changes in market share almost always set the stage for a price war. The more quickly you grab share from your key rivals, the higher the likelihood that they will respond with an aggressive price move, igniting a price war.

2. AVOID ALL POSSIBLE MISREADS OF COMPETITIVE AND MARKET DEVELOPMENTS

Misreads will kill you. Invest in understanding the qualifiers—and comparability—of competitors' prices. Similarly, do not react until you understand the reason behind your competitor's price cut. If what your competitor is doing seems senseless, you probably do not understand it well enough to react wisely. In other words, delay your response until you are confident of the facts. If you are not sure, do not react with a lower price. In particular, strive for a balanced reading of the full range of prices offered by your competitor. Never base a reactive price cut on just one or two competitive quotes. They might not be representative; they might be plain wrong. Find out. The cost of a delayed reaction is always lower than that of a misread that triggers a price war.

3. AVOID OVERREACTION

Once you get the what and why of your competitor's price cut in focus, avoid the knee-jerk response of lowering your price. Though it may sound counterintuitive, the best thing to do is often nothing. Not every competitive price initiative deserves or demands a reaction. Sometimes competitors make unintentional low price mistakes. Do not let an isolated mistake by a competitor turn into a vicious price war.

If, however, a response is required, use something other than price if possible. One successful medical supplier reacts to every competitor price cut by increasing benefit delivery—accelerating product improvements, boosting service levels, and shaving lead times—to make its price premium increasingly justifiable to customers. And if a price response is required, make it as limited and surgical as possible. If you are feeling pressure in southeast Florida, do not lower your prices across the entire country: Close just a portion of the price gap, and do it only in southeast Florida.

4. PLAY YOUR VALUE MAP RIGHT

For important market segments, invest in research to understand your value position and the amount and value of the benefit advantages you hold. Once you understand the magnitude of your advantage, make sure your price is as high as this advantage will support. Moreover, when you introduce a new or improved product, do the research to determine the value customers will assign to your incremental benefits. For example, Goodyear some years ago wisely charged a fair premium for a superior new rain tire, establishing a market position for it without placing undue downward pressure on industry price levels that were already volatile.

5. COMMUNICATE YOUR PRICE EFFECTIVELY

Price communications should be designed to minimize the likelihood that customers or competitors will misread your price levels or the reasons behind your actions. Having your own prices misread by competitors can be just as damaging as you misreading theirs; both can start a price war. While price signaling is illegal in the United States and other markets, as noted in Chapter 11, communications with a real commercial purpose are generally appropriate. If you find yourself taking actions that might be construed by your competitors as price slashing, it is proper to include in your normal price communications to the market a clear description of all qualifiers and limitations and, in some circumstances, an explanation for the action.

6. JAWBONE ON PRICING

Companies that successfully avoid price wars consistently write and speak publicly about the horrors of price competition and the virtues of benefit competition. They do this price jawboning in articles, in their own house publications and media, in analyst conference calls, and in every available public forum.

7. EXPLOIT MARKET NICHES

If you are a minor player in an industry prone to price wars, the smartest thing to do may be to find a place to hide from the crossfire. Look for a product niche, segment niche, or even distribution channel niche that is too specialized, small, or obscure for the big players. Several small computer companies have escaped being harmed by the recent PC price war because they hid in specialized, high-performance application niches.

GETTING OUT OF PRICE WARS

If all preventive measures fail, and you find yourself, through no fault of your own, in the middle of a price war, what can you do to extricate your company and limit the damage? First, continue using the seven methods we have listed for avoiding a price war. These are just plain good practices, are easy to do, and just might elicit a positive competitive response. If they fail, there are two more aggressive (and riskier) ways to get out of a price war.

First, *seek long-term contracts* with key customers. If at all possible, try to get your major customers out of the crossfire of a price war by signing them up early to extended supply contracts. This, of course, is hard to do once your customers realize there is a price war raging. Such contracts also allow prudent suppliers an extended opportunity to demonstrate benefit superiority to key customers and to create a sustainable barrier to future price incursions by competitors.

As a last resort, *actively engage the enemy* with a tit-for-tat strategy. Whenever your competitor makes an aggressive price move, immediately and publicly match it. If your rival steals one of your biggest customers, immediately go after one of its major customers in the same market. The point is to demonstrate that price aggression is a no-win proposition. You want to make it crystal clear that you will match your competitor's every move. Similarly, you should immediately act in kind to support any return to rational price behavior by that competitor, so that it knows there is no risk attached to more responsible pricing behavior.

That this strategy is fraught with risk cannot be overemphasized. Your competitor may take an inordinately long time to realize that its actions can do it nothing but harm; rivalry across the entire industry may escalate precipitously; and as the tit-for-tat game plays itself out, all of a price war's detrimental effects on customers will occur. Only take this step with extreme care, and after all else has failed.

Just as the causes of price wars are highly variable, their severity spans a broad range. Simple competitive misreads are quite different from a situation where competitors are hell-bent on putting you out of business. It is vital, therefore, that you align your response with the level of severity. The worst thing you can do is to take a high-severity response like tit-for-tat in a low-severity circumstance. Such action will quickly escalate an isolated skirmish into all-out price war.

So, before plotting your response, do a careful assessment of just how severe the situation really is. Be cautious: Price wars can become highly emotional, and it is easy for those involved in them to overestimate their severity drastically. More than likely, this will lead in turn to an excessive response, which then throws a company and its industry into a truly severe and devastating price war.

WHEN A PRICE WAR MIGHT MAKE SENSE

Given the sustained negative profit and market effects of most price wars, situations are *extremely* rare where aggressive price cuts that might ignite a price war make sense. These conditions, which are similar to those described in Chapter 6 in the discussion of penetration pricing, fall into two major categories. The first is situations where significant latent demand exists at the lower price level. Back in the late 1990s when home PC prices broke below the $1,000 barrier, huge latent demand was unleashed. This rare discontinuity in the demand curve may have allowed the combatants in this price action to, at least in the near to medium term, gain both revenue and profits.

The second category is situations where competitors are structurally unable or unwilling to react fully and quickly to your price cut. These may include circumstances where a company has a significant cost advantage (having costs that are 30 percent or more lower) or an insurmountable technology advantage. Circumstances where a rival has a lot more to lose by responding also fall into this category—for instance, if a competitor with a dominant share position would have to lower prices across the board to respond to a minor competitor's price cut.

Even these situations are fraught with pitfalls. The surge of latent demand that draws in price combatants is often not sustained. In the PDA case cited earlier, market demand ultimately flattened after swelling only temporarily. Latent demand is all too often quickly soaked up in a price war that leaves industries structurally unable to thrive because, for instance, prices are too low, costs too high, and demand too flat to sustain long-term viability.

If structural barriers make a price war tempting, you should remember that it is often difficult to predict how competitors will react, even when faced with a rival company that has a dominant cost or technology advantage. As we mentioned earlier, price wars often become very emotional and managers react in illogical ways that may not be in the best interest of their companies' financial and market performance.

*   *   *

What does all this mean for today's management teams, who must deal with the threat of price wars daily? An interesting, albeit bleak, analogy may apply. Price wars are a lot like heart disease. Heart disease is serious, and it can kill you. We all are at risk. Some of us have higher inherited risk than others, just as some industries have an inherently higher risk of price wars than others. Still, however great the risk, you can reduce that risk by the way you behave every day: your diet, whether you smoke, how much you exercise, and so on.

In much the same way, your day-to-day pricing behavior will affect your risk of a price war. You increase it with every competitive misread, with every market misread, with every overreaction, with every failure to charge an adequate premium for your superior benefits. Prevention is the best cure. Each and every pricing action needs to be passed through a price war screen. Managers must constantly ask themselves, "Will this action contribute to the creation or extension of a price war in my industry?" If the answer is yes—or even maybe—don't do it.

Ultimately, it will be a string of seemingly insignificant but correct day-to-day pricing actions that provides the firewall to keep your company from suffering the ravages of a price war. Building that wall and keeping it strong is a disciplined and endless struggle—but a struggle well worth confronting and winning.

Expanding the Boundaries

Technology-Enabled Pricing

Pricing done well is hard work. The price advantage requires a rich arsenal of knowledge to make informed decisions—detailed facts about customers, competitors, and your own capabilities and economics. Pricing technology plays an essential role in delivering the right information to those who make pricing decisions, whether a salesperson negotiating a price for a large customer, a product manager contemplating a price repositioning on a key line, or a general manager evaluating the opportunity to assume price leadership in an industry.

Getting this information accurately and continuously is not a luxury; it is an essential component of building the ongoing pricing capabilities of a company.

Unfortunately, getting the right facts to the right place at the right time is challenging. The effort required simply to access the appropriate historical information could be monumental. But recent advances in technology hold great promise for removing the obstacles to data collection and analysis and to policy implementation. Also, the widespread use of the Internet has enabled more efficient data collection in many areas and made it possible to experiment with pricing changes and get real-time reaction. While the technology will continue to evolve, the fundamental pricing issues that need to be addressed should remain constant.

Technological advances mean that price changes can be made quickly with few errors. Also, it is now possible to get regular reports on profitability by channel and segment, data necessary to analyze pricing effectiveness. Some systems can even recommend a price to optimize margins by analyzing real-time price elasticity and current supply conditions. In addition, new pricing technology gives companies better information about their customers and gives these companies the ability to set prices at the maximum customers are willing to pay, and to adjust these prices rapidly as circumstances change.

We have never seen a company make significant progress on the pricing front without upgrading its information systems, generally with new applications or software. But this does not mean that companies must make a multiyear, multimillion-dollar investment in IT to excel in pricing. In many cases, for example, rudimentary databases managed by one or two analysts can capture and report pocket price waterfalls and price bands routinely, getting a company 80 percent of the way toward building transactional pricing capabilities.

But before running out and buying the latest pricing software package, a company pursuing the price advantage must first understand the roles technology can play in enhancing pricing performance and which improvements are most relevant. Then it must evaluate internal and external options for delivering the technology that best targets these improvements.

THE ESSENTIAL ROLES OF TECHNOLOGY

As technology has evolved, pricing software has enabled advances in three essential areas: delivering the right price to each customer with greater precision; creating greater flexibility to respond to changing market conditions; and allowing more granular market segmentation. The priority given to each role will vary by industry, and even in some cases by company. By understanding how technology can contribute, managers can better target their investments to areas that hold the greatest promise for their company.

GREATER PRECISION

In our experience, companies can lose up to a percentage point in ROS from pricing errors alone. Although mistakes can creep in almost anywhere, they are most often caused by completed deals that are not properly coded into a system or by sales promotions that remain in the system after they have ended. Statistically, errors should average out: A company would overcharge about as often as it undercharges. But in reality, incorrect bills drain revenue. A customer who is charged too much will usually complain and have the bill adjusted, while a company will rarely hear from a customer who is charged too little. A good rule of thumb is that the amount a company is losing to billing errors is about equal to the adjustments it makes to overcharged customers who complain.

In addition to the erroneous invoice price itself, companies lose money by holding accounts receivable open longer, since customers with an incorrect bill generally delay payment until the matter is settled. Many companies also spend significant amounts on labor and IT to rectify pricing errors. Exhibit 10-1 shows how pricing errors affected a durable goods company with about $2 billion in annual sales. Direct revenue losses each year came to about $20 million, while other costs totaled $1.4 million.

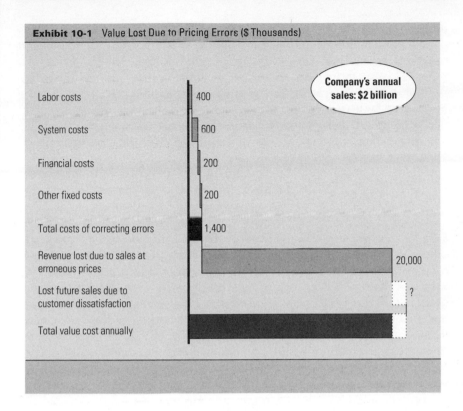

Exhibit 10-1 Value Lost Due to Pricing Errors ($ Thousands)

Labor costs	400
System costs	600
Financial costs	200
Other fixed costs	200
Total costs of correcting errors	1,400
Revenue lost due to sales at erroneous prices	20,000
Lost future sales due to customer dissatisfaction	?
Total value cost annually	

Company's annual sales: $2 billion

And these figures do not include lost business from dissatisfied customers who dropped the company because of billing problems.

The greater precision offered by pricing technology also increases the accuracy of pricing analysis. As discussed in Chapter 4, all products have a zone of pricing indifference, a range of prices within which a price change will not affect customers' choices. Zones of indifference can range from 17 percent for branded consumer health and beauty products to as little as 2 percent for some financial products. A product's location within this zone can dramatically affect a company's profits. For example, a financial services company moving from the middle to the top of its indifference zone for personal loans would increase the operating margins it earns from those products by 11 percent.[1]

In the past, determining the boundaries of these zones has been difficult, expensive, and time-consuming. Traditional price sensitivity research for a

---

[1]For example, a 2 percent zone of indifference for an 8.5 percent personal loan would range from 8.33 percent to 8.67 percent.

product category could cost up to $250,000 to complete. Few companies conducted such research. In addition, only a few sectors, such as airlines and other reservation-based industries, offer enough price variability to create a statistically significant demand curve that can be subjected to historical regression analysis. Market behavior defines the extremes of a product's price range, but the fear of losing sales has prevented most companies from actively testing the upper bounds. Some new pricing technologies, which we will discuss later, can measure customer tolerance for different price levels, allowing more precision in keeping near the top of an indifference zone.

GREATER FLEXIBILITY

Changing a price can take a lot of time. B2B markets may need several months to a year to communicate changes to distributors, to print and send new price lists, and to implement systemic changes. Even consumer prices can be very rigid and held to levels set far in advance of the actual sale—for example, tickets embossed with the price or marketing literature that quotes checking account fees. New pricing technology lets companies make more frequent adjustments, allowing them to profit from even small fluctuations in customer demand and behavior. In addition, technologies that automate price approvals for individual accounts can greatly improve a company's responsiveness to specific customer requests.

With increased flexibility and speed in setting and communicating prices, a company can react rapidly to shifts in industry supply and demand. For example, when overall capacity utilization is high, order lead times short, or inventory levels low, prices can be raised temporarily. But when demand sags, a company might use targeted short-term promotions to optimize volume and profit under the new conditions. The electronics supplier mentioned in Chapter 5 realized about $25 million in increased profits by adjusting prices faster than its competitors after an overseas production shortfall led to temporary shortages of a key component.

BETTER SEGMENTATION

Most marketers know that some customers will pay more than others for a product because they desire its benefits more. But still, most companies have difficulty tailoring prices to customer segments because they cannot identify which customers to target before a purchase, or because it is difficult to customize offerings. On the front lines, salespeople often have few tools to identify customers by segment—whether, for instance, they generally buy high-priced or discounted items.

New technologies allow companies to segment customers quickly by drawing upon multiple sources of information—historical pocket price data, buying histories, or responses to online questionnaires, for example. The experience of one electronic components company with a large customer base shows how this can work. The company relied on purchase histories to segment core customers, who bought a majority of their components from the company, from fill-in customers, who bought a majority of their components from a competitor and came to this company only in emergencies. Through segmented pricing, this supplier regularly charged fill-in customers a premium of up to 20 percent compared to the price its core customers paid. Fill-in customers, who gained the added benefit of an assured supply in a crisis, willingly paid the additional amount.

PRICING TOOLS

To profit from greater pricing precision, flexibility, and segmentation, an astute pricing organization can select from a variety of tools, as shown in Exhibit 10-2. Administration tools help efficiently set and communicate the right price for each transaction, as well as easing the approval process. Reporting and performance management tools focus on keeping score and

Exhibit 10-2   The Software Tools across the Three Sources of Value

	Administration	Reporting	Market Research	Optimization
Greater precision	• Configure complicated orders automatically • Automatic notification of exceptions	• Transaction profitability reporting to single sale, account, or product level	• Real-time data on current demand elasticity • Real-time data on competitor prices and availability	• Optimized prices based on multiple data sources • Full basket of goods optimized with unlimited incremental price changes
Greater flexibility	• Automatically codify any list price adjustments or discount changes	• Daily reports on key metrics	• Up-to-date notification of elasticity and competitor price changes	• With real-time data streaming, optimization engine can recommend price and product bundle changes automatically
Better segmentation	• Permit deployment of multilayered discount or list price schedule	• Transaction profitability reports by any segment • Identify opportunity areas by segment	• Market research to identify buying behaviors by defined segments	• Engine can be set to run optimization model with different rules and targets for each segment

allow companies to scrutinize closely customers, segments, products, regions, and salespeople to identify untapped pricing opportunities or problems. In addition, market research and optimization tools are developing rapidly. Both types are prescriptive in recommending a price based on massive data analysis.

ADMINISTRATION

To the uninitiated, the processes of assigning a price to an individual transaction or customer may seem almost trivial, but setting individual prices is quite cumbersome for many organizations. *Pricing configuration* is the process of establishing the list price and the possible discounts as applied to individual orders.

Pricing Configurators.   Many companies use a two-dimensional table to administer prices: Essentially every SKU has an assigned price. This would be a straightforward system if, for example, a company with 1000 SKUs sold these to every customer at the same price, leaving only 1000 prices to manage. But complications develop when the company wants to differentiate prices based on channel, customer segment, geographic market, or some other attribute.

Say the company with 1000 SKUs has four different distributor classes, each under a different pricing program, and four different levels of volume discounts. Now there are 16,000 unique prices to manage. In addition, if the company runs unique promotions across 10 regional markets, there are suddenly 160,000 different prices to administer. Not only is there a greater likelihood of error, but the sheer plethora of possible prices makes it more difficult to respond to changing market conditions or to pursue a segmented approach to pricing—for instance, by lowering prices in the Northwest for large customers in response to a local threat.

New technology has simplified the task by enabling rules-based pricing configurators that build up a price based on groupings of customers and products. In the case above, the company would start with the base of 1000 prices, then use calculations instead of tables to assign a price to a particular customer. Instead of 160,000 prices in its tables, the company would have to administer 1,018 variables: 1000 prices, four channel discounts, four volume discounts, and 10 regional possibilities. The configurator would calculate a customer's price based on these variables, basically multiplying the base price by the appropriate discounts.

If the technology stopped here, a configurator would be little more than an elaborate spreadsheet that could quickly create pricing tables based on a handful of easily changed variables. But in action, configurators handle dozens of discount possibilities and price arrangements, which could easily result in millions of potential prices that a company could charge for its range of products. Also, a configurator can target special pricing actions based on a combination of attributes, such as customer size, geographic market, and order history, which becomes more complicated than changing variables in a formula.

Price configurators allow a company to approach segmentation from several directions, combining attributes as necessary, with a process that is less prone to administrative error. Companies offering many product permutations that can be made to order or mixed and matched, such as computers or custom-built bicycles, are especially good candidates for pricing configurators because of the great potential for an unmanageable number of price points.

Pricing Approval Workflow Tools. The pressure to respond quickly to a customer's quote request or offer can hamper strict oversight of individual deals, but a new generation of pricing approval workflow tools has made the challenge easier to confront. While the episodic nature of pricing decisions at the industry and product/market levels allows fairly routine approval processes through, for instance, strategy review meetings with senior management, the volume and frequency of decisions at the transaction level can make appropriate management difficult. Companies have found it necessary to sacrifice due diligence and oversight to gain the competitive advantage of quick responses to customer inquiries. Fortunately, many ERP and pricing software packages now include workflow capabilities that hasten the approval process, for example, by automatically routing deals requiring approval to the proper managers. This can allow better competitive responses, faster reaction to market changes such as supply or demand fluctuations, and quicker and more robust negotiations without diminishing the amount of oversight of transactions.

REPORTING

There is an old adage: You cannot manage what you cannot measure. This is especially germane to pricing. Pricing reporting tools enable companies to measure and pinpoint pricing opportunities at many different levels of an organization—from a chief executive or vice president of marketing setting the high-level product and segment strategy, to individual sales reps making sure that their increases in volume amount to profitable growth and that their performance compares favorably to their peers.

Frontline Decision Support. As we have emphasized throughout this book, in many businesses the sales force has a monumental job that must often be accomplished with limited information. New generations of databases that are easier to manipulate and access, as well as other new technologies, have enhanced the ability of companies to provide frontline decision support. Traditionally, when faced with a competitive negotiation, most sales reps have relied on their own experience and knowledge when deciding how to price a deal. In many cases, the collective memory of the organization is absent from the decision, although even the best sales reps could benefit from this knowledge.

In businesses where list prices and standard terms and conditions are merely starting points for negotiated deals, new software and database management tools can help pricers, salespeople in the field, call center representatives, and anyone else working on the sell side of a negotiation optimize each deal. Depending on the abilities of the system, new technology can find answers to questions along multiple dimensions that have not previously been available amid fast-moving negotiations, such as

- What is the pocket margin for the products being quoted?
- Are there substitute products that would deliver more margin without sacrificing quality or customer satisfaction?
- Based on this customer's history (or the history of similar customers), what is the likelihood that the current offer will be accepted?
- Can this deal be improved by changing shipping or delivery terms, upfront volume requirements, penalty clauses, or terms of sale?
- If the deal requires special approval, who has the authority to give that approval?

More robust applications might also answer these additional questions:

- How quickly can the product be delivered considering current inventory and supply-chain dynamics?
- How does the proposed price compare with the latest prices given to similar customers?
- What are the opportunities for cross-selling (offering additional products) or up-selling (shifting the customer to a higher-margin product), particularly in light of the company's customer relationship management strategy?

Getting the unique set of prices and terms right for a specific customer can be eased by aggregating the appropriate data behind the scenes and using pricing software to deliver specific counsel to the front lines precisely when needed.

Performance Reporting and Diagnostic Tools. Performance reporting and diagnostic tools offer a company the ability to evaluate pricing performance continuously and to identify opportunities for improvement. A company will find it very difficult to create the price advantage without a clear set of timely performance metrics, and new software can aggregate transaction data using a variety of measurements. For example, such software may examine pocket margin data by region, by deal won against specific competitors, by sales rep, by customer industry or size, or by whether the deal was the first sale to this customer. With any criterion for analysis, differences in performance across categories will be highlighted, and these differences may point to improvement opportunities that may be easily captured, such as pulling low-performing sales reps in for additional training in negotiations skills or investing in building a brand in a region with low performance.

As shown in Exhibit 10-3, pricing performance reports can run the gamut from straightforward to rather complex, depending on the sophistication of the software and the needs of the company. Along with crunching the data itself, automating these reports can bring a range of additional

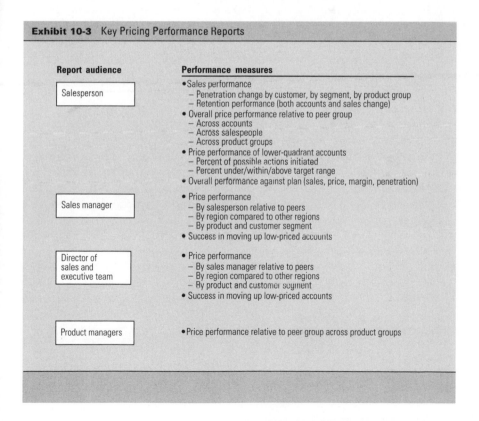

Exhibit 10-3 Key Pricing Performance Reports

Report audience	Performance measures

Salesperson	• Sales performance
	  – Penetration change by customer, by segment, by product group
	  – Retention performance (both accounts and sales change)
	• Overall price performance relative to peer group
	  – Across accounts
	  – Across salespeople
	  – Across product groups
	• Price performance of lower-quadrant accounts
	  – Percent of possible actions initiated
	  – Percent under/within/above target range
	• Overall performance against plan (sales, price, margin, penetration)

Sales manager	• Price performance
	  – By salesperson relative to peers
	  – By region compared to other regions
	  – By product and customer segment
	• Success in moving up low-priced accounts

Director of sales and executive team	• Price performance
	  – By sales manager relative to peers
	  – By region compared to other regions
	  – By product and customer segment
	• Success in moving up low-priced accounts

Product managers	• Price performance relative to peer group across product groups

benefits. Uniformity forces a company to use the same nomenclature across functions, geographies, and units. Simply put, everyone will know what *pocket price* means. Goals and individual contributions needed to achieve those goals are easier to articulate and monitor. Also, managers are looking at the same reports, although some may look at a companywide perspective and others unit by unit. This ability to make apples-to-apples comparisons also adds to peer pressure, which can be a significant motivation toward performance.

MARKET RESEARCH

Price precision requires that a company continuously test the market's zone of indifference. Few companies test different price levels for their products because administering a pilot or traditional survey-based research can cost as much as $250,000 and take up to three months.

Real-Time Testing. New technologies, however, allow real-time testing of different prices, with customer response available immediately for analysis, and can cost as little as 5 percent of the price of traditional testing. If, for example, a financial services institution wants to determine the sales impact of a 10-basis-point (0.1 percentage point) increase in mortgage rates, it might test the response by quoting the higher price to every fiftieth caller to its call center and comparing the purchase rates. These tools can be used on the Internet, through a call center, or by adjusting price recommendations given to a salesperson during face-to-face negotiations.

Such testing can have dramatic results. For example, one software services company conducted online price tests for an electronics company. Prices on four products were cut by 7 percent. For three of these products, sales volume rose by 5 to 20 percent, not enough to justify the price reduction. But sales of the high-end model more than doubled. Data from the test showed that most of that increase came from high schools and universities. The price reduction had uncovered significant latent demand from this segment, and as a result the company created a Web site to cater to these buyers, offering them prices that were not available to other groups. In addition, the company rethought its off-line approach to selling its products to the academic market.

Web-Based Elasticity Surveys. Unlike real-time price testing, which watches as customers make actual purchases, Web-based price elasticity surveys ask customers to respond to a series of potential real-world purchase situations. The cost and time required for such market research has kept many companies from really understanding how customers would react to different combinations of prices and benefits. New Web-based tools can cut the cost and time required for such analysis to about one to two weeks and $30,000, compared with up to ten weeks and $250,000 for traditional research. Early fears that Web-based surveys may be flawed because the sample base would be biased toward higher-income individuals (the demographic of early Internet users) have been alleviated by market research vendors that maintain consumer panels that are closely representative of the general population.

Web-Based Pricing Intelligence.   Along with helping analyze customer demand patterns, new technology allows Web-based competitive pricing research, which can give companies a more up-to-date picture of the market environment. Using software known as Web-bots, companies can comb the Internet automatically and gather data on competitors' prices. An electronics retailer, for example, may want to track prices offered on key product lines by a specific rival in order to ensure that it maintains its price parity on those products against that competitor. These tools can provide companies with price and availability information on competing, substitute, and complementary products, and are particularly useful for products with highly price-sensitive demand or in sectors distinguished by aggressive markdown strategies and short product life cycles.

OPTIMIZATION

Price optimization tools analyze customer buying behavior and market supply to provide recommendations for list prices, customer-specific negotiated discounts, markdowns, and other pricing elements to maximize profit potential. Powerful modeling algorithms using internal and external data can forecast pricing trends throughout the life cycle of a product.[2] Optimization tools go beyond other technology we have discussed by suggesting specific price points rather than just presenting data.

List Price Optimization Tools.   As discussed in Chapter 6, companies often struggle to set initial prices that will maximize the profits for a new product. List price optimization tools attempt to model the expected demand elasticity for new products. By breaking a product down into its characteristics—size, color, features, functionality—list price optimization engines try to predict how the market will react to a new offering. When a major computer manufacturer introduced a new line of servers, it analyzed the

---

[2]For a detailed discussion of yield management, see Robert G. Cross, *Revenue Management: Hard-Core Tactics for Market Domination* (New York: Broadway Books, 1998).

price sensitivities of individual components and configurations based on historical price and volume data to model expected demand patterns. The overall solution produced a 1.4 percentage point increase in ROS within the first year of its implementation. The software also forecast the cross-elasticities between the new line of servers and its existing products, which was useful in managing cannibalization.

Transaction Optimization Tools.   In addition, transaction optimization tools recommend discount mixes offered to customers on individual orders. Based on historical order data, market conditions, and competitor behavior, these tools can suggest price and discount levels that would maximize the margin gained on each sale. Beyond these waterfall elements, however, transaction optimization tools can also highlight opportunities for cross-selling or up-selling.

One industrial manufacturer traditionally processed by hand about 250,000 sales requests a year. With such volume, the company could not evaluate each request based on historical competitor prices, past orders, current inventories, market trends, or other relevant data. A transaction optimization system automated the process and brought these factors into play. Now, when a request arrives, the system not only routes it to the appropriate managers, but may also spot, for example, opportunities to suggest a warranty service, substitute a higher-margin product, or increase the pocket price without increasing the risk that the order would fall through. Among the benefits brought by the optimization solution was that the company was able to shorten the time needed to respond to purchase inquiries by 42 percent and to cut the time needed for negotiations by 60 percent.

Markdown Optimization Tools.   Markdown optimization tools are also available that can help companies decide how much and when to cut prices in order to clear inventory while still maximizing profits, particularly on products with a short life cycle, such as seasonal fashions and perishable goods. The software not only estimates the shift in margin and demand brought by the lower prices, it also considers carrying costs, marketing costs, and seasonal effects, among other factors. A Canadian specialty clothing chain using an optimization system increased its gross margin by a percentage point by marking down its seasonal fashions weeks later. In addition, the system gave managers real-time information on sales and inventory, which helped them make decisions for each store or style category about promoting excess inventory and selecting new merchandise. Previously, such decisions were time consuming, since paper documents had to be exchanged and analyzed and were made for the entire chain.

PUTTING THE RIGHT TECHNOLOGY IN PLACE

Advances in technology have opened opportunities for more precise pricing and segmentation and for responding more quickly to market shifts. But how does a company devise and execute a pricing strategy that takes full advantage of these advances? The goal should be to create a system that exploits these opportunities, rather than to invest in IT for IT's sake.

In approaching a technology-enabled pricing system, companies must be careful not to let the possibilities offered by these new systems conflict with key strategic objectives, core business principles, or brand promises. For instance, an optimization system might suggest that there would be short-term profit gains if a new product's price were lowered, but a company would want to reject the suggestion if its long-term strategy were to position the product as a high-benefit, upscale offering. Similarly, a retailer with a core brand image that promises consistency might not want to treat different customers in different ways. The online bookseller Amazon.com released a fury of bad press and customer frustration when an online marketing test in 2000 conflicted with its brand reputation. To test different price levels, the e-tailer offered discounts of 30, 35, and 40 percent off DVDs to online shoppers. Electronic chats on a Web site helped expose the test, and customers were angered at the idea of being treated differently. Amazon ended the test once complaints began arriving.

Pricing technology should follow pricing strategy, and not the other way around. For some companies, rudimentary tracking and testing initiatives can provide a strong foundation for a pricing strategy with an investment of no more than a dedicated analyst, computing time, and standard spreadsheet software. If a company decides a more sophisticated system is warranted, managers should evaluate the tools that have already been created and determine whether they might make the foundation for an enterprise-class solution. A company's IT department should also be scrutinized to see whether it has the skills necessary to take disparate pieces of software created for different groups within the organization and weave them into a cohesive whole that can support cross-functional goals.

In looking for technological solutions, most companies will have to evaluate offers from outside vendors as well as weigh options developed internally. A three-step process can help managers judge the numerous possibilities being presented and pinpoint the appropriate technology for their needs.

STEP 1: "PAIN POINTS"

The essential first step in selecting a pricing solution is for a company to conduct a self examination to list its *pain points*—the key inefficiencies, redundancies, and gaps in the overall planning, management, and analysis of prices. Specifically, the internal diagnostic should assess whether the right information is being used by the right people at the right time to make effective price decisions.

Asking certain types of questions can help in evaluating pricing practices and identifying key pain points:

- How are prices and price changes administered? Are prices and pricing decisions properly administered? Are there clear rules and objectives for pricing? How are deals approved?
- Are there regular reports on pricing and sales effectiveness? Are there regular reports on account and product profitability, order compliance, and exceptional sale terms?
- What kind of information is leveraged to set and manage prices?
- Do pricing analysts examine alternative scenarios based on different prices and different market situations?

Once these pain points have been identified, the universe of possible solutions will shrink according to which capabilities are needed to address key failings.

STEP 2: BEST-IN-BREED VS. ONE-STOP SHOP

The next step is to narrow the external options by determining whether best-in-breed providers or a one-stop shop would be more appropriate.

A best-in-breed approach means that one or more vendors with distinctive expertise are hired, and their products will be integrated into a coherent infrastructure. For instance, one vendor might be picked because of its markdown optimization software, while another would be chosen to handle transaction profitability analysis. This approach will likely create a more sophisticated and robust solution than the one-stop approach, and it prevents a company from becoming too dependent on one vendor for all its business IT needs. On the other hand, a best-in-breed approach requires effective system integration, which can be a significant expense.

The best-in-breed approach is most appropriate for companies that have well-defined IT implementation processes, have experience working simultaneously with multiple vendors, and have problems that require highly sophisticated solutions to derive maximum benefits. Companies that meet these conditions can best take advantage of the cutting-edge functionality that aligns with their critical needs, without the headache of a complicated and unfamiliar implementation process.

A one-stop approach would focus on vendors who already provide or can provide broader enterprise software suites for a company. For instance, a company already using one vendor's ERP system may decide it is most convenient to buy a pricing module from that same vendor. The advantages to this approach are mostly greater efficiencies—easier integration, one point of contact with a vendor, and potentially less internal training—while the main disadvantage is the potential opportunity cost from using a less robust system. This approach is best for companies that have less need for sophisticated features and have limited experience with software integration.

STEP 3: SIX CRITERIA FOR FINAL SELECTION

Vendors or internal systems that survive the first two steps should face a final evaluation based on the criteria shown in Exhibit 10-4. Both internal and external solutions should be evaluated on technological fit, functionality, the level of ongoing service and support needed, and total costs. In addition, the corporate profile and references of external vendors must be considered carefully. External vendors should be ranked through face-to-face meetings; examination of publicly available materials, including analyst and industry reports; interviews with current customers; and a review of the company's financial statements and other reports.

Exhibit 10-4 Companies Should Evaluate Systems across Six Criteria

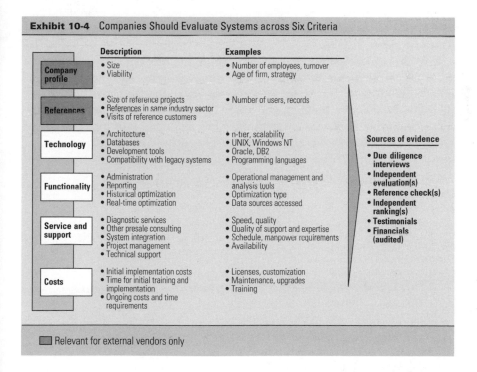

	Description	Examples	
Company profile	• Size • Viability	• Number of employees, turnover • Age of firm, strategy	
References	• Size of reference projects • References in same industry sector • Visits of reference customers	• Number of users, records	
Technology	• Architecture • Databases • Development tools • Compatibility with legacy systems	• n-tier, scalability • UNIX, Windows NT • Oracle, DB2 • Programming languages	**Sources of evidence** • **Due diligence** **interviews** • **Independent** **evaluation(s)** • **Reference check(s)** • **Independent** **ranking(s)** • **Testimonials** • **Financials** **(audited)**
Functionality	• Administration • Reporting • Historical optimization • Real-time optimization	• Operational management and analysis tools • Optimization type • Data sources accessed	
Service and support	• Diagnostic services • Other presale consulting • System integration • Project management • Technical support	• Speed, quality • Quality of support and expertise • Schedule, manpower requirements • Availability	
Costs	• Initial implementation costs • Time for initial training and implementation • Ongoing costs and time requirements	• Licenses, customization • Maintenance, upgrades • Training	

▇ Relevant for external vendors only

Individual companies will give varying importance to the different criteria. For example, one might value the experience of a third-party vendor and another the desire to develop an in-house solution. But by methodically examining the finalists along these criteria, managers will more effectively understand the tradeoffs between competing vendors as well as internal solutions, and the decision that is best for that particular company should become clearer. Ranking the solutions along these six dimensions will help guide managers toward the right provider.

*   *   *

Technology is a key enabler for the price advantage. Without the proper technical foundation, companies will find progress toward pricing excellence limited. But while pricing technology has improved rapidly in recent years, few companies have been able to reap the full benefits from these advancements. And as technology continues to evolve, these missed opportunities will only multiply.

For many companies, however, using IT to supplement pricing initiatives may not require substantial investments in new technology. Current systems may be able to support new applications that add transparency, speed, and accuracy to the pricing process and allow managers to act decisively and confidently. The key is to identify carefully how technology can support a pricing initiative and focus on those areas that have the potential for the greatest benefits.

Whether developing an in-house solution, buying software off the shelf, or working closely with a vendor to develop a customized solution, most companies striving to attain the price advantage will have to upgrade their ability to access pricing data, share insights, and respond to opportunities. But wise investment here that allows a company to move closer to creating the price advantage will yield disproportionate returns.

CHAPTER 11

Legal Issues

More than 60 years ago, the U.S. Supreme Court said restrictions on price competition are threats "to the central nervous system of the economy."[1] Consistent with this view, governments throughout the world have sought to curtail practices that interfere with market-based price competition, even as they pass conflicting legislation such as farm price supports and minimum wage laws that effectively rein in market forces.

While the laws impact many aspects of pricing behavior, they provide relatively little black-and-white guidance, but many shades of gray. In most cases, legitimate business objectives can be achieved by adjusting the approach to correspond with the degree of risk a company wishes to assume. More often than not, this risk is manifested in trade relations issues or sometimes civil litigation and adverse publicity, rather than full-scale government investigations. Pricing strategies followed by almost all businesses are affected by the law, but many respond by closing their eyes to the implications unless called to task or by adopting an ultraconservative approach that misses many opportunities.

Avoiding or exaggerating the legal realities obscures the potential of price as a powerful lever of performance. Many companies shun pricing programs that are lawful because they believe, sometimes falsely, that there is even a slight chance of legal repercussions. Indeed, it is relatively easy for those affected by a pricing decision to complain and even to take legal action, while it is much harder to prevail in court. Many companies view handling these complaints as a cost of doing business. Even more prevalent is a risk-averse mindset in pricing strategy brought by a desire to remain well within the most narrow, conservative reading of the law, foreclosing the possibility of even considering a valuable price program. Along with appetite for risk, other factors—intensity of industry regulation,

---

[1] *United States v. Socony-Vacuum Oil Co.*, 310 U.S. 150, 224 n. 59 (1940).

previous legal problems, the stature of the company, and its general cul-
ture—will help determine a company's willingness to embark on an aggressive pricing program.

There are ways to accomplish just about any reasonable strategic pricing objective within a range of legal risk that most companies would find
acceptable. Yet, among businesspeople, legal issues are probably the least
understood pricing parameter. This is not surprising, given that pricing is
one of the more complex, specialized areas of law. Recent changes in the
laws governing pricing—changes that challenge or effectively eliminate
some convenient rules of thumb—have created an environment that allows
more flexibility in pricing but adds even more complexity. To accomplish
pricing objectives, executives must understand the legal parameters of pricing and choose among the many lawful approaches to capture the maximum value from a pricing program.

In this discussion of some of the legal considerations surrounding pricing programs, we are not attempting to offer an exhaustive treatment of
the issues, legislation, and rulings relevant to pricing. We also have no in-
tention of offering legal advice. Such a treatment is beyond the scope of
this book. The law is constantly in flux, and companies should always consult specialized attorneys if they believe their actions might conflict with
applicable law. This book is descriptive and does not constitute legal advice. However, by addressing the subject, we hope to show managers that
there is more room than many might assume to pursue the price advantage
within the letter and spirit of applicable laws.

The legal parameters discussed here are broadly applicable to most
management decisions involving pricing, particularly in the United States
and the European Union. Pricing issues in the United States are generally
addressed by the Sherman Antitrust Act of 1890 and the Robinson-Patman
Act of 1936. The European Union is also watchful of practices that may inhibit competition, particularly by companies that are viewed as dominant
in their markets. The relevant EU statutes in this area are Articles 81 and
82 of the European Community Treaty (formerly Articles 85 and 86). (See
Appendix 2, "Antitrust Issues," for a fuller discussion of U.S. and EU
statutes from a business perspective, as well as contact information for antitrust authorities in many markets.)

In other markets, Japan has begun more active enforcement of its competition laws, which are similar to U.S. laws. The rules and enforcement
levels in Australia are generally similar to those in the European Union. In
emerging markets like Eastern Europe or China, there is currently not a
high level of enforcement in anticompetitive behavior. This situation is
changing rapidly as countries like Brazil, for example, are becoming much
more aggressive in enforcing competition laws. In addition, the 10 Eastern
European countries scheduled to join the European Union in 2004, and

others that aspire to join, will likely take actions to bring domestic regulations up to EU standards more quickly. Companies competing in different markets will obviously have to be familiar with the applicable local laws. In general, however, globalization is pushing a trend toward somewhat greater uniformity in antitrust laws of individual nations.

In this chapter we will cover three topics: first, the areas in pricing strategy that might trigger particularly close scrutiny; then, ways to minimize the legal risk while pursuing legitimate objectives like market segmentation, regional pricing, and reducing the threat of price wars; and finally, considerations a company should weigh when calling in internal or external experts in pricing law.

PRICING DECISIONS THAT RAISE RED FLAGS

Legal issues can arise at each of the three levels of pricing. At the industry strategy level, laws generally forbid companies from price fixing either by directly colluding with competitors to affect industry prices or by indirectly reaching an agreement through the inappropriate use of price signaling. Monopoly pricing laws prohibit companies from undertaking pricing practices that serve to establish or exploit power derived from dominance in a given market. At the product/market level, vertical price fixing laws constrain a manufacturer's ability to maintain consistency in prices set by its resellers. At the transactional level, price discrimination laws can constrain the ability to charge different prices to different customers based on willingness to pay or perceived benefits.

There are also certain situations when the likelihood of legal scrutiny is increased, which could limit pricing flexibility. These situations are not necessarily illegal nor do they automatically prompt legal review, but their presence usually requires a company to proceed more cautiously. They include the following:

- *Dominant position.* A company occupies a dominant position in its industry or market. This can involve monopoly power, where a company has the ability to control prices or exclude competition, such as local telephone companies and utilities, or market power, where a company has the ability to maintain prices above competitive levels for a significant time period.
- *High visibility.* A company's actions draw attention because of a perceived disproportionate economic effect or its attractiveness as a political target. Examples include major airlines and pharmaceutical companies.
- *New visibility.* A company makes a substantial change in the way it does business, such as redoing its distribution system or making a

significant acquisition. For instance, U.S. agricultural and construction equipment manufacturer Case had to defend itself against
charges of anticompetitive conduct when it dropped dealers following its 1985 acquisition of International Harvester's agricultural machinery businesses.

■ *Previous behavior.* A company or industry has a history of antitrust
problems, particularly in the pricing area.

In addition to these issues focused on a company's posture within an
industry, certain customer-specific pricing actions should be undertaken
with a very clear understanding of the legal boundaries. On their own,
these actions are not necessarily illegal and they could all be part of a responsible pricing program. Such actions include the following:

■ *Account-specific pricing.* A company sells at different prices or offers
varying incentives to different customers. For many companies, this is
a way of life as they try to differentiate their offerings or respond to
the demands from powerful buyers.

■ *Performance-based discounts.* A company emphasizes performance-
based discounts for resellers to make channels more efficient, which
may cause actual or de facto distributor, dealer, or end-user termina-
tions or, at the very least, create "winners" and "losers."

■ *Exclusivity and loyalty arrangements.* A company offers exclusivity
agreements or loyalty rewards that decrease total cost of ownership
for some customers. U.S. beer giant Anheuser Busch, for example,
was challenged by a group of small brewers in 1997 over its "100%
Share of Mind" program, which gave rebates, attractive payment
terms, and reimbursement for some marketing activities to loyal
wholesalers. Seven years later, the case remained open, but early court
decisions favored Busch.

■ *Product bundling.* A company offers special prices for bundled products or services or does not sell individual products or services separately. This can be an issue when one component of the bundle is not
available from competitors, effectively extending a monopoly to the
entire bundle.

■ *Resale price setting or influencing.* A company formally sets or influ-
ences resale prices. Recently, particularly as large resellers have aggressively used their market power to push prices lower, many
manufacturers in diverse industries have taken a much more active role
in dictating or influencing the ultimate price of their products.

■ *Global price differences.* A company varies its prices by country or region in order to address differing brand positions, markets, demand,
and other factors. This can be particularly difficult within the Euro-

pean Union where, for instance, Nintendo was fined €149 million in 2002 for taking action to prevent the lower prices that it was charging in the United Kingdom from undermining its higher prices on the European continent.

In addition to customer initiatives that may raise red flags, there are also moves dealing more directly with competitors that could increase the legal risks of pricing programs. Two of the more common are these:

- *Joint activity.* A company forms a joint venture or engages in joint bidding with one or more actual or potential competitors, or it participates with competitors in efforts to exchange data or set standards. Also, membership in industry cooperatives or trade associations, which may provide forums to discuss pricing issues, could increase the chance of regulatory scrutiny, unless such discussions stay within rather narrow bounds.
- *Price or price strategy transparency.* A company communicates its prices or pricing intentions to the market. For example, in the 1980s, DuPont and other manufacturers of gasoline additives provided advance public notice of price increases that went beyond the requirements of their contracts with customers. In 1984, a U.S. appellate court overruled a decision of the Federal Trade Commission (FTC) and upheld this practice, among other reasons because such advance notice was useful to customers and permitted them to plan for such increases.

A better understanding of the areas that may raise legal challenges should not prevent a company from embarking on a sensible pricing program. But with this understanding, a company can seek ways that minimize its legal risk while pursuing its pricing objectives.

MINIMIZING RISKS WHILE MEETING PRICING OBJECTIVES

The trend in legal regulation of pricing over the last several decades has been to move away from judging behavior based on economic assumptions and toward focusing on demonstrable economic effect. As a result, in order for a legal challenge to a company's pricing policies to succeed in court, it must be backed more often by hard data rather than economic theory. This trend has unleashed a great deal more flexibility and opportunity for companies that want to use price to improve performance.

Companies can consider and pursue legitimate business purposes through the use of pricing. But since pricing has often been the focus of antitrust laws and other regulations that seek to maintain or create a competitive market, a manager would be wise to know what approaches have been deemed lawful in the past. By understanding the flexibility that legislatures and courts have allowed, companies can confidently develop and pursue meaningful pricing objectives based on the degree of risk they wish to assume. In this section, we will consider some of the more common pricing objectives and how the law has been applied. (For a discussion of legal parameters in postmerger pricing, see Chapter 8.)

MARKET SEGMENTATION

As detailed in Chapter 4, companies are justified and smart to consider the perceived benefits customers place on their products and to price according to these benefits, segmenting the market into groups of customers with different benefits perceptions. In addition, companies may wish to charge different prices based on the near- or long-term profitability to the company of particular customers or segments. To embark on such a program, it is important to understand how value pricing can be implemented without violating the laws against price or promotional discrimination. Note that while some practices may be well within the law, they may cause tensions with customers, and, as with any business decision, their effects on trade relations should be carefully considered when deciding whether to adopt them.

One method that has been generally deemed acceptable is to make price tiers universally available. For example, use share-of-wallet discounts instead of those based on volume. Activity-based discounts available to all customers, such as incentives for prompt payment, also have typically met with little opposition.

Since, in the United States, the Robinson-Patman Act does not cover services, it has also been generally safe here to price services differently to different customers based on benefits delivered. (Some laws in individual states, however, purport to cover service pricing.) This approach can also extend to bundled product and service offerings, such as the sale of a server along with a maintenance contract, where the benefits of the services predominate. However, these approaches could be illegal for dominant companies in the European Union.

Another acceptable segmentation approach is to create real differences in products to appeal to the different needs of customer segments. One element in determining unlawful price discrimination in the United States is whether products within the same grade or quality were sold at different prices. When products have true functional or physical differences (different branding is not enough), then the resulting price discrimination is not considered unlawful. This approach has also been ruled acceptable in the European Union.

Companies can also charge different prices based on cost-to-serve differences, if the actual savings and nothing more are passed on to customers. Companies using this approach must be able to quantify clearly the cost-to-serve differences among customers.

U.S. companies have also been able to argue successfully that discriminatory prices were necessary to meet a competitor's price and that doing otherwise would have risked losing a customer or breaking from traditional price parity. It was important to have a reasonable basis for believing the discounted price was necessary at the time the decision was made and to establish firmly what the competitive price was. While this approach may work in the United States, it may not be legal for dominant companies in the European Union.

DIFFERENT PROMOTIONAL INCENTIVES

Companies often wish to provide incentives to resellers that market their products in certain ways or that put sufficient resources behind promoting the sale of their products. In so doing, they must consider the parameters of the law regarding promotional discrimination in the United States or the law governing price discrimination in the European Union. A dominant supplier has less flexibility under EU law, and the same may be true in the United States.

Providing different promotional benefits to intermediaries that sell a supplier's services is lawful under the Robinson-Patman Act, as the statute does not apply to service providers. In addition, purchasers that use the supplier's product in making their own product are outside the law's scope because they are generally seen as an end user rather than a reseller. The Robinson-Patman Act may become relevant, however, if the end user actively promotes the fact that its product was made using the supplier's product and is then compensated for its marketing efforts. As usual, dominant companies in the European Union have less leeway.

Companies are also on firmer ground if they make incentives available to everyone. This way, if a reseller does not receive a certain promotional benefit, it is because the reseller chose not to take advantage of an incentive that was available. Segmentation is accomplished by designing programs that could be used by all competing customers, but, due to the requirements, certain customers are less likely to participate.

Promotional incentives can also be linked directly to the value received by the supplier. For example, the size of the incentive payments can be based on the number of units purchased (an additional $10 in promotional funds for every case purchased), the actual cost of the marketing media (more money for television ads than local newspaper ads), or the relative value of the promotion (more money for advertising on shopping carts, which is more effective than window advertisements).

REGIONAL AND INTERNATIONAL PRICING

When a company sells its products in different markets, it often does not make sense to charge the same price in each. The markets could be different regions of the same country, different countries, or different global regions. Apart from tariff, tax, and currency considerations, costs in one market, for example, may be higher because more has been invested there in brand building. Corporate objectives may also be different. For instance, a company may want to focus on building market share in Greater China, while its goal in Southeast Asia is to increase profit. Such variances in pricing strategy across markets can call attention to a company's practices, and a clear understanding of the legal parameters is necessary.

In the United States, regional (or even account-specific) pricing is lawful as long as competing customers are treated alike or there are lawful reasons to differentiate. In the European Union, this strategy historically has been troublesome if the different prices are enforced by mechanisms that inhibit the movement of goods or services between countries or into the European Union. Discriminatory prices, like territorial and other restrictions on product or service movement between EU countries, are viewed as fundamentally suspect and less likely to qualify for an antitrust exemption or defense.

However, companies in the European Union can keep lower prices outside the Union from threatening a higher-value position within the Union. Companies that own the trademark attached to their products can bring trademark infringement proceedings to prevent the resale within the European Union of goods that were first sold outside the European Union. This can work if the buyer outside the European Union was not given permission to import the product into the Union. This way, the seller can establish its distribution and pricing policies in such a way as to allow differentiated prices within and outside the European Union.

PRICE LEADERSHIP AND PRICE WARS

Price leadership can unlock tremendous value in an industry, while price wars generally hurt everyone involved. (These issues are covered in Chapters 5 and 9, respectively.) But while companies might want to engage in leadership or avoid a war, they are often held back by prohibitions against price agreements with competitors. Most are appropriately cautious about even the appearance of such an agreement. However, in ways that do not run afoul of laws against price fixing, companies can inform the industry that they will vigorously act against poor pricing behavior and will pursue and support good pricing conduct.

Simply imitating a competitor's pricing behavior, a tactic known as *conscious parallelism*, is lawful in the United States and the European Union as long as there has been no agreement among the companies involved. For example, airlines frequently announce price increases and, in some cases, competitors match those changes within hours. To casual observers, this may look like collusion. But the move is economic, rather than collusive. Armed with new information (one carrier has raised it prices), the followers have recognized that profits would increase more with a higher price than with the additional volume that continued lower prices might bring.

Communicating prices or pricing intentions publicly to stakeholders is lawful, even if a competitor sees and reacts to it, although there is an important caveat: The communication should have a real commercial purpose. This purpose cannot be merely to signal intentions to competitors, but could be, for instance, to give customers needed information for their own budgeting or to inform shareholders of a likely impact on earnings. An important limitation is that the communication should not be speculative; it cannot be a trail balloon that says a company is "thinking about" raising prices. A company must announce what it is doing, rather than what it might do.

Companies are allowed to explain the reasoning behind a pricing change in their public announcements. Such clarity, for example, would have helped a packaged food manufacturer when it lowered its prices in the early 1990s to clear its inventory in response to a regulatory change. (This case is also discussed in Chapter 9.) To avoid a price war, the company could have communicated the reason behind the new prices.

A company can also combat destructive competitive behavior by establishing credible retaliatory mechanisms that clearly convey the futility of a price war. Such efforts go beyond talk and can change a competitor's calculation of the attractiveness of its own action. Two common weapons to accomplish this are meet-the-competition and most-favored-customer clauses.

Meet-the-competition clauses commit a company to match any lower price offered by competitors. This can discourage rogue competitors from undercutting prices in key accounts or key markets. Although price-matching practices have been challenged as anticompetitive, the practice has generally prevailed in the United States and the European Union since it is similar to the lawful practice of following a competitor's prices. In addition, price matching that lowers prices is less likely to trigger an antitrust challenge, since lower prices are seen generally as a sign of healthy competition.

Under a most-favored-customer clause, a supplier guarantees a key customer that it will be charged the lowest price offered anyone by the supplier. Such a commitment helps assure the industry that the supplier is unlikely to use price as a lever against rivals since any price reduction would have to be passed along to the supplier's core customers. In the United States, such clauses (also sometimes called most-favored-nation clauses) have generally been allowed, although in the health care industry the government has challenged them, saying they foster coordinated pricing or discourage price cutting. These provisions may be unlawful in the European Union for dominant companies, but are permitted for nondominant companies.

GUARDING AGAINST EXCESSIVE RESELLER DISCOUNTING

As the power of resellers grows in many industries, suppliers increasingly want to protect against heavy discounting of their brands by resellers, potentially resulting in brand dilution and channel conflict. For example, a company wanting to maintain a premium brand image would not want its products heavily discounted by a large retailer. As a result, suppliers often seek to set price floors or otherwise encourage their resellers to price at certain levels. At the same time, they need to ensure that they do not violate the laws governing vertical price fixing.

In the European Union, suppliers have very little room to try to influence or control the prices charged by resellers. In the United States, however, there are several programmatic approaches a company can use to influence resell prices and protect its market position, including the following:

- *Direct dealing programs.* A company can negotiate directly with the end user and dictate the price, even if an intermediary is used to facilitate the transaction. As long as the intermediary does not take title of the product, there is no vertical price fixing involved. (This is one of the few methods that can also be used in the European Union.) In a variation of this practice, a U.S. supplier can agree with the end user on a purchase price, then find a willing intermediary that would take title to the product and fill the order at that price. This approach is common when it is necessary to have inventory in the field, but where direct negotiations with the customer are needed because of the size or complexity of the project.
- *Minimum, maximum, or exact price policies.* A company can generally establish a resale pricing policy as long as there is no agreement with

the reseller to follow the policy. The policy can be enforced by dropping the reseller if it charges prices that are outside the range allowed by the policy.

- *Minimum advertised price (MAP) programs.* A supplier may encourage a certain resale price by offering a promotional allowance if the reseller agrees that the advertised price will not be less than the price set by the supplier. Such programs were challenged in the United States until 1987, when the FTC began permitting them on the basis that they were voluntary and only the promotional allowance was threatened if a reseller did not join.
- *Retail price support policies.* The reseller can receive an allowance, usually in the form of cash back, based on the proximity of its selling price to the supplier's suggested or target prices. Like MAP programs, resale support allowances in the United States are allowed as long as they are voluntary.
- *Shared price advertising.* For a specific promotion, a supplier can advertise in a particular market and offer to mention the reseller in the ad if it sells at the advertised price during the promotional period. This is a variant of MAP programs, and is allowed because it is voluntary.
- *Price waterfall engineering.* One of the most efficient ways of influencing the price that a reseller charges is to change the price that the reseller is charged. Price waterfall engineering, which is sometimes called buy-price engineering, refers to adjusting the price or price model offered a reseller to drive a desired resale price behavior. This could be simply raising the price or it could be something more complicated, such as shifting on-invoice discounts to off-invoice. Since price waterfall engineering can result in price differences between competing channels and customers, companies must take care that their practices are consistent with the legal requirements of the local price discrimination laws.

Companies in the United States, the European Union, and elsewhere can also turn to a more fundamental approach to influencing resell prices: fact-based persuasion. Using market research and economic analysis of the reseller, a supplier can demonstrate the advantages to the reseller of increasing (or even decreasing) the resale prices of the supplier's product. Then the reseller makes an independent decision. While the conversation raises few legal risks, care must be taken that there are no illicit agreements with the reseller, such as a promise to extend preferential treatment if a reseller prices in a certain way.

CALLING IN THE ATTORNEYS

Since little in the law is black and white, most business decisions carry at least some legal risk. By and large, a company that decides to take this risk, in pricing or any other area, is not purposely ignoring, much less violating, the law. More likely, it believes that its interpretation of the law is reasonable and would likely prevail if challenged.

When there is the possibility that a pricing program or decision will trigger enhanced legal scrutiny or will venture into an area where customers, competitors, or the government may question the legality of the move, it is crucial to bring in attorneys early in the process to assess the legal risks. Legal counsel with experience in pricing can provide important guidance regarding both the legality of the actions and the process the company should follow to chart the safest course.

At many companies, attorneys will work with business managers collaboratively to outline the limits of pricing policies or to structure approaches to business objectives in a manner that is consistent with the risks the company wishes to take. However, in some cases, internal (or external) attorneys may be quite conservative in evaluating strategic decisions or may try to eliminate risks completely, even in cases where company executives, armed with accurate information, would choose to assume some risk to pursue a valuable pricing program.

Where the advice of counsel historically tends toward eliminating risk or has not attempted to balance potential risk with potential reward, it is especially important for executives to think carefully about how to use and involve both internal and outside attorneys. Executives pushing toward the price advantage must be confident of the legal advice they are getting from their attorneys. The following questions can help in assessing the experience and qualifications of attorneys, whether internal or external, who are charged with evaluating potential changes to pricing policies.

■ Do the attorneys discuss both sides of an issue, balancing both the risks and the potential rewards, or do they focus only on risk and how to minimize it?
■ Is it constructive to engage the attorneys in the early stages of strategic planning? Do they bring useful insight that helps to shape the outcome, or do they take a "can't do" stance?
■ Do the attorneys have significant experience in the laws governing pricing? Does their advice reflect an understanding not only of the elements of illegal behavior, but also the myriad defenses and how to make a strong case in favor of pricing action?

■ Do the lawyers have incentives to improve shareholder returns and make real risk/return tradeoffs, or is the department measured solely on avoiding all legal and public relations risks and never being wrong?

■ Does your internal legal department or law firm have a healthy turnover, with attorneys coming from or leaving for private practices or competition authorities, or is it insular, without a great deal of experience in competition matters outside your company or industry? Are there lawyers on staff with significant antitrust experience?

In addition, it is important to consider the concept of legal privilege. Under this protection, companies cannot be forced to disclose in court and to antitrust authorities the contents of communications seeking legal advice and communications providing legal advice. In the United States, communications with both external and internal counsel are privileged, while in the European Union only communications with external, EU-admitted counsel benefit from such privilege.

*   *   *

It goes without saying that managers need to ensure that their company's pricing practices are consistent with the current relevant laws. Unfortunately, all too many companies avoid otherwise sound pricing efforts because of a misguided assessment of the legal risks they may face. There are ways to achieve just about any reasonable pricing objective while still being in compliance. Ensuring that overly conservative—or worse, incorrect—interpretations of pricing laws do not inappropriately restrict management decisions on pricing requires managers to think creatively through different pricing options. They must also ensure that internal or external attorneys have the right background and expertise to help develop and evaluate such options properly. Companies with the price advantage maintain a superior understanding of the relevant pricing laws and assure that pricing strategy and execution always meet the letter and intent of those laws.

Bringing It Together

Pricing Architecture

An architect, when designing a building, usually pursues objectives in two areas—some around form and others around function. The form objectives relate to the desired visual impression and *perception* of the building, while the functional objectives address the *performance* requirements of the building, like the electromechanical and climate control systems, total square footage, and room sizes. In much the same way, there is an architecture to pricing that, when executed well, can actively shape customers' *perception* of price and even drive *performance*—that is, the desired behavior of end customers and such intermediaries as retailers, wholesalers, and other channel partners.

The thoughtful pricing architect has many design elements with which to work. They include the list price level and how it might vary by segment, the discount components to include in the pocket price waterfall, and the specific policies and guidelines to apply to each of these components. Additional design elements include the unit of sale (for instance, whether a telephone service is priced per minute used or with a fixed monthly fee) and the approach for communicating price.

In this chapter, we will explore how companies that have achieved the price advantage use these and other design elements to create price architectures that most positively influence customers' perceptions of price and most effectively induce customers to behave in ways that are best for those companies. We will address separately the special challenges and added degrees of design freedom that arise in creating the price architecture for an offering that is a package of products, services, or both, rather than just a single product or service.

MANAGING PRICE PERCEPTION

Skillful pricers appreciate that just as benefit perceptions can be actively shaped, price perception can be influenced as well, as the following example illustrates.

To research the impact of price communication, a term life insurance provider that markets primarily by mail sent three sets of solicitations that were identical except for how price was communicated in the brochure headline. In the first set, the price was conveyed as $360 per year; in the second, $30 per month; and in the third, $1 per day. The annual price was, of course, identical in all three cases. And in each case, the same payment of $180 was due twice a year. Amazingly, respondents were three times more likely to buy the policy when given the monthly quote compared with the annual quote, and almost ten times more likely to buy when the price was quoted on a daily basis rather than an annual basis.

In a case from the financial services industry, a retail bank wanted to increase the price of an interest-bearing checking account it offered, while minimizing customer defections. The bank test-marketed two price increase alternatives that, while different in form, resulted in the same monthly price increase for customers in a specific segment. In the first alternative tested, the monthly account service fee paid by the customer was increased by $3 and the interest rate paid on account balances was held constant. In the second, the monthly service fee was only raised $1 but the interest paid on account balances was decreased by 0.2 percentage point. Although these two options generated an equal price increase, nearly four times as many customers defected when presented with the first price increase alternative versus the second.

These two cases illustrate how consumer price perceptions can be influenced through pricing architecture. So, too, can the price perceptions of intermediaries. Exhibit 12-1 shows the pocket price waterfall for a microwave oven manufacturer selling to appliance retailers. The price structure was complicated, with 10 on- and off-invoice discounts in play. Thinking that its price structure had grown too complex, the microwave oven company commissioned a market study to determine retailers' satisfaction with its price structure.

In interviews, retailers said they found the company's price structure somewhat complex, but no more complex than that of most other appliance manufacturers. Retailers indicated that competitors' waterfalls were quite similar to the company's *on the invoice*. It was off the invoice where competitive price structure varied widely, with volume rebates, promotional programs, and payment terms having very diverse designs. Furthermore, retailers stated that this off-invoice diversity made price comparison across microwave manufacturers difficult. So most retailers compared manufacturers' prices on an *invoice price* basis when choosing which microwave brands to carry; they assumed that the totals of each competitor's off-invoice discounts were about the same.

Exhibit 12-1 Pocket Price Waterfall—Microwave Oven (Percent of Base Price)

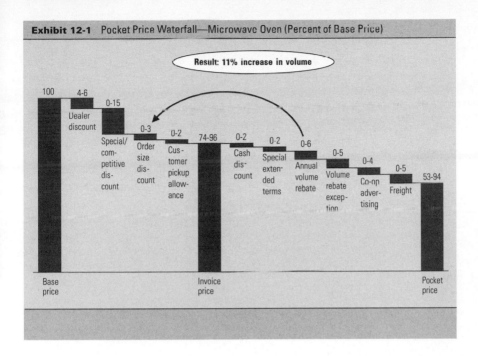

Knowing now that retailers paid much more attention to on-invoice discounts, the microwave company made a simple change to its price structure. It moved its largest off-invoice discount, the annual volume rebate, onto the invoice. In other words, it estimated each account's annual sales volume, projected the account's year-end rebate, and then included this as a discount on each invoice. If account volume at the end of the year differed significantly from the estimate, a year-end adjustment to the rebate would be made. This reduced invoice price by up to 6 percent and left pocket price unchanged, but it increased sales volume to this category of retailers by 11 percent. This volume increase was not the result of lowering price. Rather, it came from changing pricing architecture, from refining price structure to make the company's price look better against the yardstick that retailers used to compare competitive supplier prices.

For both consumers and trade intermediaries, the design of pricing architecture can significantly sway perception of price. As the examples above show, pricing architecture alternatives can be explored through market research, just like customer benefit perceptions. In fact, companies that excel at pricing regularly bundle price perception research with their general customer value research.

INFLUENCING CUSTOMER BEHAVIOR

Beyond influencing customers' impression of price level, well-designed price architecture can drive a host of customer behaviors that may be crucial to a company's success. The first principle of price architecture is that your pocket price waterfall should *work* for you. In other words, every element of your waterfall should be viewed as an investment designed to drive a specific customer behavior. For instance, a company would pay a cash discount to encourage customers to pay their invoices in a timely fashion and minimize receivables carrying costs. Or a company would provide an order-size discount to encourage customers to order in quantities that are logistically and economically attractive.

Exhibit 12-2 shows a partial list of the numerous and diverse customer behaviors, some of which are relevant only for resellers rather than direct customers, that can be influenced by price architecture. Let us explore sev-

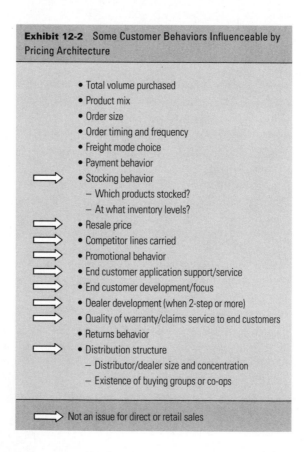

Exhibit 12-2 Some Customer Behaviors Influenceable by Pricing Architecture

- Total volume purchased
- Product mix
- Order size
- Order timing and frequency
- Freight mode choice
- Payment behavior
- Stocking behavior
  - Which products stocked?
  - At what inventory levels?
- Resale price
- Competitor lines carried
- Promotional behavior
- End customer application support/service
- End customer development/focus
- Dealer development (when 2-step or more)
- Quality of warranty/claims service to end customers
- Returns behavior
- Distribution structure
  - Distributor/dealer size and concentration
  - Existence of buying groups or co-ops

⇨ Not an issue for direct or retail sales

eral of these desirable customer behaviors and see how they can be affected by a thoughtfully designed and well-executed price architecture.

TOTAL VOLUME PURCHASED

Some of the largest discounts along the pocket price waterfall can be the least effective at influencing desired customer behavior. Annual volume bonuses—discounts paid at the end of the year, tied to total annual volume purchased—are often large waterfall elements that just do not work for companies; they seldom stimulate as much sales volume and growth as expected. An auto parts supplier's annual volume bonus program illustrates what so frequently goes wrong.

This company sold its line of products to auto parts wholesalers and retailers. Exhibit 12-3 shows the structure of its annual volume bonus program. Accounts with annual purchases of between $100,000 and $200,000 would receive a bonus equal to 1 percent of their volume at the end of the year. Those with annual purchases of between $200,000 and $500,000 would receive a 2 percent bonus, and so on.

Exhibit 12-3 Auto Parts Company: Annual Volume Bonus Structure

Account volume ($ thousands)	Volume bonus discount (percent)
<100	0
100–200	1
200–500	2
500–1,000	3
1,000–2,000	4
2,000–3,000	5
>3,000	6

A look at how this company's accounts were distributed based on annual volume, illustrated in Exhibit 12-4, shows why this volume bonus
structure was not working. Since the business was stable and mature, account growth greater than 20 percent was almost impossible. As a result,
any account that had to increase its purchases by roughly 20 percent or
more to reach the next bonus level was entirely unmotivated by the volume bonus structure. For example, if an account's volume was in the
$300,000–$400,000 range, as was the case for 17 percent of the accounts,
it would have to grow by 25 percent or more to reach the next volume
bonus hurdle at $500,000. That was too large a volume jump for those
accounts, which are shaded as "unmotivated accounts" in the exhibit.
More than half of this company's accounts, representing nearly 75 percent
of the company's sales volume, fell into the unmotivated category. Each
account, of course, gladly accepted its annual volume bonus check at the
end of the year, even though the bonus often had no impact on actual volume purchased.

It is no wonder that the auto parts company's expensive annual volume bonus program, which paid accounts up to 6 percent of sales, was not
working and was not providing an adequate return on the sizeable investment. Following this analysis, the company refined its annual volume
bonus program by realigning its volume bonus break points to better
match the distribution of its accounts' sales volumes.

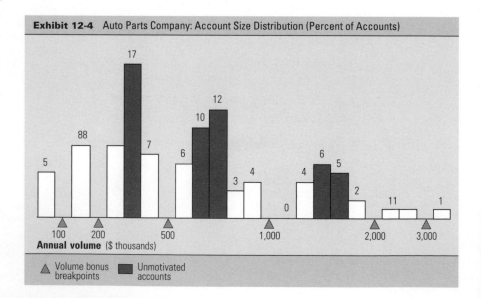

Exhibit 12-4   Auto Parts Company: Account Size Distribution (Percent of Accounts)

PRODUCT MIX

For companies that sell multiple product lines, large variations in profitability across those product lines are common. One company that manufactures hydraulic equipment had six major product lines that it sold through industrial distributors. As Exhibit 12-5 shows, its most profitable lines (Mark I, Mark II, and Crestline) regularly generated pocket margins that were two to four times higher than its low-margin lines (Advent, C-Line, and Nova). The company was not aware of this extreme profit variability across lines until it created its first pocket margin transaction database. A host of factors, including which plant made the product, design efficiency, and the level of market competition, contributed to this wide average pocket margin variation by product line.

In this situation, a mere 5 percent shift in product mix to high-margin products would increase total pocket margin dollars for this company by more than 8 percent. However, the company's price structure was blind to product mix, providing no incremental award to distributors who chose to purchase a richer mix of product lines. All discounts, allowances, rebates, terms, and conditions applied equally to all lines.

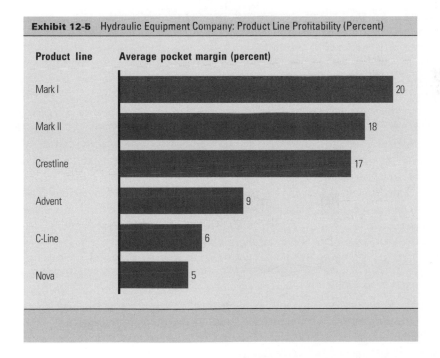

Exhibit 12-5 Hydraulic Equipment Company: Product Line Profitability (Percent)

Product line	Average pocket margin (percent)
Mark I	20
Mark II	18
Crestline	17
Advent	9
C-Line	6
Nova	5

With such a high payoff for improving product mix, the company decided to refocus its price structure to stimulate sales of the higher-margin product lines. It rebalanced its annual volume bonus program to pay a higher reward for Mark I, Mark II, and Crestline sales, and a lower reward for Advent, C-Line and Nova purchases. It concentrated all of its cooperative advertising and promotional discount programs on the high-margin lines. Furthermore, it allowed slightly longer payment terms on the three high-margin product lines, allowing 45 days to pay while still qualifying for a 1.5 percent cash discount, rather than the usual 30 days. These more generous terms caused distributors to stock greater inventory levels of the high-margin lines and ultimately to sell more as a result. This thoughtful reengineering of the pocket price waterfall yielded huge returns for the company. While total dollars invested up and down the pocket waterfall remained virtually unchanged, the hydraulics company increased its high-margin product mix by 14 percent within one year and increased operating profits by 23 percent.

RESALE PRICE

As discussed in Chapter 11, the price at which a trade intermediary resells a supplier's product has strategic importance. If a retailer charges a price that is too high relative to competitive offerings, then sales volume may be insufficient. If the retail price is too low, the desired premium position and brand strength of the supplier's product may erode. A supplier's price architecture provides a powerful tool for influencing prices that resellers charge for its product.

Most trade intermediaries trigger their resale price off of the *invoice* price that they see from their suppliers—not the pocket price. In other words, they take the supplier's invoice price and add a specific margin to it to come up with the price to charge their customers. Thus, the lower the invoice price, the lower the resale price. By shifting discounting between on and off the invoice, a supplier can change invoice price without affecting its pocket price.

With that in mind, if you want to influence your resellers to sell your products at a higher price, you should shift discounting from on-invoice to off-invoice. This will increase the invoice price that the reseller sees and, in most cases, engender higher resale prices. If, on the other hand, you want resellers to sell your products at a lower price, you should do the opposite—shift discounting from off-invoice to on-invoice. This will lower the invoice price and usually result in lower resale prices as well. Care should be taken, however, to manage competitors' perceptions of this move.

In addition to the balance of on- and off-invoice discounting, consistently managing list prices can also help influence resale prices. Discounting that occurs between starting point list price and invoice price can often be large and vary widely. As a result, too many companies assert that "my list prices don't mean anything, since none of my direct customers buy at list price anyway." This attitude can result in list prices not being managed consistently and the loss of a potential opportunity to influence resale prices constructively.

Price-advantaged companies actively manage list price and use it to communicate price to the market. While *list price* may take on different meanings for different companies—"suggested retail price," "the day-to-day price that a certain class of resellers pays," or "the price, when 20 percent is subtracted, at which the best retailers buy"—the point is that list price is not just a random starting point for negotiation, but rather a price level that has tangible meaning in the market. When list prices are managed with consistency and diligence, then changing list price can deliver important and credible messages to the marketplace, messages about industry price direction and even about the desired value repositioning of specific products.

Total volume, product mix, and resale price are just a few examples of the wide range of customer behaviors that can be influenced through price architecture. In our experience, we have seen companies successfully influence customer conduct in all the areas we have mentioned and more, using thoughtful design and careful execution of price architecture.

INFLUENCING PERCEPTION AND PERFORMANCE WITHIN A PACKAGE

Crafting a pricing architecture becomes an even more intricate challenge when a buying decision encompasses more than one product or service from an individual supplier. As we have seen in Chapter 7, these packages can take several forms. In the most straightforward, multiple products are bundled together and sold at the same time—for example, by a distributor. At the other extreme, a company may offer a carefully composed package of components that are engineered to work optimally together. Examples of such solutions include a surround-sound entertainment system or a telecommunications infrastructure package comprising integrated hardware, software, and services.

Whatever type of package is sold, a company must be careful to apportion the overall package price among the elements of the offering in a way that best communicates the benefits being delivered while also driving the desired buying behavior, or performance, of the customer. Even seemingly simple shifts in how price is allocated across a packaged offering can change the message buyers receive about the offering's benefits and the elements driving those benefits. As a result, these shifts can prompt significant changes in purchasing behavior.

PERCEPTION

A supplier offering razors and razor blades to the market provides a familiar example of one of the more common ways of using pricing architecture to communicate price—and to extract optimal profits from a packaged offering. If a supplier prices its razors too high—even if this reflects its real benefits—and its blades quite low, customers might hesitate to try the product because of the high perceived price driven by the initial price of the razor. Instead, razor makers tend to price the razor lower, expecting to recoup the missed revenue through blades that are priced slightly higher. This structure encourages potential users to try the product and experience its benefits.

This particular architecture is commonly used for paired products when an initial purchase of one leads to a steady stream of volume for the second product. Often the high margins from the second product provide the manufacturer with a secure revenue flow over the life of the first product and more than outweigh the initial discounting. In addition, this architecture creates a barrier to switching or trying a competing product.

Crafting a package's pricing architecture becomes more complex when different segments of the market have quite different perceptions of the relative benefits of its various elements, even if the final package is the same. As a result, a skillful pricer will not only look at the aggregate view of price allocation, but will seek ways to communicate these allocations that resonate among the specific segments.

The experience of a global data network systems provider shows how using price architecture to emphasize the benefits offered by portions of the package can cater to particular market segments. A leader in the high-end market for integrated networking systems, this supplier was being attacked in the mid-tier market. Traditionally, the company had placed a single price on its networking package to highlight the benefits offered by integration. But as the market evolved, several competitors from the lower end of the market began to attack the mid-range market using lower price as their primary weapon. The attackers only offered portions of the total package, but they compared their hardware and software prices to the aggregate price the incumbent supplier charged for the full package (in essence comparing their apples to the incumbent's orange), creating a large gap in price perception. Since mid-tier customers did not always appreciate the full suite of benefits included in the integrated offering, they would often see the competing systems as operationally similar. As a result, the attackers rapidly began growing share.

Realizing the problem was price perception and not an inherent flaw in the actual offering, the networking supplier recrafted its pricing structure for this segment. It explicitly assigned prices to the core portion of the integrated package, the hardware and software operating system, which could be compared directly with the attackers' offerings. The incumbent also differentiated the pricing of the remaining, more advanced feature functionality, so that these benefits could be articulated separately. This allowed customers to compare apples to apples and removed the perceived price gap from the market. The move halted the company's share loss almost immediately.

PRICING A MIXED BAG

Pricing a packaged offer, whether a bundle, an integrated offering, or a solution, becomes especially difficult when the components are fundamentally different in nature. This situation is commonly faced by high-tech suppliers, who must juggle a package that includes a physical component (the hardware), an intellectual property component (the software), and a human component (the service providers). But the challenges are relevant to anyone trying to price such a mixed bag. Whatever type of package is being offered, suppliers must carefully weigh the advantages and disadvantages of how they apportion the total price among the components. Even if the customers see just one price, this internal exercise is important because it can validate the price of a system by constructing it from the bottom up, and it can ensure that, should the price be disaggregated, minimum price levels are reached for each component.

One obstacle to allocating price effectively can be a company's tradition. For instance, a company founded as a hardware manufacturer may face internal resistance to a pricing architecture that highlights the value of software or services. A company can push forward, however, by understanding how the customer perceives the benefits being delivered by the package, and setting prices in line with that benefit perception. As we have seen repeatedly, benefit perceptions can shift dramatically from one market segment to another, so pricing policies for integrated packages should keep such differences in mind.

(Continued)

PRICING A MIXED BAG *(Continued)*

In addition, other factors come into play when offering a package of diverse components. The economics of individual pieces could differ, with prices rising for some and falling for others. In this case, allocating an additional portion of the price to the component on an upward trend might make sense. Also, if different components of the package are delivered at different times, the pricing architecture should probably be created to time payments as value is delivered. If, for instance, the hardware (usually the first component delivered) included in a package is not distinctive, a buyer may be reluctant to make a large up-front payment, even if it reflects the value of the full package that will eventually be delivered.

PERFORMANCE

Just as packaged offerings provide new opportunities for influencing price perception, they also open up unique opportunities to use pricing architecture to drive customer buying behavior, as well as the supplier's revenue capture. From being a one-stop source for all maintenance, repair, and operations (MRO) items to offering outsourced IT services, packaged offerings integrate to varying degrees directly into a customer's business system. Consequently, they can allow suppliers to use more robust pricing mechanisms that share business risk, increase the formal tie between supplier and customer, and close the door to competitors.

These pricing mechanisms tend to fall into one of two categories: pay-per-use and pay-for-performance.

Pay-per-Use Arrangements. A pay-per-use approach is a common way to share business risk. In essence, payments escalate as the buyer increases its use of the offering—for instance, a software application that is installed on multiple PCs. This approach is effective when it is hard to quantify the direct benefits of a product, such as increased IT security; when the benefits offered by the product are realized as part of a greater whole; or when the customer has principal control over whether the benefits are captured.

Related to pay-per-use agreements, pay-as-you-grow deals link payments to increases in sales, unit volume, or some other clear growth measurement. Many software companies have turned to this method, which would commonly allow payments to increase as a company grows or to decrease if the company shrinks. Pay-as-you-grow plans could be more appropriate if it is difficult to identify or count individual uses of a product or if the benefits delivered are delayed.

Pay-by-Performance Arrangements. Performance-based pricing is more complex than pay-as-you-grow or pay-per-use approaches. At its core, a customer and supplier agree to a set of performance metrics, and payments are made as specific targets are reached. The best candidates for this structure offer benefits that are clearly measurable, such as revenue directly tied to the package installed (a telecommunications system, for example) or the number of cars coming out of an outsourced paint shop. Performance-based pricing should be considered only if the supplier has significant influence or actually controls whether the offerings' benefits will be delivered. As we saw in Chapter 7, this is the most common architecture used when a true "outsourced" solution is offered.

The building industry offers another good example of how performance-based pricing can work. One contractor offered to retrofit its customers' infrastructure—internal lighting, heating, ventilation, air conditioning, fire and security systems—with a building automation system at no initial cost. Instead, payments were based on the energy savings generated by the integrated offering. The customer and supplier agreed to a baseline of energy costs. As the energy costs went below this baseline, the supplier was paid the difference; the more energy saved, the more money the supplier made.

While performance-based pricing can be attractive, its advantages for both the buyer and the seller can disintegrate quickly amid disputes over how to measure the benefits. Problems can also develop if the customer fails to use the product adequately to drive performance improvements. One process automation supplier spent more time and effort wrangling with a customer over the definition and measurement of excellent performance and, ultimately, establishment of blame for the system failures, than in designing, installing, and maintaining the system.

* * *

As we have shown, there is an architecture to pricing that can be more important than absolute price level itself in driving customer behaviors and perception. Too many businesses fail to recognize price architecture for the powerful market tool that it can be. They leave price structure, policy, and communication unchanged year after year, feeling bound by tradition and industry convention.

Businesses that have achieved the price advantage take a very different and dynamic view of price architecture. Whether selling components or packages, they set specific market and customer objectives that can be reached through price architecture. They regularly reassess those objectives and always make sure that their price structure is working for them—that their waterfall elements are not just entitlements to customers, but rather are efficiently driving desired customer behaviors.

CHAPTER 13

Driving Pricing Change

Deciding to pursue the price advantage launches a company on a transformational journey that can touch almost every aspect of its business system. Capturing the price advantage is not about a handful of clever pricing tips and tricks. Instead, it requires a change in mindset and capabilities in marketing, sales, operations, finance, and any other part of the organization that touches pricing decisions.

Managers invariably encounter cultural and even emotional resistance along the journey. The freedom to set price can be seen by individuals in marketing and sales as central to their personal power and authority within the organization. When empowered with pricing authority, a sales rep or sales manager ultimately has the power to decide who the company's customers will (or will not) be. Pricing authority may even heighten the customer's perception of the importance of an individual in the seller's organization. So, when that authority is controlled more tightly, which often occurs as an organization moves to create the price advantage, some resistance is unavoidable.

As with most sustained change programs, commitment and stamina are necessary to create the price advantage. While some quick wins are usually found early in the journey, the real returns are typically seen over several years, as a company develops and institutionalizes its pricing knowledge and continually improves its pricing capability. Time and again, we have seen that pricing success breeds upon itself. As initial targets are reached, successful teams pursue and attain increasingly aggressive targets. But before this virtuous cycle takes hold, a company must embark on a deliberate agenda to assure that constructive pricing change occurs and is maintained.

THE CHANGE AGENDA

In our work with hundreds of companies over the years, we have found four common cornerstones in the most effective pricing change agendas, as shown in Exhibit 13-1: fostering understanding and conviction, reinforcing the change with formal mechanisms, developing talent and skills, and role modeling. We will explore each of the four cornerstones in some detail and conclude with a discussion of failure modes—the most frequent break-downs that cause pricing change agendas to come up short.

FOSTERING UNDERSTANDING AND CONVICTION

Before stepping up to their role in creating the price advantage, individuals first need to understand what they are being asked to do and why. Senior executives must build throughout the organization a strong sense of align-ment behind the price advantage vision, make a credible case for success, and point to the path that goes there. As Exhibit 13-2 shows, price leaders can foster understanding and conviction throughout a company in a num-ber of ways, including proving the merit of the opportunity, crafting a compelling change story, aligning the leadership team, choosing a cham-pion, and establishing consistent targets. This job cannot be delegated. Only top managers can clearly and convincingly make the case—through

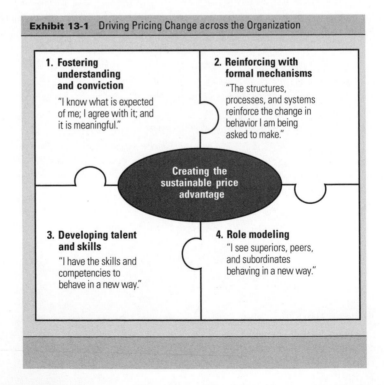

Exhibit 13-1   Driving Pricing Change across the Organization

1. Fostering understanding and conviction

"I know what is expected of me; I agree with it; and it is meaningful."

2. Reinforcing with formal mechanisms

"The structures, processes, and systems reinforce the change in behavior I am being asked to make."

Creating the sustainable price advantage

3. Developing talent and skills

"I have the skills and competencies to behave in a new way."

4. Role modeling

"I see superiors, peers, and subordinates behaving in a new way."

Exhibit 13-2 Driving Pricing Change: Fostering Understanding and Conviction

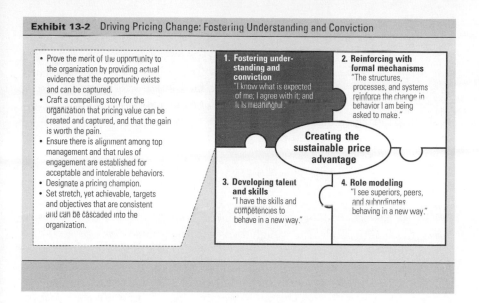

- Prove the merit of the opportunity to the organization by providing actual evidence that the opportunity exists and can be captured.
- Craft a compelling story for the organization that pricing value can be created and captured, and that the gain is worth the pain.
- Ensure there is alignment among top management and that rules of engagement are established for acceptable and intolerable behaviors.
- Designate a pricing champion.
- Set stretch, yet achievable, targets and objectives that are consistent and can be cascaded into the organization.

1. Fostering understanding and conviction
"I know what is expected of me; I agree with it; and it is meaningful."

2. Reinforcing with formal mechanisms
"The structures, processes, and systems reinforce the change in behavior I am being asked to make."

Creating the sustainable price advantage

3. Developing talent and skills
"I have the skills and competencies to behave in a new way."

4. Role modeling
"I see superiors, peers, and subordinates behaving in a new way."

frequent and consistent communications across the organization and to all stakeholders—that the aspirations can be achieved.

Prove the Merit. Creating a clear, believable, and respectable success story for the organization is the best way to show that the impact from pricing excellence is real, substantial, and attainable. So too is choosing a subset of a business—for example, a product category, a distinct customer segment, or an isolated geographical region—to create an insulated pricing pilot program that is sufficiently resourced with leadership, sales and marketing insight, IT support, and funding. Once complete, this successful pilot can become the rallying point and guiding light for pricing improvement initiatives across the remainder of the organization.

A Compelling Story. Once a credible case has been established, the next challenge for senior management is to craft a compelling and credible story that will drive the broader organization to work hard to change. By *story* we do not mean a fairy tale, but rather a tangible, fact-based explanation of why the company is upgrading its pricing capability, what needs to be done, and what rewards lie at the end of the journey. The ease of creating the compelling story can vary. For example, if a company is in significant financial trouble, that alone may be enough to rally the employees to take on pricing excellence to improve its profitability.

Leadership Alignment. For an organization to rally around pricing change, top management must be firmly aligned behind the program and committed to achieving a price improvement target. Any disagreements within the leadership will spread quickly down the ranks. The team will face hard choices along the way: Some unprofitable customers will be let go, other customers might be angered by tougher enforcement of pricing policies, some favored customers may receive lower service levels that align with their willingness to pay, and entire markets might be abandoned. If the top executives responsible for each affected area are not ready to face these challenges with a single voice, employees at all levels will quickly sense the misalignment and splinter along internal silos of inconsistent support.

Pricing Champion. Along with the shared commitment of the executive team, there should also be a high-level figure assigned with personal responsibility for overseeing the change program and longer-term responsibility for assuring that the changes are hard-wired into the organization. Think of this individual as a "chief pricing officer" who tracks specific improvement targets for pocket price, watches closely how product/market pricing is evolving relative to the competition, or identifies opportunities for industry price leadership.

Stretch Targets. A successful pricing change program must be anchored in realistic, though challenging, aspirations that translate into credible stretch targets. These targets are often expressed in quantified pocket price or pocket margin goals that cascade across all levels of the organization. In other words, the pocket margin goals of all the sales representatives in a region would add up to the pocket margin goal for the region; the sum of all the region goals would equal the pocket margin goal for the division, and so on. These targets should be weighted in a way that provides a healthy tension among competing company goals, such as share or market growth.

FORMAL MECHANISMS

The next cornerstone is to create the structure, processes, and systems that form the backbone of a pricing change program. As shown in Exhibit 13-3, these formal mechanisms can be catalogued into four specific groups: tools and processes, organization and structure, key performance indicators, and incentives and compensation.

Tools and Processes. In Chapter 10, we took a close look at the IT tools that can be used to support pricing excellence. A change program can be quickly swept away in a flood of data if the development of these tools and

Exhibit 13-3 Driving Pricing Change: Reinforcing with Formal Mechanisms

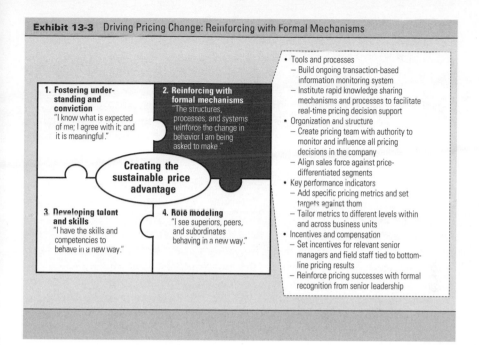

processes is not monitored closely. Or it can be mired in a vain pursuit of accuracy to the nth degree.

There are endless permutations for configuring the tools and processes that underpin a winning pricing change program. While an exhaustive discussion is beyond the scope of our book, a few core guidelines are listed below:

- The right pricing data needs to be in the hands of the relevant decision makers. From real-time negotiation support to crafting a new product's release price, the right data in the right hands at the right time is central.
- Pricing data must be just accurate enough to guide good decisions. For example, 0.1 percent accuracy in pocket prices is not needed when the pocket price band width is 60 percent.
- Pricing data should be aggregated to a level of managerial usefulness. Managers must be able to make decisions on a page of data, rather than be forced to wade through reams of figures.
- Appropriate discounting authority must be set and enforced. Profits are too sensitive to even small movements in prices for field authority to be too extreme.

■ A pricing performance management system must define a performance metric for each unique role in the pricing effort. Underperformance by even a few individuals can cripple the most well-designed pricing improvement initiative.

Organization and Structure. Pricing change programs often require organizational and structural changes. While there is no one-size-fits-all organizational template, there are several guiding principles that most price-advantaged companies have lived by:

■ Pricing is owned by an executive champion within each business unit—a "chief pricing officer," if you will—who leads a specialized pricing group.
■ The charter of these pricing groups is to support actively, to coordinate, and, occasionally, to deliver the myriad pricing decisions. These can range from setting prices for new products and ensuring the highest pocket price possible is realized transaction by transaction, to reviewing pricing performance. Exhibit 13-4 shows how such pricing decisions can be interwoven throughout a company.

Exhibit 13-4   Linkage between Pricing and Other Business Functions

Pricing decisions		Involved business functions					
		Business unit/ marketing	Sales	Pricing	Finance	IT	Operations
Product/ market pricing	• Segment ID and positioning	●	○	◐			
	• Product/system development	●		◐			◐
	• Product/system pricing and position	●	◐	●			
	• Competitive intelligence	●	◐	◐			
	• Pricing structure	◐	◐	●			◐
Transaction policies	• Transaction guidelines and thresholds		◐	●	◐		
	• Customer ID and prioritization	◐	●	◐			
	• Account-specific negotiation		●	◐			
	• Exception identification*		●	●			
	• Exception approval	●		●	●		
Performance management	• Data gathering/integrity, reporting			◐	●	◐	
	• Price performance monitoring/dialogue		◐	●			
	• Sales force compensations/ incentives	●	◐	◐			

*Threshold levels, order of involvement jointly determined   ○ No involvement   ◐ Some involvement   ● Primary responsibility

■ Formal linkages and interfaces are spelled out between the pricing organization and other affected groups. A pricing group that has no hard wiring into actual decision making processes will simply add no value.

■ As the unbiased fiduciary conscience of the organization, the pricing group constantly screens for potentially destructive pricing decisions.

■ As the primary driver of the pricing performance management system, this group is tasked with making actual pricing performance visible while, at the same time, continuously looking for untapped opportunities to do even better.

■ The group's structure balances the need for central governance and oversight with the need for intimate knowledge of the local market situation. While all pricing decisions at a global semiconductor supplier might be made centrally, it would be impossible for headquarters to guide pricing decisions at a local plumbing distributor without deep knowledge of the local market conditions.

Key Performance Indicators. Performance metrics, or key performance indicators (KPIs), must be established that allow a company to monitor an individual or group's progress toward specific pricing goals. These KPIs must reflect the company's stated objectives as well as the nature of an individual's responsibilities. Effective KPIs involve both output metrics, such as comparing actual pocket prices achieved against target values, and input metrics, such as the number of total deals reviewed by the pricing group.

Effective KPI designs share a number of characteristics. First, the metrics should be robust enough to be used at different levels within the organization with minimal change. For example, a pocket price ratio (PPR), which compares pocket price to target list price, can track the performance of an individual account, of a salesperson, or of a sales region. Next, a company should try to maintain a relatively small number of KPIs that allow comparability across different products, markets, or even business units. And finally, pricing KPIs should complement other marketing and operational KPIs, which may be in conflict with each other, to create a healthy tension in the performance review process.

Incentives and Compensation. A careful choice of compensation and incentive structure is one of the principal mechanisms that a company can use to link the behaviors of individuals with a desired set of business actions. To some extent, the old maxim holds: People do what they are paid to do. While a comprehensive review of this topic would be impractical, there are some rules of thumb that companies that price well use when crafting their compensation and incentive systems:

■ Incentives that promote good pricing behavior must be established for all roles that touch the pricing process, not just the frontline sales force. Driving the desired behavior in sales management and product marketing, for example, is as critical as in the frontline sales force.

■ When developing the compensation and incentive package for the sales force, a balance must be struck between volume and price realization. This balance will vary by role (prospecting new accounts compared with servicing existing accounts, for example) and over time.

■ Compensation plans should usually avoid threshold structures. Pricing performance incentives that do not kick in until a minimum volume threshold is reached are undesirable because they tend to drive dramatically different behaviors before the threshold is met, compared with after, which can confound customers, confuse competitors, and damage industry price levels.

■ Comprehensive incentive plans should thoughtfully leverage nonfinancial motivators. A salesperson's behavior can change quite drastically simply from knowing that once a month the sales force will be force-ranked against their peers on price realization.

DEVELOPING TALENT AND SKILLS

Just giving someone a hammer, nails, wood, and a blueprint does not create a carpenter. Similarly, just providing an individual with pricing tools and guidelines does not create a world-class pricer. The process of building pricing skills takes time and must be coordinated across all levels of a company, from senior management through to the frontline sales force. In general, as shown in Exhibit 13-5, there are at least four requirements for building these new capabilities: defining the pivotal jobs, managing and acquiring key talent, developing targeted training and learning, and disseminating knowledge and information.

Pivotal Jobs.   For each core pricing process, for example new product or transaction pricing, there will be a small handful of jobs that are absolutely critical. Often at multiple levels in an organization, those jobs are the linchpins to a process that, when well executed, ensures that the pricing function transcends the barriers of a traditional support function to become a true performance driver. As the appropriate pricing jobs within a company are defined, managers must be clear about which skills and other attributes are necessary for outstanding performance. For example, if a company creates a pricing manager position to support negotiations, the individual given that role must not only be well acquainted with the benefit profiles of the company's products and how they rate against the competition, but must also have a clear understanding of negotiating processes and strategies. Most importantly, field reps must respect that person enough to accept the negotiating advice being offered, especially in tough situations.

Exhibit 13-5 Driving Pricing Change: Developing Talent and Skills

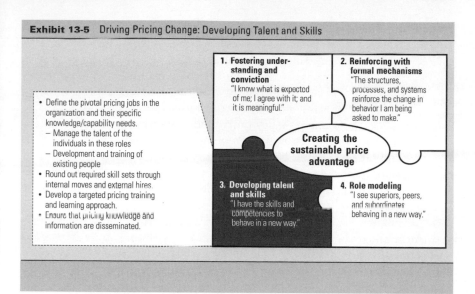

Key Talent. Managing key talent covers two principal elements: finding people with the right talent and developing that talent. Pricing talent can sometimes be found within the company itself. Along with nurturing abilities already on hand, developing internal talent carries the implicit message that pricing skills are valuable to career advancement. In one high-tech firm, aspiring sales managers were expected to spend up to two years as a national pricing manager before being promoted to higher-level positions.

Training and Learning. Once the needed skills are defined—for instance, large account pocket price management, competitive pricing intelligence, value-based new product pricing—training and learning become vital components of a development program. One of the first steps is to identify sources of relevant knowledge. While external benchmarking or outside experts can provide useful insight, the best sources are often right inside your own organization—your best practitioners. These best pricers may either be already resident in the organization or they may need to be developed further through targeted pricing training. Once these best pricers have been identified, a company can bring them together in workshops to codify those skills that are at the core of their distinctiveness. When recognized for their skills, these pricers can also inspire a company's entire team to better performance.

Disseminating Knowledge and Information. Spreading this knowledge can be accomplished through a number of formal and informal mechanisms, including external training, sharing internal best practices, online knowledge modules, and real-time learning. Management workshops and role-playing exercises, led by the most skilled employees as part of larger training sessions, can make these tasks easier. Knowledge is retained best when it is shared and then used in real customer situations.

ROLE MODELING

Role modeling, at its core, is a demonstration in words and deeds that individuals across the organization, from a company's most senior executives to the frontline sales force, are behaving in new ways. Exhibit 13-6 highlights four elements of effective role model creation: sharing risk, promoting a performance dialogue, reinforcing good behavior, and penalizing poor behavior.

Share the Risk.   Few change programs carry as much personal risk as pricing. After all, if the wrong decision is made, a customer may be lost. A sales rep who takes the risk of holding firm on price must know that senior management is sharing that risk. In contrast, it is a running joke at some companies that the quickest way for a customer to get an additional 5 percent off the price of a major deal is to go straight to a senior executive. It is, of course, the customer who indeed laughs all the way to the bank in these situations. Even if a logical reason is offered for senior management's capitulation on price (it is a strategic account, the new market segment is attractive), word will spread quickly that senior management is not truly committed to pricing excellence, and commitment throughout the organization will suffer accordingly. A visible act of strength—senior manage-

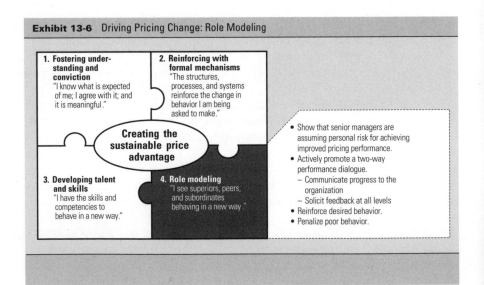

Exhibit 13-6   Driving Pricing Change: Role Modeling

1. **Fostering understanding and conviction**
"I know what is expected of me; I agree with it; and it is meaningful."

2. **Reinforcing with formal mechanisms**
"The structures, processes, and systems reinforce the change in behavior I am being asked to make."

Creating the sustainable price advantage

3. **Developing talent and skills**
"I have the skills and competencies to behave in a new way."

4. **Role modeling**
"I see superiors, peers, and subordinates behaving in a new way."

- Show that senior managers are assuming personal risk for achieving improved pricing performance.
- Actively promote a two-way performance dialogue.
  - Communicate progress to the organization
  - Solicit feedback at all levels
- Reinforce desired behavior.
- Penalize poor behavior.

ment holding the line on pricing at a large account, for example—has the opposite effect. Word will spread like wildfire through an organization when senior management shows the courage to risk losing a major account in the name of pricing excellence.

Promote the Performance Dialogue. There should be an ongoing, two-way performance dialogue between the executive team and those individuals involved in pricing. This performance dialogue is the process by which a baseline is established, specific pricing targets are set, visibility is brought to actual pricing performance, corrective measures are defined, rewards are established, and pressure is continuously applied to find the next wave of pricing opportunity.

But more than holding the organization's feet to the fire, top managers should also listen to and learn from the front lines. The entire company—senior management and the front line alike—must stay in touch with changes in the marketplace. Top executives must be as eager to solicit feedback on real pricing challenges in the market as they are to pressure the organization for results.

Reinforce Good Behavior. Role models of pricing excellence must populate every level of a company. And as good pricers emerge, either from the executive ranks or the front lines, their efforts must be acknowledged and reinforced. A series of questions can help determine whether a company is doing enough to recognize and advance its best pricers:

- How are the best salespeople identified and publicly acknowledged? Are they praised because they stood firm in the face of intense competitive pressure, holding the line on pocket price (even if a deal fell through in the process), or only because they brought in the most revenue?
- What criteria go into deciding promotions? When announcing promotions, is pricing excellence cited as a factor or is volume growth? Does the reputation of the promoted manager match the company's pricing objectives?

Along with public recognition of jobs well done, good behavior can also be reinforced more subtly, but with similar wide-ranging impact. At one large services company, the CEO began calling personally the top three salespeople based on margin percentages at the end of each quarter and congratulated them for excellent work. The praise was specific and private. Still, the first time the calls were made, the entire sales force knew about them by the next morning.

Penalize Poor Behavior. Of course, with responsibility come consequences, and one of the more unpleasant tasks during a change program is to enforce the new direction when the organization resists. Without clear enforcement of the new direction, even if their short-term compensation suffers, employees will begin second-guessing a company's priorities if they sense that career advancement is not linked to meeting the objectives of the new program. As surely as penalties are noticed, the absence of penalties will also be noted.

FAILURE MODES

The four cornerstones of an effective price change agenda should seem straightforward and logical. Still, our experience indicates that there are a handful of common failure modes—shortcomings that throw otherwise well-designed price change programs off track and that result in lower pricing performance improvement, improvements that are not sustained, or both. Some of the most common failure modes to avoid are reviewed below:

- *Believing it is enough for the CEO to assert that pricing is a priority.* Senior management needs to back up that assertion with repeated reinforcement to assure that pricing is not perceived as a "flavor of the month" improvement priority. Conviction and commitment to achieving the price advantage are built by clear and repeated messages, over a number of years, on the importance of pricing distinctiveness. It must be stressed that pricing excellence is not just a one-time project but rather part of the lifeblood of a company and the way that a company routinely does business from now on.
- *Overemphasizing the building of pricing systems and processes, while underemphasizing the building of requisite pricing skills and conviction.* The emotional nature of pricing decisions and the fundamental behavior and mindset shifts required to build the price advantage require a fair balance of the change management effort to focus on nurturing capability and conviction.
- *Thinking a couple of training sessions are enough to build adequate pricing capability.* Structured training sessions can only lay the foundation. Real pricing skill is best learned over time, reinforced through regular coaching and mentoring. Furthermore, the mentors and coaches should continually refresh their pricing excellence knowledge base with learning gleaned from the most current pricing successes across the company.
- *Inadequately rewarding pricing excellence in the incentive system.* As we have asserted, pricing done well is hard work that entails real risks.

Inadequate incentives make pricing superiority worth neither the work required nor the risk incurred.

■ *Openly rewarding individuals whose pricing performance is substandard.* If the "Salesperson of the Year" award is given to a sales rep who excels at selling high volumes of products but whose pricing performance is mediocre, then management assertions on the importance of pricing excellence lose all credibility.

■ *Senior management caving in on pricing under pressure.* As mentioned earlier, few things undercut a pricing improvement initiative more quickly than senior managers capitulating to price discount demands from large customers and failing to act as role models of the new approach to pricing.

*   *   *

Any company pursuing the price advantage is embarking on a journey of operational and cultural change—a journey during which the hearts and minds of many must be won. Making pricing change happen is the result of building broad understanding and conviction, reinforcing this with appropriate tools and processes, finding and developing the required skills, and creating role models of the new behavior throughout the organization. A breakdown in any of these four cornerstone areas can prevent the price advantage from becoming a lasting reality in your company.

CHAPTER 14

The Monarch Battery Case

Throughout this book, you have read in-depth discussions of a number of specific pricing topics. We have covered the three levels of price management in considerable detail, showing the approaches and tools at each level and demonstrating their application with targeted cases. We have also devoted chapters to a number of special pricing topics, including new product pricing and postmerger pricing, as well as topics that apply more generally to most businesses trying to create the price advantage, such as the legal issues and driving price change.

In this chapter, we will share a more comprehensive pricing case study that cuts broadly across many of the topics covered thus far, bringing many of our pricing fundamentals together and illustrating how these fundamentals worked in concert in a real-life pricing situation.

THE MONARCH BATTERY COMPANY

The Monarch Battery Company makes replacement lead-acid batteries used in automobiles. As Exhibit 14-1 shows, Monarch's direct customers are auto parts distributors (who resell to smaller auto parts retailers), regional and national auto parts retail chains, and several national general mass merchandisers who have automotive departments within their stores. These various retailers and mass merchandisers then sell Monarch batteries directly to car owners.

Exhibit 14-2 shows Monarch's economics and profit structure. With an ROS of 5.2 percent, Monarch's profitability is extremely sensitive to even small swings in price. A 1 percent increase in price with no volume loss would increase operating profit by 19 percent. As this figure also shows, that is almost three times the impact of a 1 percent increase in volume, assuming no decrease in average price levels. So, as is usually the case, the payoff for Monarch for improved price performance would be enormous.

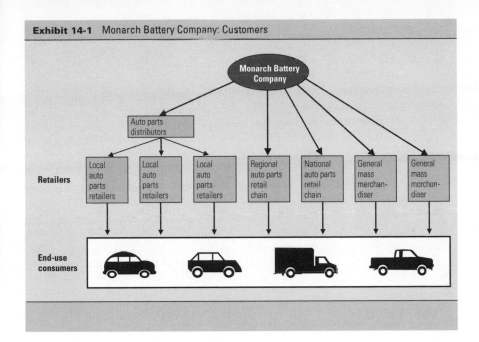

Exhibit 14-1 Monarch Battery Company: Customers

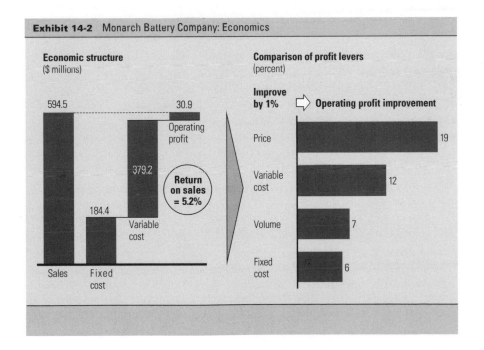

Exhibit 14-2 Monarch Battery Company: Economics

Despite successful cost-cutting programs across the entire Monarch organization, including efforts in manufacturing, distribution, sales, and administration, Monarch's operating profits had declined 50 percent over a period of five years. With a cost structure that was already lean and better than the competition, Monarch had limited room to cut costs further. Unfortunately, the cost improvements it had achieved were more than offset by a steady drop in the average prices that Monarch received from its customers. Monarch managers finally realized that they would be unable to return Monarch to acceptable levels of bottom-line profitability without improving their performance in pricing. Monarch senior managers decided to tackle pricing head-on and to look vigorously across all three levels of price management for opportunities.

We will go through each of the three levels, starting with the transaction level, to show how Monarch identified potential sources of price improvement. We will follow this with a description of the integrated set of actions Monarch took at each level to capture the identified pricing opportunities.

TRANSACTION

Transaction complexity at Monarch was relatively high, given the variety of Monarch's customer base and a price structure whose components had grown in number and size over the years. Exhibit 14-3 shows the typical pocket price waterfall for one of Monarch's common battery models, the Mega-Lite. From a dealer list price of $28.40, Monarch deducted several discounts to get to invoice price. There was a standard retailer/distributor discount that differed by account type and averaged $4.26 per battery. Monarch also provided an order size discount that could reach 5 percent, depending on the total dollar value of an order. On average, it was 71 cents per battery, 2.5 percent of list price. Additionally, many transactions included an on-invoice exception discount, negotiated on a customer-by-customer basis to meet the competition in each account. With these discounts, the average invoice price for the Mega-Lite model was $21.16. What little attention Monarch paid to transaction pricing was targeted almost exclusively on the invoice price.

That focus by Monarch management ignored all of the discounting and revenue leaks occurring off-invoice. Monarch allowed a cash discount of 1.2 percent for prompt payment of invoices. Additionally, Monarch granted extended payment terms of 60 or even 90 days from delivery as part of promotional programs and on an exception basis for select accounts. The extra cost of carrying these extended receivables averaged 22 cents per battery. Cooperative advertising, where Monarch contributed to the funding of Monarch products in its accounts' local and regional adver-

Exhibit 14-3 Monarch Battery Company: Mega-Lite Pocket Price Waterfall

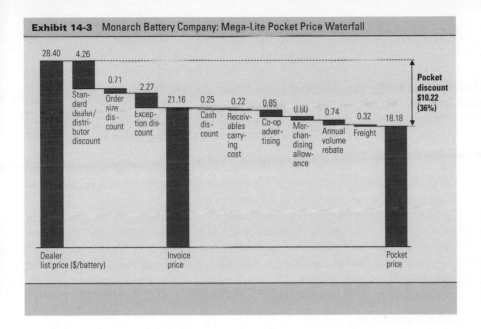

tising, cost an average of 85 cents. A special merchandising program that supported in-store promotions featuring Monarch products resulted in an average merchandising allowance discount of 60 cents. An annual volume rebate, based on total volume that an account purchases across all product lines, represented 74 cents in additional off-invoice discounting per battery. And finally, freight paid by Monarch for shipping batteries to the retailer cost an average of 32 cents.

The invoice price minus this host of off-invoice discounts, allowances, and costs resulted in an average pocket price of only $18.18, a full 14 percent less than the invoice price. The pocket discount, which is the total revenue drop from dealer list price down to pocket price, averaged $10.22, a 36 percent drop from dealer list price.

As is typical, not all transactions for the Mega-Lite had the identical pocket price. Accounts from different channels qualified for different standard dealer discount levels. Accounts ordered in different quantities, which resulted in variations in order-size discounts. And the on-invoice exception discounts were just that—exceptions negotiated on a one-off basis.

Further variability extended into the off-invoice items. Accounts paid invoices with varying levels of promptness, resulting in major differences in cash discounts and receivables carrying costs. Not all accounts used all of the cooperative advertising allowance available to them. The merchandising allowance was only paid to retailers who featured Monarch's products with special displays in their stores, and not all did. Account size, which varied greatly, drove the level of annual volume rebate, and freight paid by Monarch varied extensively based on retailer location and order pattern.

The result of all of these differences across on- and off-invoice discount elements was the wide pocket price band shown in Exhibit 14-4. While the average pocket price was more than $18, units sold for as high as $26 and as low as $14 on a pocket price basis—an 86 percent difference from the lowest to the highest. This wide pocket price band triggered the usual transactional questions: What are the underlying drivers of the price band's shape and width? Does this pocket price variability make good management sense and align with Monarch's market strategy? Why are pocket prices so variable, and can that variability be managed?

To begin to answer a few of these questions, Monarch performed the analysis shown in Exhibit 14-5 to see if the wide price band was somehow explained by the volume of batteries that customers purchased. Each point on this chart represents an individual Monarch distributor or retail account. The horizontal axis shows annual dollar volume of sales through each account. The vertical axis shows pocket price as a percentage of dealer list price for Mega-Lite batteries sold to each account. It is clear from Exhibit 14-5 that there is no overall correlation between account

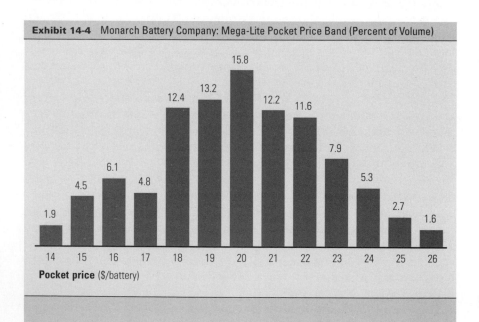

Exhibit 14-4 Monarch Battery Company: Mega-Lite Pocket Price Band (Percent of Volume)

Pocket price ($/battery)

Exhibit 14-5 Monarch Battery Company: Pocket Price vs. Account Size

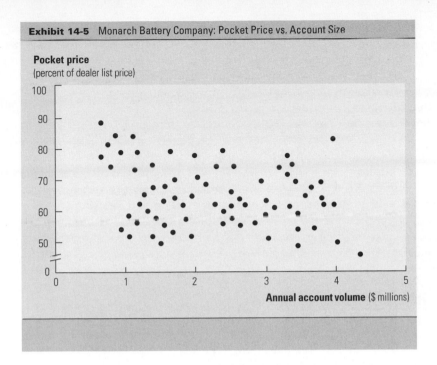

size and pocket discount. A number of relatively small accounts were receiving very low pocket prices (lower left on chart), while a number of larger accounts were buying at rather high pocket price levels (upper right on chart).

Further analyses were conducted to determine if there were other characteristics of accounts that might better explain the wide pocket price band. Variables tested included customer channel, geographical location, local competitive intensity, and other battery brands carried by each account. However, none of these variables helped much to explain the extreme width of the pocket price band. The apparent randomness of pocket price levels baffled Monarch managers, who had thought that they were quite careful about setting prices.

Further study showed this randomness had its roots in a transaction pricing process that actively managed only a portion of the pocket price waterfall and paid little attention to the ultimate pocket price level for each account. The standard dealer/distributor discount level was clearly defined and enforced. Order size was also well defined, but a number of "preferred accounts" were allowed to take the maximum order size discount on all orders, regardless of magnitude. Some general rules of thumb existed for the on-invoice exception discount (for instance, retail accounts with annual purchases less than $2 million should never receive an on-invoice exception discount of more than 5 percent), but these guidelines were neither clearly articulated nor carefully enforced.

The situation was even worse for off-invoice elements of the pocket price waterfall. Rules of thumb for these discounts were even less specific, and Monarch's information systems provided individuals in sales and marketing with no report on these items by individual transaction or even by account. This systems shortfall, of course, made it impossible for Monarch to pay any incentive to sales and marketing people for pocket price realization.

This assessment led Monarch senior management to recognize that its transaction pricing process was out of control, that decision making up and down the waterfall lacked unambiguous rules and discipline, and that no one was focusing on the end results of those decisions as represented by pocket price.

PRODUCT/MARKET STRATEGY

Monarch managers had for years been laboring under the assumption that the battery industry was becoming increasingly commoditized, making it ever more difficult for Monarch to distinguish its products from competitors. They assumed that price was the most critical factor driving consumer selection of battery brand, saw low-priced competitive offerings as real threats to their market share, and believed that any attempt to raise prices would result in a significant loss of volume and profit. Against this backdrop, they thought it was futile to invest in market research to understand better the Monarch value position in key markets and as a result had gone nearly a decade without conducting research on consumer value perception and price sensitivity. However, fundamental shifts in where consumers were choosing to purchase their replacement batteries, along with the merger of two of Monarch's smaller competitors, convinced managers that it was time to update their understanding of their current value position. To gain richer understanding at the product/market strategy level, Monarch conducted new consumer price research that exposed some eye-opening information.

The objective of this market research was to gain an up-to-date perspective on Monarch's current price/benefit positioning for major products and the likely impact of price changes at the retail level. They used discrete-choice analysis to simulate the customer battery buying experience and test the effect of changing price and other attributes on consumer brand and retailer choice.

The market research was conducted as follows. Researchers identified a sample group of 1,200 people who had recently purchased Monarch or other battery brands and were willing to participate. The research began with a series of background questions about the respondents' demographics, vehicles, circumstances around their last battery purchase, and retailers they had considered. Based on these answers, each respondent was put in front of a computer screen, given a set of three discrete choices for buying a battery, and asked a series of questions (see box).

DISCRETE CHOICE AT MONARCH

Discrete-choice analysis is one of several advanced market research tools that can help a company look at the potential impact of price levels and benefit offerings across several market segments. Monarch used the analysis to get a clearer picture of its position on the market.

Exhibit 14-6 shows the nature of the choices that were presented to respondents. Choice attributes included where the respondent might shop, the brand of the battery available at that retailer, and features of the various batteries being offered. The price that the retailer charges for that battery was also included with each choice. This initial set of choices is designed to mirror the brands, features, and prices that the respondents would actually see if they were to shop at their

Exhibit 14-6 Monarch Battery Company: Discrete-Choice Research

	Choice 1	Choice 2	Choice 3
Retailer	ABC Auto Parts	Auto King	Mass-Mart
Battery brand	Monarch	Everest	Qualco
Battery features			
• Cold cranking amps	700	700	650
• Warranty	60 months	60 months	48 months
• Nationwide replacements	Yes	Yes	No
Retail price	$64.95	$69.95	$59.95

(Continued)

DISCRETE CHOICE AT MONARCH *(Continued)*

chosen retailers in the local market. Presented with these choices, the respondents were asked to select which they would purchase.

Suppose in this case that the respondent had selected Choice 1 in Exhibit 14-6, which was the Monarch battery bought at ABC Auto Parts for $64.95. At this point, the discrete-choice software would generate a slightly different set of choices for the respondent—for instance, the same choices as in Exhibit 14-6, but with the retail price for Choice 1 raised to $66.95. The respondent would then be asked to choose again. If Choice 1 were selected again, the next set of choices might have the Choice 1 price raised to $68.95. If the respondent then made a different choice, such as the Everest brand battery at Auto King for $69.95, then the program might change the pattern for the next set of choices put before the respondent. For instance, the warranty period under Choice 3 might be increased to 60 months or the nationwide replacement availability might be changed from "no" to "yes." Each research respondent might be taken through a sequence of up to 15 of these modified discrete-choice scenarios, with individual choices at each stage generating a slightly different set of choices for the next stage.

The underlying discrete-choice program tracks the choices each respondent makes over the course of the research and analyzes the changes in choice attributes that cause respondents to make different selections.

The research gave Monarch managers a fresh outlook on their markets and allowed them to create up-to-date value maps for their key products and market segments, like the Mega-Lite map shown in Exhibit 14-7. Among the insights gained were these:

■ In most product categories, Monarch batteries were priced at or near value equivalence with competitors.
■ Suggested reductions in Monarch prices of up to 10 percent failed to attract many customers from the economy end of the market being served by Qualco. The research made it clear that there was a small, very price-sensitive set of customers who would not consider switching from Qualco until a competitor's price nearly matched Qualco's price.

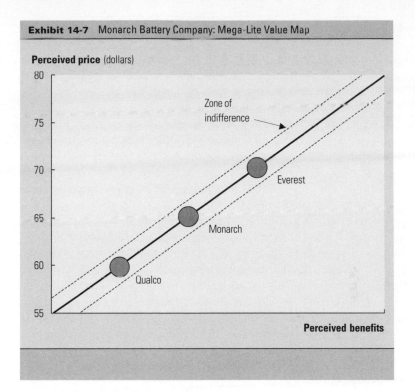

Exhibit 14-7 Monarch Battery Company: Mega-Lite Value Map

There was a small but notable zone of indifference around Monarch prices for most of its models. In almost every product category, Monarch retail prices could be raised as much as 2 percent with virtually no loss of consumer choice for the Monarch brand. This was valuable to know, considering the impact of a 1 percent increase shown earlier in Exhibit 14-2.

Monarch had underpriced its new stress-resistant, high-performance battery, the Ultra, by as much as 20 percent. In the demanding application niche targeted by Ultra, the innovative battery provided performance attributes that were far superior to Monarch's own in-house estimates.

These findings unveiled exciting and unexpected opportunity at the product/market strategy level for Monarch's managers and triggered a number of high-payoff market actions.

INDUSTRY STRATEGY

A number of trends in the replacement automotive battery industry had conspired over the years to place destructive downward pressure on overall industry prices. Improvements in battery design had caused the average life of an automotive battery to increase by more than 15 percent over a decade, resulting in flat unit demand from consumers. Over that same period of time, the three major battery manufacturers had streamlined their manufacturing processes and increased industry production capacity by 11 percent without building a single new manufacturing facility. These trends in demand and supply had resulted in current industry capacity exceeding demand by more than 22 percent.

Furthermore, distribution channels that sold replacement batteries were consolidating drastically. Growing regional and national auto parts retail chains were buying out many of the smaller auto parts retailers. At the same time, an increasing number of consumers were purchasing replacement batteries from the national mass merchandisers and discounters. Battery manufacturers—Monarch and its competitors—found themselves selling to a smaller number of increasingly powerful retail and wholesale customers who were only too willing to exercise their purchasing power to extract lower and lower prices.

The mass merchandisers and national auto parts retailers aggressively advertised their low prices for Monarch batteries, which fostered intrabrand competition between retailers and further depressed Monarch retail prices. Competitors were facing the same channel dynamics. Even the remaining smaller auto parts retailers would pressure Monarch to give them a price that would allow them to compete with the very low prices advertised by the national retailers.

The combination of chronic excess industry capacity, ongoing consolidation in distribution channels, and aggressive intrabrand competition had driven average retail prices paid by consumers for batteries down a real 9.6 percent over five years. As is usually the case, these retail price reductions were basically matched by lowered prices that battery makers could charge their retail and wholesale customers. In the wake of these price declines, profit margins for Monarch and its competitors were squeezed to unacceptable levels.

Attempts by both Monarch and its largest competitor, Everest, to relieve this profit squeeze and lead industry prices higher had been totally ineffective. When Everest tried to take prices up at some of its largest direct customers, they threatened to leave Everest and move their business to Monarch and Qualco. When Monarch tried to raise prices across the board to small retailers, the most costly channel for Monarch to serve, the small retailers rebelled, saying they could not compete with low-priced national retailers if Monarch increased its prices. In both cases, Everest and Monarch relented. Meanwhile, Qualco marketed itself as the lower-priced alternative to Monarch, contributing to the belief that replacement batteries were undifferentiated commodities.

Mindful that they could do little on the pricing front that would have lasting positive impact unless declining industry prices could be slowed, Monarch managers conducted a thorough assessment of their industry. Their objective was to understand better the real sources of the price freefall and to devise a plan to stop it. Among their revelations were these:

- Very few consumers shopped across different retail channels. In other words, a consumer who goes to a small auto parts retailer to purchase a battery seldom even considers a national mass merchandiser as a viable retail alternative. That consumer values the expert advice of a knowledgeable local retailer. In much the same way, the consumers who purchase their batteries from a mass merchandiser seldom consider the small auto parts retailer.

- While Everest and Qualco's cost structures were different from Monarch's, the price/volume/profit tradeoffs (as shown earlier in Exhibit 14-2 for Monarch) worked essentially the same for all three. In other words, easing downward price pressure was just as attractive for Everest and Qualco. Furthermore, Monarch's discrete-choice research showed that if Everest or Qualco were to cut prices further, they would not gain nearly enough consumer volume to offset the price cut and gain profit margin.

- Although Monarch liked to see itself as a constructive industry player, Qualco apparently perceived it as a very aggressive price competitor. The impression came from "introductory prices" Monarch had offered some of Qualco's high-profile retail accounts during competitive bids for supply contracts. While Qualco retained the customers, it was forced to lower its prices significantly to match Monarch's bid. As a result, Qualco leaders were dubious whenever Monarch tried to lead prices higher.

- Excess production capacity would probably remain a fact of life for the foreseeable future. There were no anticipated developments on either the demand or supply side that would affect that imbalance significantly.

These findings at the industry strategy level of price management provided fresh perspective and indicated greater freedom for Monarch to try to relieve some of the downward pressure on pricing that had damaged the industry so much over the past several years.

CAPTURING THE MONARCH PRICING OPPORTUNITY

So far, we have highlighted the findings of what might be called a pricing diagnostic across the three levels of price management. As we have shown, crucial pricing issues and opportunities emerged at each of the three levels. Armed with this new knowledge, Monarch took specific steps to capture and sustain the pricing opportunities it had identified. Although many of the price improvement actions taken by Monarch touch more than one of the three price management levels, we will summarize these actions within the level that is most appropriate, starting with the transaction level.

ACTION STEPS: TRANSACTION

Monarch took several specific steps to begin to bring control and discipline to its transaction pricing. First, Monarch decided to orient its entire transaction pricing process around pocket price realization. With input from sales, marketing, and pricing managers, Monarch set overall pocket price targets by account channel and size. These targets were aspirational with the dual intentions of actively shaping Monarch's pocket price band and setting a higher bar, account by account, for pocket price realization. Smaller accounts generally were assigned higher pocket price targets—that is, less total discounting—than large ones; full-service dealers and distributors who were developing and growing markets for Monarch were given lower pocket price targets than those who were not.

Next, Monarch compared target pocket price to actual pocket price, account by account. It identified underperforming accounts where the gap between target and actual pocket price was large and devised specific account plans to bring their pocket price levels into line. To help account managers focus on the individual elements of price that were excessive for these accounts, Monarch created an average pocket price waterfall for similar higher-performing accounts and compared it to the waterfall for the overdiscounted accounts. The price discount elements that were excessive became clear to account managers, who then understood which parts of the pocket price waterfall to focus on for improvement. This targeted approach to fixing outliers allowed Monarch to bring the majority of its outlier accounts in line within a year.

Simultaneously, Monarch mounted a program to grow sales volume in select accounts where actual pocket price was already *greater* than the target. The higher pocket prices made growth in these accounts extremely profitable, so much so that Monarch earmarked these attractive accounts for special treatment. A marketing and sales team investigated them to determine the nonprice benefits that were most important to these accounts. Monarch significantly increased unit sales to these accounts, not by cutting price, but by providing the benefit attributes that were most critical to each: more targeted promotions for some, higher levels of service for others, preferential order fill rates for still others.

Finally, Monarch instituted an aggressive program to bring greater overall discipline to the transaction pricing process. Beyond the pocket price targets discussed above, this program included setting clear guidelines and decision rules for each element in the pocket price waterfall. Monarch's IT department created new information systems to support and monitor transaction pricing decisions, and Monarch instituted pocket price as the companywide metric of price performance in all of these systems. It began measuring and assigning, transaction by transaction, all the significant off-invoice waterfall elements that were previously collected and reported only on an aggregate basis. Finally, compensation for salespeople, sales managers, and even product managers was tied to pocket-price realization against account-specific targets.

ACTION STEPS: PRODUCT/MARKET STRATEGY

Actions at the second level of price management were driven directly from the rich set of consumer and market insights drawn from the discrete-choice market research. Knowing now the width of the zone of price indifference for each of Monarch's product lines, the company launched its first broad increase in dealer list prices in years. While the list price increase was a modest 1.5 to 2 percent for most lines, Monarch could commit itself to these increases because it was confident consumers would not switch from the Monarch brand with the new prices. Monarch even shared market research results with skeptical retailers to help encourage them to charge justifiably higher retail prices in their stores.

Again based on market research results, Monarch relaunched the innovative new Ultra product line with a 16 percent increase in dealer list price. They placed additional advertising emphasis on the benefit attributes that market research had shown to be most important to customers purchasing the Ultra model. And, to help reinforce the high-price, high-benefit positioning of the Ultra line, virtually all requests for special or discretionary discounting of the product line (both on- and off-invoice) were denied.

Also in the category of actions to avoid, Monarch management no longer even considered requests from the field to discount any Monarch product lines to approach the price levels of Qualco, the low-end economy competitor, since discrete-choice research had shown Qualco's customers to be the most price-sensitive and unlikely to switch unless Monarch prices matched or beat Qualco's.

Finally, the abundant insights drawn from the market research clarified to Monarch the value of up-to-date consumer behavior information.

Monarch managers realized that they had been flying blind for years without these insights, and decided to commission similar market research every year or two, or whenever a major discontinuity occurred in their markets. These recurring research efforts not only prescribed specific price positioning actions for Monarch, but also established Monarch as the most informed and credible adviser to retailers on consumer buying behavior for automotive batteries.

ACTION STEPS: INDUSTRY STRATEGY

The action steps at the transaction and product/market strategy levels were, in most cases, quite direct and explicit, and the impact could often be seen immediately. Actions taken at the industry strategy level had less direct and immediate effect but were among the most important taken by Monarch. If industry prices continued their fall uninterrupted, the hard-fought gains at the transaction and product/market strategy levels might be wiped out by industrywide price declines.

The first steps taken at this level were designed to decrease the destructive Monarch intrabrand competition across the different types of retailers. Monarch took its research on consumer buying behavior to its retailers to demonstrate that the various retail battery channels—mass merchandisers, national auto parts retailers, and small auto parts retailers—were seldom competing for the same customers. The small auto parts retailer did not share customers with the national auto parts chains and did not have to be overly concerned with their advertised prices for Monarch batteries. Likewise, the national auto parts chains did not have to worry much about mass merchandisers' advertised prices; consumers in their customer base seldom shopped the mass merchandisers for auto parts.

Next, Monarch designed and executed a thoughtful communications program around its across-the-board list price increase. Monarch was upfront that the increase was indeed market-based. Monarch issued press releases explaining the logic and intent of its price increase and the benefit that it expected Monarch and its retailers to gain. Monarch trained its salespeople on how to sell the price increase to retailers and how to respond constructively to their questions and unavoidable objections. Monarch's president and CEO took every opportunity to explain and reinforce the rationale behind the price increase, and even accompanied salespeople on calls to select key accounts where the price increase had encountered some resistance. Again, Monarch's commitment to making the price increase stick was clear and unwavering.

Finally, Monarch marketing and sales management went on high alert to make sure that Monarch was not taking any actions in the marketplace that might be construed as counter to the price leadership that they were trying to exhibit. Extra care was taken to avoid aggressive transactional discounting in accounts shared by or visible to Everest and Qualco. All promotional programs were carefully assessed to assure that the market would not perceive them as price cuts counter to the spirit of price leadership. It was clear to Monarch managers that any market action taken that might be misread by the market could completely undermine their industry price leadership initiative.

HARD-WIRING THE CHANGE

Monarch's efforts to create and sustain improved performance in pricing went well beyond specific action steps across the three levels of pricing. As discussed in Chapter 13, reaching for the price advantage requires a tremendous transformational effort. The four primary tasks needed to shift pricing behaviors and mindset were each explicitly addressed in Monarch's pricing change program:

1. *Fostering understanding and conviction.* The CEO and president augmented his external market communications on pricing with an ongoing internal dialogue. Pricing became a routine agenda item at all monthly and quarterly management meetings. It was clear to everyone that senior leadership was unambiguously committed to the creation of a sustained price advantage for Monarch.
2. *Reinforcing with formal mechanisms.* In addition to all the pricing process and systems changes described earlier and incentive compensation changes, Monarch senior management took many symbolic steps to further reinforce a positive pricing mindset. For instance, each month the CEO and president made personal commendation calls to the salespeople who had achieved the most significant improvements in individual account pricing performance. These calls made the priority of pricing excellence across Monarch unmistakable.
3. *Developing talent and skill.* One of Monarch's most talented marketing managers was assigned the position of pricing director. She not only helped orchestrate the upgraded Monarch pricing process but also took the lead in building pricing capability across marketing and sales. She pushed the development and execution of training sessions on all of the new transactional pricing tools. She led regular field workshops with sellers to brainstorm and share a growing arsenal of pricing improvement ideas that was being created across Monarch.
4. *Role modeling.* The CEO and president provided a positive pricing role model to the Monarch organization by personally taking very tough stands with even very large customers who were asking for excessive

discounting. Furthermore, care was taken that the "salesperson of the year" award be given only to an individual who displayed exemplary pricing performance in addition to high-revenue volume performance.

*   *   *

The Monarch Battery Company case illustrates the intertwining set of initiatives and change programs that usually cut across all three levels of price management when a business gets serious about creating the price advantage for itself. The journey to create the price advantage was a rewarding one for Monarch. In the first year of full implementation, an ROS increase of 2.1 percentage points was attributed to price performance improvement. Incremental improvements continued in the second and third years, resulting in a cumulative ROS increase of 5.4 percentage points from the pricing program. Monarch more than doubled its operating profits—and has sustained that improvement—through thoughtful, disciplined actions and changes across all three of the price management levels. Monarch management remains to this day convinced that no other initiative could have yielded the lasting profit impact of their enthusiastic creation of the price advantage.

CHAPTER 15

Epilogue

So is now the time to begin to make the price advantage one of your advantages—to make excellence in managing the prices you charge for the goods and services you provide a cornerstone of your ongoing success and profitability? Should you strive to execute routinely the pricing function at a level of skill and professionalism that exceeds your industry peers and serves as a source of sustainable competitive advantage?

The reasons to excel at pricing are diverse and compelling. No single management lever available to you can boost profitability more quickly than even a slight improvement in average price levels. As we have discussed earlier, a 1-percentage-point improvement in price can drive huge increases in operating profits. Just as importantly, however, excellence in pricing requires and pulls along in its wake excellence in other essential management disciplines.

It requires you to understand your customers more richly than ever, to know the benefits that are most important to them, and to deliver those benefits in a manner that is so superior that your customers can easily justify any price premium that you seek. It requires you to understand how customers compare your prices to those of competitors, and to determine the pricing architecture that causes your prices to be perceived most positively by customers.

Excellence in pricing also requires you to understand your competitors better, to comprehend the price/benefit tradeoffs they are offering in your markets, so that you can consistently maintain a position of value equivalence and even value advantage in the eyes of the customers you most want to serve. It requires you to understand with greater clarity the price initiatives and price levels of your competitors, so that the misreads that invariably lead to price wars can be avoided.

And finally, it requires you to understand yourself better, to understand your economics of serving individual customers with greater precision, and to understand your benefit delivery capability—both what it is and what it could be—so that you can target the market segments and customers that are truly best for you. It requires you to take a hard look at your own competitive behavior to assess and potentially improve on conduct that places unnecessary downward pressure on industry price levels in your markets.

Achieving the price advantage and all the benefits that come with it, however, does not happen by accident. To excel at pricing is hard work. It compels you not just to react to market and competitive prices but *to manage pricing actively*—with organizational commitment and discipline and structure. We hope that with this book, we have convinced you that the price advantage is indeed an advantage worth pursuing aggressively and worth the effort required to achieve it ultimately. We hope also that we have provided you with an integrated and structured approach that will help you begin to capture routinely the full complement of pricing opportunities that remain by and large untapped by most businesses today, and to begin to make the price advantage *your* advantage.

Sample Pocket Price and Pocket Margin Waterfalls

I n Chapter 3 we introduced the pocket price and pocket margin waterfalls. Here, we offer a collection of waterfalls from disguised client situations to illustrate how revenue can leak through a wide variety of
mechanisms. This collection not only shows how waterfall elements can
proliferate (often unintentionally) and how they can trigger large differences between base and pocket prices, but also how the waterfalls differ
across a broad sweep of businesses.

Please note that these waterfalls reflect the situation for a specific product at a specific company during a particular time period. They are not
meant to be broadly applicable examples. Also, all list and base prices have
been indexed to 100.

CONTENTS

Athletic Shoe	Pocket Price	Automotive Aftermarket Part	Pocket Margin
Breakfast Cereal	Pocket Price	Automotive Glass	Pocket Margin
Data Communication Service	Pocket Price	Business Line of Credit	Pocket Margin
Dishwasher	Pocket Price	Construction Equipment	Pocket Margin
Electrical Controls	Pocket Price	Custom Manufacturing System	Pocket Margin
Elevator System	Pocket Price	Enterprise Computer	Pocket Margin
Executive Recruiting	Pocket Price	Enterprise Software and Service	Pocket Margin
Fabricated Aluminum Product	Pocket Price	Plastic	Pocket Margin
Furniture	Pocket Price	Rolled Steel	Pocket Margin
Laboratory Services	Pocket Price		
Passenger Car	Pocket Price		
Personal Computer	Pocket Price		
Polymer	Pocket Price		
Surgical Supplies	Pocket Price		
Television	Pocket Price		
Vinyl Flooring	Pocket Price		

POCKET PRICE WATERFALLS

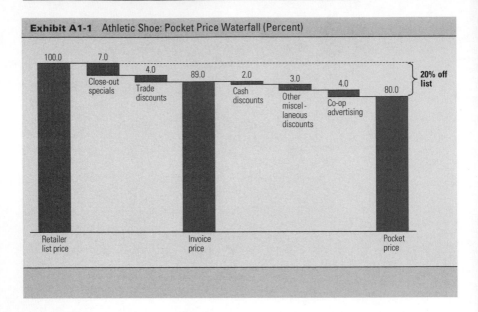

Exhibit A1-1 Athletic Shoe: Pocket Price Waterfall (Percent)

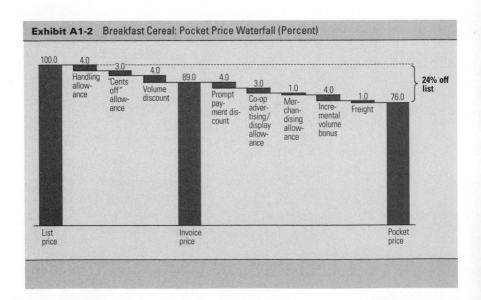

Exhibit A1-2 Breakfast Cereal: Pocket Price Waterfall (Percent)

Exhibit A1-3 Data Communication Service: Pocket Price Waterfall (Percent)

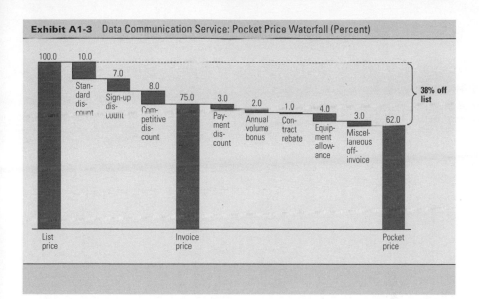

Exhibit A1-4 Dishwasher: Pocket Price Waterfall (Percent)

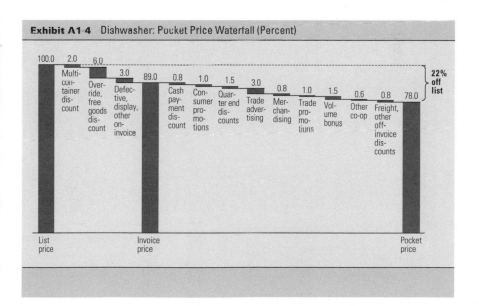

Exhibit A1-5   Electrical Controls: Pocket Price Waterfall (Percent)

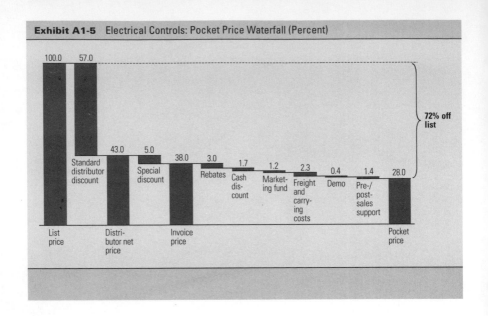

Exhibit A1-6   Elevator System: Pocket Price Waterfall (Percent)

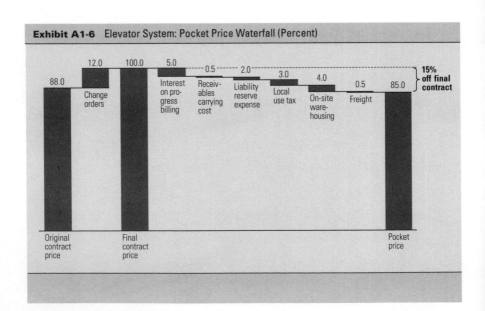

Exhibit A1-7   Executive Recruiting: Pocket Price Waterfall (Percent)

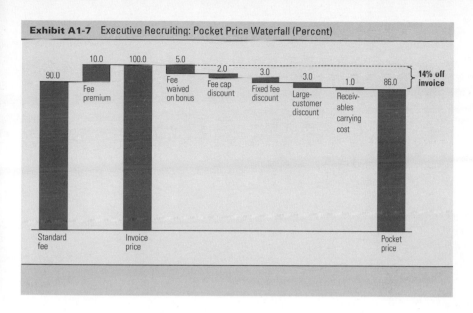

Exhibit A1-8   Fabricated Aluminum Product: Pocket Price Waterfall (Percent)

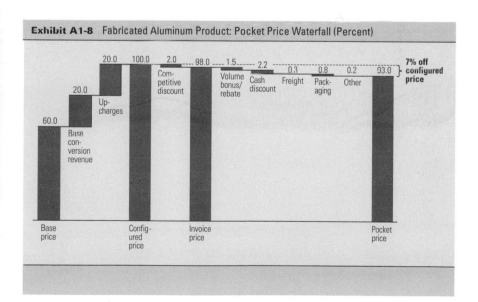

Exhibit A1-9 Furniture: Pocket Price Waterfall (Percent)

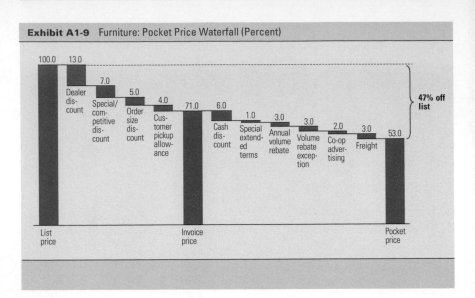

Exhibit A1-10 Laboratory Services: Pocket Price Waterfall (Percent)

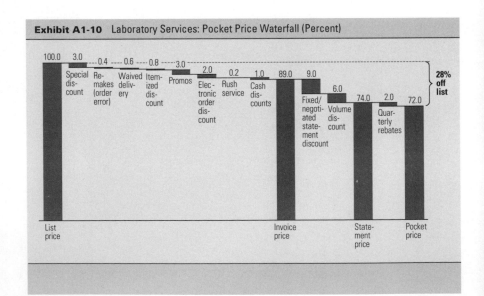

Exhibit A1-11 Passenger Car: Pocket Price Waterfall (Percent)

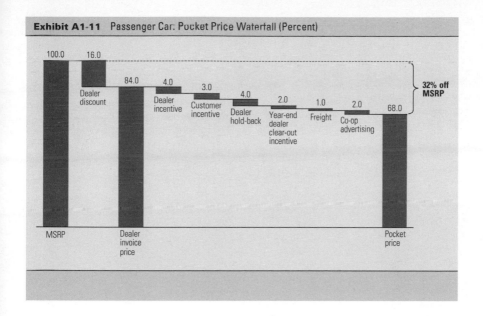

Exhibit A1-12 Personal Computer: Pocket Price Waterfall (Percent)

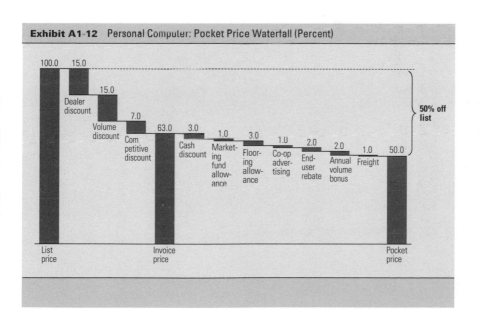

Exhibit A1-13   Polymer: Pocket Price Waterfall (Percent)

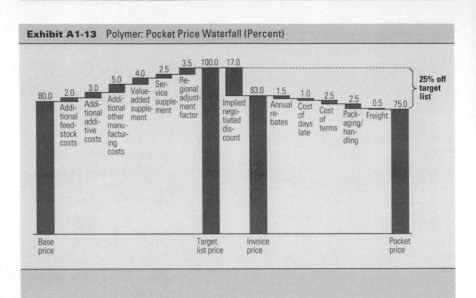

Exhibit A1-14   Surgical Supplies: Pocket Price Waterfall (Percent)

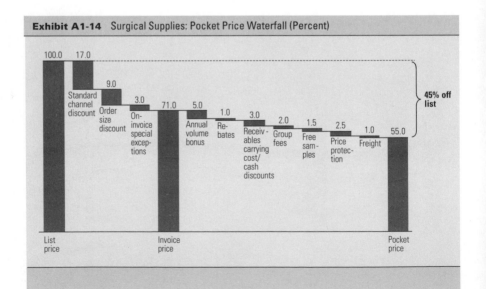

Exhibit A1-15 Television: Pocket Price Waterfall (Percent)

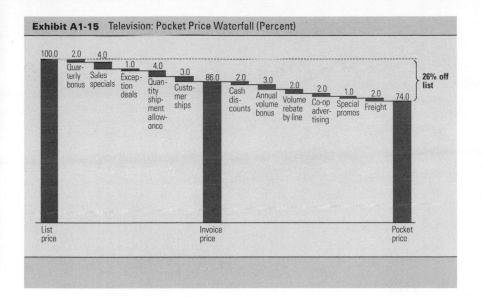

Exhibit A1-16 Vinyl Flooring: Pocket Price Waterfall (Percent)

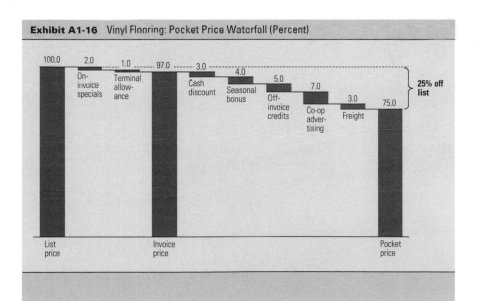

POCKET MARGIN WATERFALLS

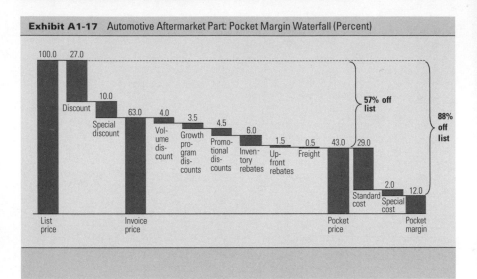

Exhibit A1-17 Automotive Aftermarket Part: Pocket Margin Waterfall (Percent)

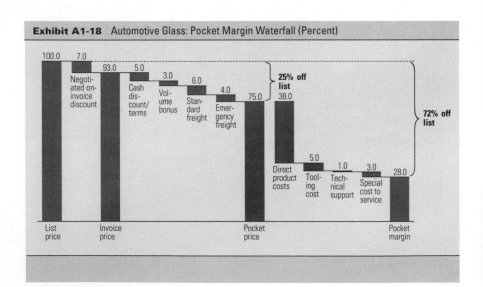

Exhibit A1-18 Automotive Glass: Pocket Margin Waterfall (Percent)

Exhibit A1-19 Business Line of Credit: Pocket Margin Waterfall (Percent)

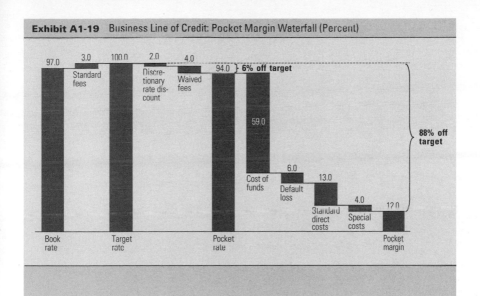

Exhibit A1-20 Construction Equipment: Pocket Margin Waterfall (Percent)

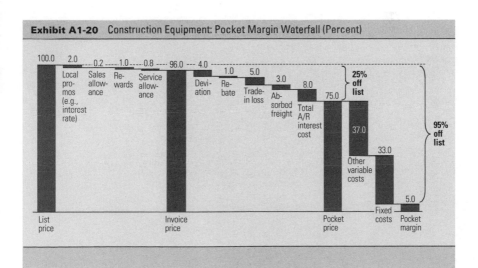

Exhibit A1-21   Custom Manufacturing System: Pocket Margin Waterfall (Percent)

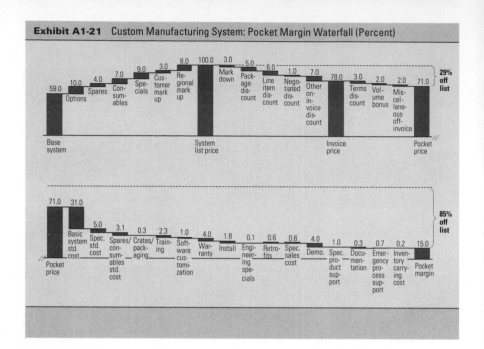

Exhibit A1-22   Enterprise Computer: Pocket Margin Waterfall (Percent)

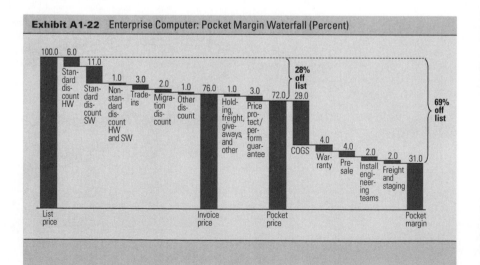

Exhibit A1-23 Enterprise Software and Service: Pocket Margin Waterfall (Percent)

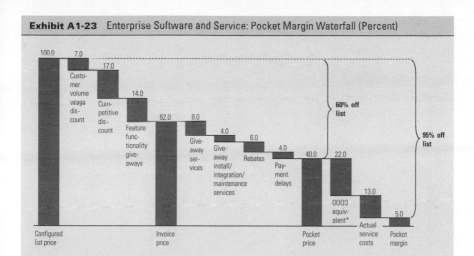

*Derived by apportioning product-specific R&D and other costs over expected volumes.

Exhibit A1-24 Plastic: Pocket Margin Waterfall (Percent)

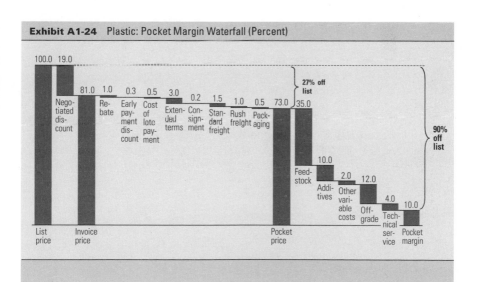

Exhibit A1-25   Rolled Steel: Pocket Margin Waterfall (Percent)

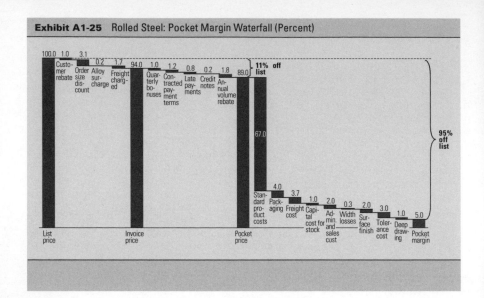

Antitrust Issues

In this appendix we will highlight some of the major U.S. and EU statutes and regulations relevant to pricing strategy. The descriptions are not meant to be exhaustive. The law is continuously in flux, so companies should always consult with legal counsel to obtain advice on the current state of the law, how it has been applied, and whether actions being discussed comply with relevant laws. This book is descriptive and does not constitute legal advice.

U.S. PRICING LAW

The U.S. experience with federal antitrust statutes has developed over more than a century and has influenced the law in other jurisdictions, such as the European Union and Japan.[1] A common thread that runs through much of U.S. antitrust law is that some practices are always anticompetitive and are therefore considered to be *per se illegal,* while others may be good or bad depending on the circumstances, so they are judged under the *rule of reason.*[2]

---

[1]This section will examine U.S. laws of general applicability at the federal level. Individual states also have antitrust statutes that tend to be consistent with the federal statutes, but there are exceptions. Industry-specific laws and those at the state level are beyond the scope of this appendix.

[2]Antitrust laws in the United States are enforced by the government and private parties. At the federal level, the Justice Department may file civil and criminal actions, while the Federal Trade Commission (FTC) and private parties may bring civil cases. While criminal violations are felonies, such penalties usually are used only in per se cases of price fixing and hardcore cartel activity. Civil plaintiffs often pursue injunctions to stop objectionable behavior, and private parties, if successful, are entitled to three times their actual economic damages (called *treble damages*), plus their legal fees and court costs.

Under the per se test, courts require only that the presence of the objectionable activity be proven, along with antitrust injury and damages. In contrast, the rule of reason adds a third element—that the conduct is unreasonably anticompetitive. Due to this additional point, it generally is more difficult to prove a violation, because, among other things, there must be evidence of adverse competitive effect and the defendant is given the opportunity to justify its behavior. As a result, there tends to be more pricing flexibility afforded under this standard.

Significantly, U.S. antitrust law for the last 25 years or so has been moving away from per se treatment, with its reliance on economic assumptions, to the rule of reason's insistence on demonstrable economic effect. Consequently, the law has become increasingly more forgiving, as many of the old assumptions have been jettisoned in favor of a more fact-specific approach.[3]

Despite the changes in the law, it would be remiss not to mention that the most serious or "hardcore" pricing violations remain strictly prohibited, and there can still be significant consequences for companies and individuals that engage in such violations, from large fines to prison sentences for individual directors and managers. For example, a fine of more $1.2 billion was imposed by U.S. and EU authorities in the vitamins cartel price-fixing case in 2001.

PRICE FIXING OR PRICE ENCOURAGEMENT

There are two types of price fixing: horizontal and vertical. In the case of horizontal price fixing, competitors agree on the prices they will charge or key terms of sale affecting price. In the case of vertical price fixing, also known as *resale price fixing*, a supplier and a reseller agree on the prices the reseller will charge or the price-related terms of resale for the supplier's products.[4]

---

[3]Even the European Union softened its historically more structuralist approach in 2000 by creating a safe harbor that permits a supplier to control how its products are resold in certain situations, by imposing territorial and certain other vertical nonprice restrictions as long as the supplier's market share is 30 percent or less. (Case reference: OJ (L 336) 21.)

[4]Note that in the United States there cannot be any vertical price fixing when the intermediary does not take title to the goods or services from the supplier. So a supplier may tell an independent sales representative or sales agent (in an agreement or otherwise) what price to charge for the supplier's goods or services. The same is true for a party that holds the supplier's products on consignment until they are sold to the end user.

The principal points of U.S. law in this area are Section 1 of the Sherman Act, an 1890 statute that prohibits "every contract, combination . . . or conspiracy in restraint of trade," and the subsequent cases that have shaped its application. Two important points bear mentioning.

First, the "contract, combination, or conspiracy" requirement necessarily means that there must be an express or tacit agreement between two or more individuals or entities. Thus, if a company is acting alone, there can be no illegal price fixing.

Second, there are rarely written contracts or other direct evidence of price-fixing conspiracies, so evidence of agreement usually must be inferred from the actions of the parties involved.[5] For example, based on case law, courts are more likely to find illegal price fixing when there is parallel pricing behavior and one of two situations:

- Such conduct would be against the self-interest of each party if it acted alone, but consistent with their self-interest if they all behaved the same way. An example would be near-simultaneous price increases when the companies involved all have excess production capacity and there has been no corresponding increase in input costs.
- Such conduct is preceded by an opportunity to collude, such as direct communications between the parties, and the actions taken cannot be supported by legitimate business explanations.

Horizontal price fixing remains per se illegal, except when a price effect is ancillary to a legitimate purpose of competitors working together. Under such circumstances, the rule of reason applies.[6]

The law is more complex, and hence more flexible, in the case of vertical or resale price fixing. Setting minimum or exact prices by agreement is still per se illegal, but, since 1997, setting maximum prices is judged under the rule of reason.[7] However, courts have determined that setting maximum, minimum, or exact resale prices without an agreement—for example, a policy unilaterally held by the supplier—is outside the reach of the

---

[5]Without more, the practice of imitating a competitor's pricing or other moves in the market—something called *conscious parallelism*—is not illegal. There must be proof of an agreement to meet the Sherman Act standard.

[6]In *National Collegiate Athletic Association v. Board of Regents*, 468 U.S. 85 (1984), while competitors getting together in an athletic conference served many useful purposes, broadcast restrictions which affected output and price were struck down under rule of reason. See Federal Trade Commission and U.S. Department of Justice, *Antitrust Guidelines for Collaborations Among Competitors* (April 2000).

[7]*State Oil Co. v. Khan*, 522 U.S. 3 (1997).

Sherman Act and therefore lawful.[8] Many high-end brands of consumer durables have successfully adopted minimum price policies in the United States to protect their brand price positions from erosion.

The way the policy is implemented makes all the difference between legality and illegality. The supplier typically announces the desired resale price as a policy and then refuses to do business with any reseller that does not comply.[9] No contracts can be used to establish or enforce the policy. Similarly, discussions with resellers regarding this matter must be limited to explaining the policy, as no assurances of compliance can be sought or accepted. In addition, a violator of the policy cannot be placed on probation. In its least risky form, this approach is zero-tolerance, one-strike-and-you're-out, although it is entirely up to the supplier when, if ever, to reinstate the violator.

Because of the narrowness of the exception for unilateral acts, it is imperative that the supplier's headquarters and field people be instructed carefully on what they can and cannot say and do. Moreover, the policy should be applied uniformly, otherwise an inference of an illegal agreement can be created.

PRICE SIGNALING

Sometimes companies communicate pricing or other intentions to the market, which can facilitate parallel behavior on the part of competitors. While such conscious parallelism alone is not unlawful, care must be taken to avoid the inference of an illegal contract, combination, or conspiracy. Consequently, such communication should be public and should have a business purpose apart from giving early warning to the competition, such as to provide customers advance notice of a price increase or to furnish investors with some insight into the company's pricing strategy.

Two examples illustrate these points. In the first, the court found nothing unlawful in manufacturers of gasoline additives providing advance public notice of price increases beyond that required by their customer contracts and ostensibly to aid buyers in their financial and

---

[8]In such places as Canada and the European Union, this practice remains illegal. See the discussion on EU law later in this appendix.

[9]Compliance with the policy is not considered to be an agreement to maintain a price. In addition, the policy can apply to some or all products, channels, or geographic areas. Moreover, failure to comply may result in the loss of only the covered product or products upon which the violation occurred, a product line, or all of the supplier's products.

purchase planning.[10] In the second, eight major airlines and their jointly owned data company settled price-fixing charges centering on a nonpublic computerized system that was used to communicate intended fare changes and promotions and permitted later modification or withdrawal of them.[11] Such a system apparently served as a virtual smoke-filled room in which the parties privately discussed and effectively coordinated their pricing.

PRICE DISCRIMINATION

Price discrimination is simply charging different prices to different customers, but it is unlawful in the United States only under certain conditions.[12] The law in this area—usually referred to as the Robinson-Patman Act[13]—balances the economic efficiency justification for price discrimination with the goal of preserving competition by maintaining the viability of numerous sellers, but errs on the side of the latter.

In order to prove illegal price discrimination under the Robinson-Patman Act, each of five elements must be present:

- *Discrimination.* Different prices are charged to different customers. But there is no discrimination if the price difference is based on a discount or allowance available to all or almost all customers—for example, a prompt payment discount. This is called the *availability* defense.
- *Sales to two or more customers.* Different prices must be charged on reasonably contemporaneous sales to two or more purchasers.
- *Goods.* The sale must be of goods, not services or bundles where services predominate in value.
- *Like grade and quality.* The goods must be physically the same or essentially the same. For this element, the willingness to pay more for branded products is irrelevant.

---

[10]*E. I. Du Pont de Nemours & Co. v. FTC*, 729 F.2d 128 (2d Cir. 1984), decided under Section 5 of the Federal Trade Commission Act, 15 U.S.C. § 45, a statute that is more regulator-friendly than the Sherman Act. The court upheld the legality of price signaling where there was no evidence that it was collusive, predatory, coercive, or exclusionary.

[11]*United States v. Airline Tariff Publishing Co.*, 1994-2 Trade Cas. (CCH) ¶ 70,686 (D.D.C. 1994); 836 F. Supp. 12 (D.D.C. 1993).

[12]Price discrimination can also be charging the same price to different customers in different circumstances, although this situation arises much less often in practice.

[13]*15 U.S.C. § 13.* The U.S. Justice Department and the FTC may enforce this law, but neither is particularly active in this regard. By far, most cases are brought by one business against another (consumers have no standing to sue).

■ *Reasonable probability of competitive injury.* There must be substantial competitive injury or the reasonable probability of it, usually at one of two levels. First, the *primary line*: A company may file suit against a competitive supplier for the latter's discriminatory pricing, but the law requires proof that the competitor's prices are below its costs and that the market structure is such that the competitor may recoup its losses.[14] Second, a supplier's disfavored customer may sue the supplier for price discrimination, as long as the customers in question compete with each other.[15]

Even in cases where all five of the elements of price discrimination are present, there are three defenses that may be used to avoid a finding of unlawful discrimination:

■ *Cost justification.* A price disparity is permitted if it is based on legitimate cost differences.
■ *Meeting competition.* Discrimination is permissible if it is based on a good faith belief that a discriminatory price is necessary to meet (but not beat) the price of a competitive supplier to the favored customer or to maintain a traditional price difference.
■ *Changing conditions.* Special prices may be provided to sell perishable, seasonal, obsolete, or distress merchandise.

PROMOTIONAL DISCRIMINATION

Promotional discrimination is providing different benefits such as advertising allowances to different customers, effectively achieving discriminatory pricing through other means. While the Robinson-Patman Act also governs promotional discrimination, the standards here are more flexible in some respects than those for price discrimination.

Promotional discrimination is unlawful if *each* of three elements is present:

■ *"The provision of allowances, services, or facilities . . ."* The supplier grants advertising or promotional allowances or provides services or facilities, such as free display racks or demonstrators.

---

[14]*Brooke Group Ltd. v. Brown & Williamson Corp.*, 509 U.S. 209, 221-24 (1993). This standard is so onerous that the threat of a primary line case tends to be rather remote.
[15]If they don't compete, the Robinson-Patman Act does not prohibit price discrimination. The lack of customer overlap may occur naturally or it may be engineered with the use of vertical nonprice restrictions discussed later in this appendix. The customers in question can be either resellers or end users that compete.

■ "... _in connection with the resale of the supplier's goods_ ..." The law applies only to resellers and only to the sale of goods, not services.[16]

■ "... _which are not available to all competing customers on proportionally equal terms._"[17] As with price discrimination, only competing customers must be treated alike. The greater flexibility here is based on the fact that competing customers do not have to receive the same level of benefits—only benefits that are proportionally equal based on unit or dollar purchases, the cost to the reseller of the promotional activity, or the value of the promotional activity to the supplier.

Notably, there also are three ways in which the standards for promotional discrimination are more restrictive than those for price discrimination. First, the same sort of evidence of competitive injury is not required, so in certain respects, promotional discrimination is treated as a per se offense. Second, the only defense when all three elements are proven is meeting competition, as cost justification and changing conditions are irrelevant. Finally, if the supplier provides promotional benefits to direct-buying resellers, it must also furnish them to competitive resellers that buy the same products through intermediaries.

VERTICAL NONPRICE RESTRICTIONS

There are several ways in which a supplier can control how much its resellers compete with each other on price or otherwise using the suppliers products, a situation known as _intrabrand competition_. Fortunately, U.S. law has afforded suppliers a good deal of flexibility in this regard in the name of promoting competition between rival brands, or _interbrand competition_. Each of these three approaches is judged under the rule of reason (or something substantially similar) and may be implemented using the carrot approach, the stick approach, or a combination:[18]

---

[16]Due to differing standards, deciding whether a pricing action under consideration is to be judged as price or promotional discrimination is important. As a rule, price discrimination applies to the sale of goods by the supplier to the end user or reseller, while promotional discrimination applies only to the resellers of such goods.
[17]While availability is a defense to price discrimination, functional availability is required to avoid illegal promotional discrimination. The benefits or the performance necessary to earn them must be usable or attainable in a practical sense by all competing customers. If not, alternatives must be offered.
[18]Under the carrot approach, financial incentives are provided by the supplier to reward compliance. Under the stick approach, a failure to comply results in a termination of the relationship due to breach of the distribution agreement or otherwise.

- ■ *Customer restrictions*. The supplier specifies that the reseller may sell only to certain customers or may not sell to certain customers.
- ■ *Territorial or market restrictions*. The supplier defines a certain geographical area or market in which the reseller may sell and prohibits or discourages the reseller from selling outside of it.[19]
- ■ *Product restrictions*. The supplier determines which of its products a reseller may buy, prohibits reseller or end user purchases of certain products from another supplier, or ties the sale of a desirable product or service with the purchase of a less desirable product or service.

PREDATORY PRICING

A supplier engages in predatory pricing when its prices are set below its marginal cost or average variable cost, which is easier to measure, over a sustained period of time with the intent of driving competition out of business. Such practice is unlawful only if the resulting structure of the market allows the supplier to recoup its losses by raising prices. These factors make it difficult to bring predatory pricing suits successfully.

PRICE SQUEEZES

When a producer has monopoly power in an intermediary product and both sells the product to others for further processing and does such processing itself, it engages in a something known as a *price squeeze* if it prices the intermediary product and the finished product in such a fashion that its competitors are squeezed and cannot compete in the finished product market. The same effect can occur when a company sells at both the wholesale and retail levels, has monopoly power at the wholesale level, and prices in such a fashion that its wholesale customers cannot compete against it in the retail market.

EU PRICING LAW

In this section we will highlight the relevant EU regulations and the primary ways in which EU law differs from U.S. law. As with our coverage of U.S. law, the descriptions are not meant to be exhaustive, and companies

---

[19]This tactic can be combined with the grant of an exclusive distributorship, where the supplier agrees not to supply anyone but the reseller in that market. When an exclusive distributorship is combined with absolute confinement to a geographic territory, the result is referred to as an *airtight territory*.

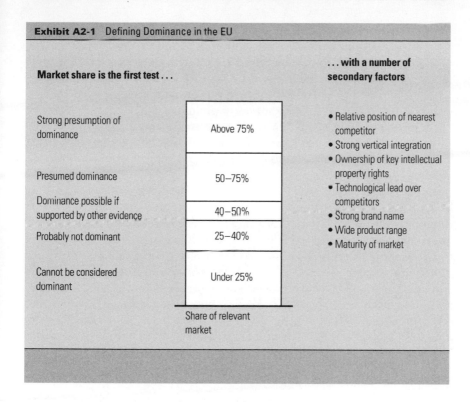

Exhibit A2-1 Defining Dominance in the EU

Market share is the first test . . .

. . . with a number of secondary factors

	Share of relevant market	
Strong presumption of dominance	Above 75%	• Relative position of nearest competitor
		• Strong vertical integration
		• Ownership of key intellectual property rights
Presumed dominance	50–75%	• Technological lead over competitors
Dominance possible if supported by other evidence	40–50%	• Strong brand name
Probably not dominant	25–40%	• Wide product range
		• Maturity of market
Cannot be considered dominant	Under 25%	

should always consult with legal counsel for specifics on whether a certain program complies with the laws described.

There are two key differences between the EU law governing pricing and U.S. law. First, there is a crucial distinction in the European Union between a company deemed to be *dominant* and a company that is not. Most EU pricing law applies only if a company is dominant.[20] Therefore, analyses of the relevant product and geographic market and the market share of the company can be key determinants of whether its pricing practices are legal or illegal. As shown in Exhibit A2-1, while a market share of 50 percent or higher raises a presumption of dominance, the European Court of Justice (ECJ) has found dominance in a company with a share as low as

---

[20]The European Court of Justice (ECJ) has defined dominance as "a position of economic strength . . . [enabling a company] to prevent effective competition being maintained on the relevant market by affording it the power to behave to an appreciable extent independently of its competitors, customers and ultimately of its consumers." Case 27/76 *United Brands* [1978], ECR 207, ¶ 65.

39.7 percent.[21] Also, the European Commission (EC) has stated that a dominant position cannot be ruled out when market share is between 25 and 40 percent. There are other factors the EC and the ECJ consider to determine dominance, including relative market share compared with competitors, barriers to entry, and period of time the company has held its market position.

Further, duopolistic or oligopolistic markets can lead to a finding of *collective dominance* and cause companies that otherwise would not be dominant to be deemed dominant for the purpose of application of the pricing laws. An explicit agreement or other legal link is not necessary for companies to be considered collectively dominant. EU law is not clear on this subject, so in situations where there is a potential oligopoly, companies should be careful even when engaging in practices that are prohibited only for dominant companies.

The second key distinction between U.S. and EU pricing laws regards the unique structure of the European market. The European Union has a strong focus on market integration of its member states, and the EC and ECJ use and support the use of the EU competition rules to promote market integration and building a single European market. Thus, there are certain actions, such as restricting export from one EU country to another, that are especially prohibited as contrary to this single-market goal.

The relevant EU statutes in this area are Articles 81 and 82 of the European Community Treaty (formerly Articles 85 and 86). Article 81 deals in general with collusive pricing, whether the companies involved are in dominant positions or not, while Article 82 addresses abuse of a dominant position and only applies to companies deemed to be dominant. Thus, for a nondominant company, price fixing and resale price fixing are restricted, but most other pricing practices are legal so long as it does not represent collusion with competitors.

At the outset, it is worth highlighting that specific national laws are not within the scope of this book. Companies operating within the European Union must comply both with EU law and also with any local laws that may be stricter. Most of these laws are similar to EU law in the areas of pricing, but in some cases national laws carry a stricter punishment for violation or provide a broader standing for others to bring a case against potential violators. The major exceptions to the similarity in legal rules are France and Germany, where the national nondiscrimination laws are more restrictive on pricing policy. In most cases compa-

---

[21]Fifty percent presumption: C-62/86 AZKO [1991] ECR-2585; 39.7 percent finding: *Virgin/British Airways*, OJ [2000] L 30/1, [2000] 4 CMLR 999.

nies will need to remain cognizant of both EU law and national laws when setting pricing policy.

PRICE FIXING OR PRICE ENCOURAGEMENT

As in the United States, horizontal price-fixing agreements are essentially per se illegal. This prohibition applies to both dominant and nondominant firms. Even in cases where participants failed to comply with agreed-upon prices, such agreements are a violation of the law.

Price uniformity among competitors does not as such violate Article 81, but it may lead to an inference that unlawful concerted action has taken place when additional factors—such as resulting conditions of competition, which do not correspond to the normal conditions of the market—are present.[22] For example, *parallel pricing* when the competitors have met or made contact has been held illegal when deemed to limit competition. While neither the ECJ nor any European court has found companies guilty of an unlawful concerted practice where they have not met, European rules take a strict approach to the notion of concerted practice, which covers communication of a company's actual or intended policies on pricing with the intent that competitors will react. If the industry is oligopolistic, price leadership and followership can give rise to suspicion of collusion or even an abuse of collective dominance.

EU law governing resale price fixing also applies to both dominant and nondominant companies and is more restrictive than U.S. law. Minimum resale prices, even if part of a stated policy and enforced unilaterally, are generally illegal in the European Union, based on the idea that any policy decision by a company toward its dealers can be seen to become automatically a part of the dealership arrangement and not merely a unilateral policy.[23] Although a recent appellate decision indicates a potential movement toward seeing some of these policies as unilateral acts

---

[22]The leading case on this subject is the *Dyestuffs* case, Decision 69/243 OJ 1969 L195/11, in which several uniform price increases in the aniline dye market throughout Europe in the mid-1960s led to a EC investigation of 17 producers. The investigations resulted in a ruling of "concerted practice" and fines for all but one company. The court ruled that "concerted practice" can be a form of coordination, without amounting to formal agreement, which purposely substitutes practical cooperation for the risks of competition.

[23]*Ford-Werke AG v. EC Commission* (Joined Cases 25 and 26/84) [1985], ECR 2725.

rather then agreements, the outcome of the case is still uncertain and the case itself covers a relatively limited set of circumstances.[24]

A minimum resale price restriction is also considered a policy that can make an otherwise legal vertical agreement illegal. Fixed resale price restrictions are equally illegal. Recommended resale prices, and in some cases maximum resale price policies, have been permitted as long as the recommendation is not reinforced by any pressure or incentives that could make the prices operate essentially as minimum or fixed resale prices.

These restrictions on resale price fixing apply equally to actions by an individual supplier and actions by a trade association on behalf of all suppliers in the trade.

National law technically governs resale price maintenance systems operating at a purely local level. However, if they are deemed to deflect likely trade between EU countries from its natural patterns, they may come under the scope of EU law.

PRICE SIGNALING

Intentionally disclosing pricing or production information in order to signal to competitors privately or to elicit an anticipated reaction from them is strictly prohibited in the European Union for both dominant and nondominant firms. If companies choose to disclose future pricing information publicly, they should have a legitimate business purpose for doing so.

While exchanges of price information between competitors, such as *open price systems*, may in some circumstances be prohibited under Article 81, published price lists that competitors can see do not alone constitute an unlawful exchange of information. In fact, it is likely that such systems would be found legal so long as they serve a clear bona fide commercial purpose. It is only when communication of prices or anticipated prices to competitors is done with an intent that they will modify their behavior that the specter of illegality is raised. For example, the EC has stated that trade associations may compute and disseminate aggre-

---

[24]In *Bayer AG v. EC Commission* (Case T-41/96) [2000] ECR II-3383, the EC found that pricing policies by Bayer regarding its Adalat product supplied to pharmaceutical wholesalers in Spain—attempting to provide lower prices than those in the UK but only providing a limited quantity to cover local market demand to prevent export—were part of a set of unlawful agreements and concerted practices. On appeal, the Court of First Instance agreed with Bayer that the action was unilateral. The case is currently on appeal to the ECJ.

gate output and sales statistics so long as individual companies and transactions are not identified.

PRICE DISCRIMINATION

Generally, so long as a company is nondominant, it may legally discount quoted prices however it chooses to each of its customers, even competing customers, as long as it does not collude with its competitors or agree with some customers as to what other customers will be charged. However, a nondominant company still may not discriminate for an unlawful purpose, such as to exert pressure or provide an incentive around resale price maintenance or to create territorial limitations or indirect restrictions on exporting or importing within the European Union. For example, a discount linked directly to products resold for local consumption was found to be an unlawful restriction. Furthermore, the laws in France and Germany regarding price discrimination are broader in scope than the equivalent EU rules, applying to both dominant and nondominant companies.

Where a company is dominant in the European Union, the rules are similar to U.S. law and prohibit discriminatory pricing to customers in the same or similar circumstances. There are two main defenses to such action. First, the discount can be based on genuine cost savings. Second, different prices can reflect differing values of services provided by the buyer, such as in IT, where value-added resellers can provide demonstrable value to the seller, or in groceries, where a supermarket can provide a favorable display location. Thus, quantity discounts (where larger orders reduce unit costs) and prompt payment discounts (where fast payments reduce financing costs) are justifiable, while a loyalty rebate is not. For example, in *Hoffman LaRoche*, the classic case on loyalty rebates, the ECJ ruled that a rebate tied to a purchaser's obtaining all or most of its requirements from a dominant seller, even when that rebate was willingly accepted by the buyers, is a violation of Article 82.[25]

Certain specific actions are likely to trigger a finding of discriminatory pricing, such as defending against a new entrant by offering loyalty discounts to those customers targeted by the new entrant. Other acts that could trigger discriminatory pricing concerns include securing a long-term, exclusive contract with a reseller, withdrawing discounts if the customer satisfied some or all of its requirements from other suppliers, and including

---

[25]Case 85/76 [1979], ECR 461.

contractual provisions that require the customer to allow the supplier to match the best prices offered by other suppliers.

It is important to note that there is no defense that the company offering the discriminatory prices had low profits or losses, or that customers requested the discounts. In other words, a meet-the-competition argument is not necessarily an acceptable justification for price discrimination in the European Union. It is also important to note that the ECJ is more likely to find price discrimination in cases where prices are not transparent, or where, if they are transparent, they are clearly unequal.

GEOGRAPHIC DISCRIMINATION

The European Union's single-market objective is a central driver of EU competition policy enforcement. As such, it affords strict treatment of both dominant and nondominant companies that engage in practices that effectively segregate countries from one another. For example, if goods are marketed in the European Union, there must be no agreement or understanding that directly or indirectly prohibits or restricts their subsequent export and trade within the Union. Such policies as pricing differently to customers from different countries, even if the prices were claimed to be "what the markets would bear," are illegal for a dominant supplier. Similarly, offering discriminatory discounts to certain customers to discourage them from importing from or exporting to certain other countries have been held illegal regardless of dominance.

A qualified territorial agreement, in which a supplier gets dealers to agree not to actively market and sell outside their territory, is sometimes allowed, so long as the agreement does not restrict passive sales (responding to unsolicited orders) that come from outside the agreed territory of the supplier.

PROMOTIONAL DISCRIMINATION

Under EU law, promotional discrimination does not have a special set of rules. Actions that in the United States might be covered by promotional discrimination laws are judged in the European Union under price discrimination law.

PREDATORY PRICING

The ECJ has adopted a two-part test to gauge whether predatory pricing is illegal as an "abuse of a dominant position." First, if prices are below average variable costs there is a per se violation, because the only justification for such prices is deemed to be the elimination of a competitor. Matching a competitor's prices is not considered to be a valid defense. Second, if prices are higher than average variable cost but below total costs, then there must be a demonstration of intent to eliminate a competitor.[26]

However, such practices as introductory offers, end-of-season sales, or other temporary price reductions with generally legitimate business purposes are likely to be legal in the European Union as long as there is no specific intent to eliminate a competitor.

EXCESSIVE PRICING

Excessive pricing can be construed to be an abuse of a dominant position, but it is very difficult for the EC to prove its case in such situations because there is no clear definition of what constitutes *excessive*. Generally the only companies found guilty of this conduct have been absolute monopolies. The ECJ has defined a price as excessive if it has no reasonable relation to the economic value of the product or service provided. It has also suggested several ways of measuring what is excessive, including comparison of prices charged for the same product in different geographies; comparison of the dominant company's price charged in its geographic market to the price charged in competitive markets in other geographies for the same product; and, where possible to measure, comparison of price to production cost.

PRICE SQUEEZING

Similar to U.S. law, it may be illegal for a dominant European company to engage in price squeezing, in which a dominant supplier of intermediary products that also produces finished products prices the intermediary products to other players in such a way that they cannot compete effectively.

---

[26]*Tetra Pak International SA v. EC Commission* (Case C-333/94P) [1996], ECR I-5951. In this case, sales below average variable costs were deemed to be part of an eviction strategy designed to eliminate competition. However, the Commission noted that not covering total costs may be economically justified in the short term if the activity still covers fixed costs in part, but that any activity for which the profits would remain permanently inadequate to cover variable costs would be illegal and must be terminated.

ANTITRUST INFORMATION SOURCES

Argentina
Comisión Nacional de Defensa de la Competencia
Ministerio de Economía y Obras y Servicios Públicos
Av. J.A. Roca 651
4 Piso, Sector 10
1322 Buenos Aires
Argentina
Tel: (54) 11 4349 4095/99; 4349 4100/07
Fax: (54) 11 4349 4225
www.mecon.gov.ar/cndc/home.htm
(Spanish only)

Asia-Pacific
Asia-Pacific Economic Cooperation
35 Heng Mui Keng Terrace
Singapore 119616
Tel: (65) 6775-6012
Fax: (65) 6775-6013
www.apeccp.org.tw

Australia
Australian Competition and Consumer Commission
P.O. Box 1119
Dickson ACT 2602
Australia
Tel: (61) 2 6243 1111/1123
Fax: (61) 2 6243 1199/1122
www.accc.gov.au

Austria
Federal Ministry of Economic Affairs
Wettbewerbsabteilung (C1/4)
Stubenring 1
A-1011 Vienna
Austria
Tel: (43) 1 711 00 5355
Fax: (43) 1 711 00 5776
E-mail: POSTC14@bmwa.gv.at
www.bmwa.gv.at/BMWA/Thema/Wirtschaftspolitik/
    Wettbewerbspolitik
(German only)

Belgium
Division Prix et Concurrence
Ministère des Affaires Economiques
Administration de la Politique Commerciale
North Gate III
Boulevard du Roi Albert II, 16
1000 Bruxelles
Belgium
Tel: (32) 2 206 51 63
Fax: (32) 2 206 57 72
E-mail: PRICE.CONC@pophost.eunet.be
mineco.fgov.be

Brazil
Conselho Administrativo de
Defesa Economica
Ministério da Justiça
Bloco T, Anexo II, 2 andar, Sala 228
70064-900 Brasilia DF
Brazil
Tel: (55) 61 218 3414/15/16
Fax: (55) 61 321 1209
www.cade.gov.br
(Portuguese only)

Canada
The Competition Bureau
50 Victoria Street
Hull, Quebec K1A 0C9
Canada
Tel: (1) 819-997-4282
Fax: (1) 819-997-0324
cb.bc.gc.ca

China
Ministry of Commerce
2 Dong Changan Jie
Beijing 100731
China
Tel: (86) 10 6512-1919
Fax: (86) 10 6519-8173
english.mofcom.gov.cn

Czech Republic
Office for Protection of Economic Competition
Joštova 8, 601 56 Brno
Czech Republic
Tel: (420) 542-161-233
Fax: (420) 542-210-023
http://www.compet.cz/Titulni_eng.htm

Denmark
Competition Council
(Konkurrenceraadet)
Norregade 49
DK-1165 Copenhagen K
Denmark
Tel: (45) 33 17 70 00
Fax: (45) 33 32 61 44
www.ks.dk/english

Egypt
Ministry of Foreign Trade
8 Adly St.
Cairo, Egypt
Tel: (20) 2 391-9661
Fax: (20) 2 390-3029
www.moft.gov.eg

European Commission
Direction Générale Concurrence
Commission Européenne
200 rue de la Loi
B-1049 Bruxelles
Belgium
Tel: (32) 2 295 32 66
Fax: (32) 2 295 54 37
E-mail: infocomp@cec.eu.int
europa.eu.int/comm/competition/index_en.html

Finland
Finnish Competition Authority
Pitkänsillanranta 3, P.O.B. 332,
FIN-00531 Helsinki
Finland
Tel: (358) 9 731 41
Fax: (358) 9 7314 3328
www.kilpailuvirasto.fi/english

France
Competition Council
11, rue de l'Echelle
75 001 Paris, France
Tel: (33) 1 55 04 00 00
Fax: (33) 1 55 04 00 33
www.conseil-concurrence.fr

Germany
German Cartel Authority
Kaiser-Friedrich-Strasse 16
D-53113 Bonn
Germany
Tel: (49) 228-949-9-0
Fax: (49) 228-94-99-400
www.bundeskartellamt.de/english.html

India
Monopolies and Restrictive Trade Practices Commission
Kota House Annex, Shahjahan Road
New Delhi 110011
India
Tel: (91) 11 3384326; 3384965
Fax: (91) 11 3385974; 3385977; 3384965

Indonesia
Ministry of Industry and Trade
Jl Gatot Subroto No. 52-53
Jakarta 12950
Indonesia
Tel: (62) 21 525-5509
Fax: (62) 21 526-1086
www.dprin.go.id/default_e.htm

Ireland
Competition Authority
14 Parnell Square
Dublin 1, Ireland
Tel: (353) 1 804-5400
Fax: (353) 1 804-5401
www.tca.ie

Italy
The Italian Competition Authority
Via Liguria, 26
00187 Rome, Italy
Tel: (39) 06-48-16-21
Fax: (39) 06-48-16-22-56
www.agcm.it/eng

Israel
Antitrust Authority
22, Kanfei Hanesharim Str.
Giva' at Shaul
Jerusalem 917341
Israel
Tel: (972) 65 56 111
Fax: (972) 65 15 330
www.antitrust.gov.il/fram_e_set.html

Japan
International Affairs Division
Fair Trade Commission
1-1-1 Kasumigaseki Chiyoda-ku
Tokyo 100-8987
Japan
Tel:(81) 3 3581-1998
Fax: (81) 3 3581-1944
www2.jftc.go.jp/e-page

Korea, Republic of
Fair Trade Commission
International Affairs Division II
1 Chungang-dong
Kwachon-shi Kyunggi-Do
427-760
Republic of Korea
Tel: (82) 2 504-5145/46
Fax: (82) 2 504-5144; 507-3544
E-mail: chan@ftc.go.kr
www.ftc.go.kr/eng

Mexico
Federal Competition Commission
Monte Libano 225

Lomas de Chapultepec
11000. México, D.F.
Tel: (52) 9140-6500
Fax: (52) 9140-0380
www.cfc.gob.mx/EnIndex.asp

The Netherlands
The Netherlands Competition Authority
P.O. Box 16326
NL-2500 BH The Hague
The Netherlands
Tel: (31) 70 330 33 30
Fax: (31) 70 330 33 70
www.nmanet.nl/en

New Zealand
Ministry of Commerce: Regulatory
     and Competition Policy Branch
33 Bowen Street
P.O. Box 1473
Wellington, New Zealand
Tel: (64) 4 472 0030
Fax: (64) 4 473 4638
www.med.govt.nz/about/rcpb.html

Norway
Competition Authority
H Heyerdalsgaten 1
N-0033 Oslo 1
Norway
Tel: (47) 2 240 0900
Fax: (47) 2 242 7336
www.konkurransetilsynet.no/internett/index.asp

Pakistan
Monopoly Control Authority
65-E, Pak Pavilions, 2d and 3d floor
Fazal-Ulhaq Road (G-7/F-7), P.O. Box 1227
Islambabad, Pakistan
Tel: (92) 51 920 59 25
Fax: (92) 51 921 18
Email: section@isb.comsats.net

Poland
Office for the Protection of Competition and Consumers
Powstancow Warszawy 1
00-950 Warsaw
Poland
Tel: (48) 22 556-0800
Fax: (48) 22 826-5076
www.uokik.gov.pl/a_organigram.phtml

Russia
Anti-Monopoly Ministry
11 Ul Sadovaya-Kudrinskaya
Moscow 123808
Russia
Tel: (7) 95 252 7653
Fax: (7) 95 254 8300

Saudi Arabia
Ministry of Commerce
P.O. Box 1774
Riyadh 11162
Saudi Arabia
Tel: (966) 1 401-2220
Fax: (966) 1 403-8421

Slovakia
Antimonopoly Office
Drieňová 24
826 03 Bratislava
Slovakia
Tel: (421) 2 43337 305
Fax: (421) 2 43333 572
www.antimon.gov.sk/eng

South Africa
South African Competition Commission
Private Bag x23, Lynwood Ridge 0040
South Africa
Tel: (27) 12-482-9000
Fax: (27) 12-482-9123
www.compcom.co.za

Spain
Dirección General de Política Económica
y Defensa de la Competencia
Servicio de Defensa de la Competencia
Paseo de la Castellana 162, planta 20
28046 Madrid
Spain
Tel: (34) 91 583 51 88/87
Fax: (34) 91 583 53 38
www.tdcompetencia.org
(Spanish only)

Sweden
Swedish Competition Authority
Malmskillnadsgatan 32
SE-103 85 Stockholm
Sweden
Tel: (46) 8 700 16 00
Fax: (46) 8 24 55 43
www.kkv.se/eng/eng_index.shtm

Switzerland
Federal Competition Commission
Effingerstrasse 27
CH-3003 Bern
Switzerland
Tel: (41) 31 322-2040
Fax: (41) 31 322-2053
www.wettbewerbskommission.cb/site/e-html

Taiwan
Fair Trade Commission
12-14F, No2-2, Sec.1, Chi Nan Road
Taipei
Taiwan, R.O.C.
Tel: (886) 2 2351-7588
www.ftc.gov.tw/english.asp

Turkey
Competition Council
Bilkent Plaza Blok B3
Bilkent, 06530, Ankara
Turkey
Tel: (90) 312 266 6966
Fax: (90) 312 266 7920
www.rekabet.gov.tr/english.asp

United Kingdom
Office of Fair Trading
Fleetbank House, 2-6 Salisbury Square
London EC4Y 8JX
United Kingdom
Tel: (44) 8457 22 44 99
www.oft.gov.uk

United States
Federal Trade Commission Antitrust Division
Office of Policy and Evaluation, Room 394
Bureau of Competition
600 Pennsylvania Ave NW
Washington, D.C. 20580
USA
Tel: (1) 202-326-3300
www.ftc.gov/ftc/antitrust.htm

Venezuela
Pro-Competencia
Superintendencia para la Promocion
Y Proteccion de la Competencia
Torre Este, piso 19
Nivel Lecusa, Parque Central
Caracas 1010
Venezuela
Tel: (58) 2 509 05 55
Fax: (58) 2 509 05 77
www.procompetencia.gov.ve
(Spanish only)

Vietnam
Ministry of Trade
31 Trang Tien, Hanoi
Vietnam
Tel: (84) 4 825-3835
Fax: (84) 4 8264696
www.mot.gov.vn/index_en.asp

World Trade Organization
Centre William Rappard
Rue de Lausanne 154
CH-1211 Geneva 21
Switzerland
Tel: (41) 22-739-51-11
Fax:(41) 22-731-42-06
www.wto.org/english/tratop_e/comp_e/comp_e.htm

List of Acronyms

ABC	activity-based costing
ATM	automated teller machine
B2B	business-to-business
CEO	chief executive officer
CFO	chief financial officer
COGS	cost of goods sold
CPG	consumer packaged good
CRM	customer relationship management
EC	European Commission
ECJ	European Court of Justice
EDI	electronic data interchange
ERP	enterprise resource-planning
FDA	U.S. Food and Drug Administration
FTC	U.S. Federal Trade Commission
IT	information technology
KPI	key performance indicator
M&A	mergers and acquisitions
MACs	moves, adds, and changes
MAP	minimum advertised price
MRO	maintenance, repair, and operations
MSRP	manufacturer's suggested retail price
PC	personal computer
PDA	personal digital assistant
PPR	pocket price ratio
PTMC	price to meet competition
R&D	research and development
ROI	return on investment
ROS	return on sales
SKU	stock-keeping unit
SUV	sports utility vehicle
VAR	value-added reseller
VEL	value equivalence line

About the Authors

MICHAEL V. MARN

Mike Marn joined McKinsey in 1977 and is a partner based in Cleveland, Ohio. Mike has developed many of the most universally used analytic approaches for identifying and capturing opportunities in pricing.

Mike is a 1974 Phi Beta Kappa graduate of Hiram College with a degree in mathematics, and he holds a master's degree in operations research from Case Western Reserve University, which he received in 1976. Mike is on the board of advisers of the Pricing Institute, and he chaired the annual U.S. Pricing Conferences in 1992, 1993, 1996, and 2001. He has written a variety of articles on pricing, appearing in such publications as *The Wall Street Journal*, *The New York Times*, *Boardroom Reports*, *Sales and Marketing Management*, the *Harvard Business Review*, and *The McKinsey Quarterly*.

ERIC V. ROEGNER

Eric Roegner joined McKinsey in 1994 and is a partner based in Cleveland, Ohio. He has helped clients in all major markets on a wide range of pricing and marketing issues.

Eric earned a joint MBA from Case Western Reserve University in the United States and the Rotterdam School of Management in the Netherlands in 1994 and a bachelor's degree in mechanical and aerospace engineering from Princeton University in 1991. He has published articles in *The McKinsey Quarterly*, *Marketing Management*, and the *OESA Journal*, among others, and has spoken at many industry conferences.

CRAIG C. ZAWADA

Craig Zawada joined McKinsey in 1997 and is a partner based in Pittsburgh, Pennsylvania. Craig's experience spans a wide range of B2B and consumer products.

Craig earned his bachelor's degree in business administration in 1992 and his MBA in 1993, both from the Schulich School of Business, York University, in Ontario, Canada. Craig is widely published on pricing strategy, with articles appearing in the *Harvard Business Review*, *Mergers and Acquisitions*, and *The McKinsey Quarterly*. He has spoken on pricing strategy at industry conferences in North America, Europe, and South America.

Accountability, 117
Accounting systems, 26
Account size, pocket discounts, 34–36, 224–225
Account-specific pricing, 180, 184, 233
Ace Computer, 48
Actual costs, 104
Administration, technology-enabled tools, 165–167
Advertising/advertising costs, 25, 32, 35, 187, 222–223. *See also* Cooperative advertising
Allen Glass Company, transaction management illustration, 37–42
Alpha Computers, product/market strategy illustration, 47–54
Amazon.com, 173
Anheuser Busch, 180
Annual volume bonus, 25–26, 33, 38
Antitrust:
    defense, 184
    EU pricing law, 260–267
    information sources, 268–277
    overview of, 140–142
    U.S. pricing law, 253–260
Australia, competition laws, 178
AutoKing, 228
Automotive:
    aftermarket, 30–37, 147, 248
    car makers, 95–97, 100–101, 114–115, 121, 145, 245
    suppliers, 37–41, 57–59, 134, 197–200, 220–236, 248

Baby boomers, consumer habits, 8–9
Bar code readers, 94–95, 100
Bargain hunters, 99
Baseco, 48
Benchmarking, 215
Benefit-bracketed customers, 67
Benefit perceptions, *see* Customer(s), generally, benefit perceptions

Best-in-breed providers, pricing software vendors, 174–175
Big number syndrome, 55
Brand dilution, 186
Brand equity, 87
Brand positioning, 96
Bundler:
    characteristics of, 116, 118, 122
    pricing model by supplier role, 119–120
Business cycles, 65. *See also* Product life cycle
Business environment, impact of, 8
Buy-price engineering, 187

Caesar, 132–133
Capacity utilization, 15
Capital investments, 15
Carrying cost, 25–26, 32
Case, antitrust litigation, 180
Cash discounts, 25
Channel partners, 53–54
Chemicals, 78–79, 181, 246, 251
Chief executive officer (CEO):
    commitment of, 218
    postmerger pricing, 142
Chief pricing officer, 210
China, legal issues, 178, 184
Cleaning out the pipeline, product cannibalization, 102
Clean teams, 141
Coexistence, product cannibalization, 102–103
Collective dominance, EU pricing law, 262
Commitment/conviction, importance of, 208–210, 218, 235
Communication skills, *see* Price communication
Compaq, 144
Compensation, management system, 212–213
    bonuses, 25–26

Competition, generally:
  awareness of, 84
  interband, 259
  intrabrand, 259
  market entry, 60
  new products, 108, 111
  penetration pricing, 108
  postmerger pricing, impact of, 131
  price cuts, reaction to, 156
  price leadership strategy, 79–80, 87
  price wars, 144–146, 152–153
  product repositioning, impact of,
    60–61
  response strategies, 65–67, 83–84,
    104, 106, 108–109
Competitive discount, 24
Competitive injury, 258
Component specialist:
  characteristics of, 116, 121–122
  pricing model, 118–119
Computers:
  hardware, 44, 68, 93, 144, 145, 245,
    250
  network systems, 45–53, 112–113,
    122
  services, 98, 241, 251
  software, 106, 165, 251
Conjoint analysis, 47, 99, 134
Conscious parallelism, 185
Consignment costs, 25
Consolidation, postmerger, 134
Consumer durables, 27–28, 134–139,
    241, 247
Consumer goods, 8, 30–37, 96,
    194–195, 240, 247
Consumer packaged goods, 132–133,
    148, 202
Contract clauses:
  input-cost, 78
  meet-the-competition, 85, 185
  most-favored-customers, 85,
    185–186
  most-favored-nation, 186
Contracts:
  clauses, *see* Contract clauses
  long-term, 155
Cooperative advertising, 25, 32, 35,
    222–223
Cost analysis, 103–104
Cost changes, 76
Costco, 8
Cost curves, 88
Cost estimates, 103–104
Cost-plus pricing, 103

Cost reductions, 120
Costs structures, 15
Costs-to-serve, 107–108, 183
Credibility, 209
Cross-product elasticity, 56, 84
Customer behavior analysis:
  product mix, 199–200
  resale prices, 200–201
  total volume purchased, 197–198
Customer(s), generally:
  benefit perceptions, 47–54, 59, 107,
    195, 204
  clusters, benefit perceptions, 66–68
  elasticity, 107
  needs analysis, 118, 124
  perceptions, 16–17, 44, 56
  postmerger pricing, impact on,
    128–129
  price perceptions:
    influential factors, 201–203
    management strategies, 193–195
    product/market strategy, 54–56
    significance of, 59
  price sensitivity, 79, 84
  satisfaction, 67
  sensitivity, 145
  on value map, 67–69
  value research, 195
  vertical nonprice restrictions, 260
Customer-relationship management
    (CRM), 112

Data accuracy, 211
Dealer/distributor discount, 31–32, 225
Dealer Partnership, 135
Deep-structure interviews, 61
Dell, 144
Demand, *see* Supply and demand
  analysis, 88
  creation of, 56–57
Demographics, impact of, 8
Destructive pricing, 80
Diagnostic tools, 168–169
Direct dealing program, reseller
    discounting, 186
Direct questioning, 61
Discount accumulation trap, postmerger
    pricing, 138–139
Discounting, *see specific types of
    discounts*
  authority, 211
  impact of, generally, 14, 28–29, 85,
    110, 119
  misreading the market, 148

Discounting *(Continued)*
  Monarch Battery Company case
      illustration, 222–226
  performance-based, 180
  postmerger, 129
  price perception, 201–202
  by resellers, 186–187
  technology-enabled pricing, 166–167
Discount retailers, 8
Discrete-choice analysis, 47, 134,
      227–228, 233–234
Discretionary discounts, 140
Discriminatory prices, 182–184
Distribution:
  channel partners, 53–54
  legal issues, 180–181
  market changes, impact on, 10
  multitiered environments, 85
Dominant position, EU pricing law,
      261–262
Down-market options, 62
Duopolistic markets, 262
DuPont, 181
Dynamic value management, 57

Early-adapter segment, 109
Eastern Europe, competition laws,
      178
Economic conditions, impact of, 11
Economic swings, 57
Elasticity, *see* Price elasticity
Elasticity surveys, Web-based, 170–171
Electronic data interchange (EDI),
      49
Employees, postmerger, 129–131
End-user rebate, 25
Enterprise resource-planning (ERP)
      system, 51, 106, 175
EU European Community Merger
      Regulation, 141
European, 138
European Court of Justice (ECJ),
      261–263, 265–266
European Union, antitrust legal issues:
  excessive pricing, 267
  geographic discrimination, 266
  overview, 178–179, 183–186,
      260–263
  predatory pricing, 266–267
  price discrimination, 265–266
  price encouragement, 263–264
  price fixing, 263–264
  price signaling, 264–265

  price squeezing, 267
  promotional discrimination, 266
Everest, 230–231, 235
Evolutionary products, 96, 103
Excessive pricing, EU pricing law,
      267
Exclusivity arrangements, 180

FastPress, 136–137
Federal Trade Commission (FTC), 181,
      187, 253
Financial services:
  banking, 122, 133, 194, 249
  insurance, 194
Financial statements, as information
      resource, 175
Fixed costs, 4, 6, 104, 151–152
Fixed prices, 74
Fixed resale price, 264
Flexibility, technology-enabled pricing,
      164
Focus groups, 61
Followership, 75, 79, 84, 87–89
Forced phase-out, product
      cannibalization, 102
Ford Explorer, new product pricing
      illustration, 100–101
France, price discrimination, 265
Free samples, 110
Freight, 25–26, 32–33, 38
Functional benefits, 49–50, 98–99

Generational shifts, impact of, 8–9
Generosity trap, postmerger pricing,
      138
Geographic discrimination, EU pricing
      law, 266
Germany, price discrimination, 265
Globalization, impact of, 9–10, 179
Global price differences, 180–181
Global 1200 economics, 4–6
Go-to-market approach, 71
Goodwill, 103
Goodyear, 154
Growth aspirations, 15–16

Handspring, 144
Hard benefits, 68
Hart-Scott-Rodino Act, 141
HemaTech, 149–150
Higher-end market, 46, 61–62
Home Depot, 8
Horizontal price fixing, 255

IBM, 44
IBM, Global Services, 112–113
Incentives:
impact of, 23, 183–184
performance management system,
212–213, 218–219
postmerger, 134–135
Income statements, as information
resource, 4–5, 65
Industry cooperatives, 181
Industry dynamics, implications of, 57,
65
Industry shakeouts, 145–146
Industry strategy:
characteristics of, 74–75, 88–89
focus of, 88
Monarch Battery Company case
illustration, 230–232, 234–235
motivation in, 80, 82–84
organizational resolve, 84–89
postmerger pricing, 131–133
price followership, 75, 79, 84,
87–89
price leadership, 75, 79–80
in price management, 15–19
price predictions, 75–79
visibility tactics, 80–82
Information sharing, 48–49, 215–216
Information technology (IT), *see*
Technology-enabled pricing
functions of, 173–174, 176
outsourced, 204
product/market strategy, 44
transaction management, 36,
173
Integrator:
characteristics of, 117–118, 122
pricing model by supplier role,
119, 121
Intellectual property, 203
Interbrand competition, 259
Internal controls, 85
International Compressors, 138
International Harvester, antitrust
litigation, 180
Intrabrand competition, 259
Inventory control, 94–95

Jackson, 149–150
Japan, competition laws, 178
Jeffrey, 132–133
Joint bidding, 181
Joint ventures, 181

Keycomp, 48, 50, 51
Key performance indicators (KPIs), 213

Labco, 149–150
Leadership, alignment of, 210. *See also*
Price leadership
Legal issues:
attorney roles, 178, 188–189
overview, 176–178
pricing decisions, red flags, 179–181
risk minimization, 181–187
Line-by-Line Printers, 136–137
List price, 105, 171–172, 201
Litigation, 177. *See also* Antitrust; Legal
issues
Loyalty arrangements/rewards, 49, 180

Management information systems, 23
Manufacturer's suggested retail prices
(MSRPs), 43, 95–96, 105
Markdown optimization software, 172,
174
Market cycles, 57
Market-development funds, 25
Market entry, new products, 109–110
Market forces, impact of:
business environment, 8
business-to-business (B2B) companies,
9–10
demographics, 8
generational shifts, 8–9
lean suppliers, 9–10
Marketing campaigns, 65
Market niches, exploitation of, 154
Market positioning/repositioning, 14,
61, 65, 154
Market research:
Monarch Battery Company case
illustration, 227–228
new product pricing, 98–100
postmerger pricing, 134
strategies for, generally, 47, 61, 73, 95
technology-enabled tools, 165,
170–171
Market segmentation:
legal issues, 182–183
market size, 100–101
purpose of, 18, 56, 70–71
technology-enabled pricing, 164–165
Market share, changes/shifts in, 62–64,
68, 108, 104
Market size, significance of, 100–101,
103

Mazda Miata, new product pricing illustration, 95
Medical products, 27, 67, 148–150, 246
Meet-the-competition clauses, 85, 185
Mergers and acquisitions (M&A), *see* Postmerger pricing
Me-too products, 96
Micro-Comp, 138
Microeconomics, 14, 74–76, 78–79, 88
Minimum advertised price (MAP) programs, 187
Misjudgments, impact of, 148–150
Misreading the market, 147–148, 153, 156
Monarch Battery Company, case illustration:
    background, 220–222
    capturing pricing opportunity, 232–235
    change program, 235–236
    industry strategy, 230–232, 234–235
    product/market strategy, 226–229, 233–234
    transactions, 222–226
    transactions strategy, 232–233
Monopoly pricing laws, 179
Most-favored-customers clauses, 85, 185–186
Most-favored-nation clauses, 186
Motivation, in price leadership, 80, 82–84
MTE, 148–149

Negotiations, 14, 35, 43, 167–168, 186, 201, 211
Networking systems, 67
New product positioning, 149, 154
New product pricing:
    benefits, assessment and quantification of, 98–100
    case illustrations, 95–96, 100–101
    characteristics of, generally, 110–111
    competitor response, prediction of, 106, 108–109
    influential factors, 93–94
    launch position, 96–97
    market entry, 109–110
    market size, determination of, 100–101, 103
    need for, 94–98

    price floor, determination of, 103–105
    product cannibalization, 101–103
    release price, 96, 105–106, 110
Nintendo, antitrust litigation, 181

Obsolete inventory, 148
Off-invoice discounting, 25, 28–29, 33, 54, 187, 194, 200
Off-the-shelf products, 105
Oligopolistic markets, 262
One-stop shop, pricing software vendors, 174–175
On-invoice discounting, 33, 38–39, 187, 194, 200
Open-book costing, 9
Open-ended questioning, 99–100
Open price systems, 264
Operating profit, influential factors, 4–6, 28
Opportunity costs, 175
Optimistic projections, dangers of, 104
Optimization tools:
    benefits of, generally, 165, 171
    list price, 171–172
    markdown, 172, 174
    transaction, 172
Order discount, online, 25
Order-size discount, 24
Organizational change, implications of, 208–210
Organizational pride, 10
Organizational structure, 212–213
Overhead costs, 104
Overreaction, avoidance of, 153

Pain points, technology-enabled pricing, 173–174
Palm, 144
Parallel pricing, 263
Parent trap, postmerger pricing, 140
Pay-by-performance arrangements, 205–206
Payment terms, benefit perceptions, 47, 49
Pay-per-use arrangements, 204–205
Penalties, performance management system, 25, 41, 218
Penetration pricing, 106–108
Perceived benefit, *see* Customer(s), benefit perceptions
Perceived price, *see* Customer(s), price perceptions
Performance dialogue, 217–218

Performance management system:
  compensation, 213–214
  importance of, 212–213
  incentives, 213–214, 218–219
  key performance indicators (KPIs),
    213
  penalties, 25, 41, 218
  performance dialogue, 217
  reinforcement, 217–219, 235
  role modeling, 216–217, 235–236
  talent and skill development,
    214–216, 235
Performance metrics, 212
Performance reporting, technology-
    enabled tools, 165, 167–170
Performance standards, 86
Pocket discount, 26
Pocket margin, transaction management:
  band, 37, 39, 41
  case illustration, 37–39
  waterfall, 37, 40, 248–252
Pocket price, transaction management:
  band, 25, 27–29, 41, 224–225
  case illustration, 35–36
  optimization tools, 172
  waterfall, 24–27, 35–36, 41, 56, 123,
    194–195, 200, 239–247
Pooling, market segmentation, 71
Postmerger pricing:
  antitrust laws, 140–142
  common traps, 137–140
  competitors, 131
  components of, 127–128
  customers, 128–129
  employees, 129–131
  industry strategy, 131–133
  product/market strategy, 133–135
  transaction pricing, 135–137
Predatory pricing:
  characteristics of, 146
  EU pricing law, 266–267
  U.S. pricing law, 260
Premium price, 82
Press releases, 82
Price advantage, generally:
  benefits of, 11–12, 237–238
  defined, 3
  market forces, impact on, 8–10
  1 percent price improvement/decline,
    4–6, 11, 27
  price/volume tradeoff, 6–7
  rarity of, 10–12
Price aggression, 155
Price/benefit point, 69

Price-capped customers, 67
Price changes/shifts:
  agenda, 207–208
  anticipation of, 77–78
  conviction, 208–210, 235
  developing talent and skill, 214–216,
    235
  failure modes, 218–219
  formal mechanisms, 210–214
  increases, 66, 89
  role modeling, 216–218
  understanding, 208–210, 235
Price communication:
  clarity in, 81–82
  consistency in, 84
  impact of, 194
  leadership plan, 85
  legal issues, 185
  methods of, 56, 71–73, 82
  postmerger, 131
  price wars and, 154
Price cuts, 63, 66–67, 102, 120, 144,
    155–156
Price differentiation, 11
Price discount, 14
Price discrimination:
  EU pricing law, 265–266
  legal issues, 182–184
  U.S. pricing law, 257–258
Price elasticity, 7, 55–56, 144
Price encouragement:
  EU pricing law, 263–264
  U.S. pricing law, 254–256
Price expectations, distorted, 144–145
Price fixing:
  EU pricing law, 263–264
  legal issues, 179, 185
  U.S. pricing law, 254–256
Price floor, determination of, 103–105
Price leadership, 75, 79–80, 210
Price management levels:
  industry strategy, 15–17, 74–89
  interdependent hierarchy, 17–18
  opportunities, identification of, 13,
    18–20
  product/market strategy, 16–18,
    43–73
  transaction, 17–18, 23–42
Price matching, 185
Price perception, *see* Customer(s),
    generally, perceptions
Price policy, reseller discounting,
    186–187
Price premium, 14

Price sensitivity, 151
Price signaling:
  EU pricing law, 264–265
  U.S. pricing law, 256–257
Price squeezing:
  EU pricing law, 267
  U.S. pricing law, 260
Price-to-meet-competition (PTMC)
    discount, 32
Price trends, 81
Price/volume tradeoff, 6–7, 148–149
Price wars:
  avoidance strategies, 150–154, 185
  beneficial, 155–157
  deliberate, 146
  getting out of, 154–155
  incidence of, 143
  postmerger, 131–133
  reasons to avoid, 143–146
  risk for, 151–152, 156
  sources of, 65, 79, 146–150
Price waterfall engineering, 187. *See also*
    Pocket margin; Pocket price
Pricing architecture:
  customer behavior, influential factors,
      196–201, 204–206
  price perception, 193–195, 201–203
Pricing configuration, 166–167
Pricing errors/mistakes, 162–163, 166
Pricing excellence, 10, 23, 237
Pricing intelligence, Web-based, 171
Pricing law, *see* Antitrust; Legal issues
Pricing talent, identification of, 214–215
Proactive management, 124, 138
Process-related benefits, 49–50, 98–99
Product bundling, 180
Product cannibalization, 101–103
Production, optimal, 78–79
Product life cycle, 75–76, 118, 151,
    171
Product/market strategy, in price
    management:
  characteristics of, 16–18, 43–44, 73
  competitor response, 65–66
  goal of, 43
  Monarch Battery Company case
      illustration, 226–229, 233–234
  opportunities, identification of, 19
  postmerger pricing, 133–135
  value map, 44–69
  value profiling, 69–73
Product mix, 199–200
Product positioning, 25, 57. *See also*
    Market positioning/repositioning

Product restrictions, vertical nonprice,
    260
Product testing, 100
Profitability:
  pocket margin, 40–41
  postmerger pricing and, 133
  significance of, 87
  solution economics, 123
Profit growth, 83
Profit motive, 83–84
Profit sensitivity, 144
Promotional discrimination:
  EU pricing law, 266
  U.S. pricing law, 258–259
Promotions:
  benefits of, 164
  new products, 110
  off-invoice, 25, 32, 35
Pulp and paper, 130

Qualco, 228, 230–231, 233, 235

Real-time inventory, 94
Real-time testing, 170
Rebates, 25, 47, 110, 195
Regression analysis, 164
Reinforcement, performance
    management system, 217–219,
    235
Relationship-based benefits, 49–50,
    98–99
Release price, 96, 105–106, 110
Reputation, 54
Resale price, generally:
  EU pricing law, 264
  setting/influencing, 180
Research and development (R&D), 15,
    103, 105
Resellers:
  discounting, 186–187
  price leadership and, 84–87
  resale price, influential factors,
      200–201
  vertical nonprice restrictions, 260
Retail price support policies, 187
Return on investment (ROI), 62, 68,
    111
Revenue losses, 163
Revolutionary products, 96, 98, 100
Risk-averse mindset, 177
Risk minimization strategies:
  international pricing, 184
  market segmentation, 182–183
  price leadership, 184–186

price wars, 184–186
promotional incentives, 183–184
regional pricing, 184
reseller discounting, 186–187
Risk sharing, 216–217
Robinson-Patman Act of 1936, 178,
182, 187, 257–258
Role modeling, 216–218
Role-playing, 215–216
Rotation Co., product/market strategy
illustration, 57–59
Rule of reason, 253

Salespeople:
incentive programs for, 23
price negotiations, 14, 35
technology-enabled pricing, impact
on, 168
Senior management:
change agenda, role in, 208–210
failure of, 219
functions of, generally, 11, 142, 167,
208–210, 218
Shared price advertising, 187
Shell Chemical, industry strategy
illustration, 78–79
Sherman Antitrust Act of 1890, 178,
255–256
Simmons, 132–133
Skills development, 214–216, 218
Slotting allowance, 25
Soft benefits, 68
Solutions:
characteristics of, 113–114
defined, 112
examples of, 114–115
false providers, 117–118
relationship options, 115–117
true providers, 117, 121–124
Soundco Radio Company, transaction
management illustration, 30–37
Southeast Asia, legal issues, 184
Special costs, transaction management,
37, 39
Spot prices, 71
Stable environment, value in, 46, 56
State Compressors, 138
Static environment, value in, 56
Stocking allowance, 25
Strategic intent, 65
Stretch targets, 210
Supplier(s):
costs-to-serve, 107–108
high-tech, 203

lean, 9–10
price leadership and, 87
product cannibalization, 102
role of, *see* Supplier roles
vertical nonprice restrictions,
259–260
Supplier roles:
bundler, 116, 118–120, 122
component specialist, 116, 118–119,
121–122
integrator, 117, 118–119, 121–122
solutions provider, 117, 121–124
Supply and demand, 14, 76–78, 167
Sure Motors, product/market strategy
illustration, 57–59, 61

Talent development, 214–216
Technology-enabled pricing:
administration tools, 165–167
advances in, 161
benefits of, 162–165
best-in-breed providers *vs.* one-stop
shop, 174–175
in-house solutions, 175–176
market research tools, 165, 170–171
optimization tools, 165, 171–173
"pain points," 173–174
performance reporting tools, 165,
167–170
software selection factors, 175–176
Third-party vendors, 176
Tooling costs, 40
Trade associations, membership in, 181
Trade relations, 177
Training programs:
importance of, 215, 218
pricing software, 175
Transaction management:
case illustrations, *see* Allen Glass
Company; Monarch Battery
Company; Soundco Radio
Company
characteristics of, 17–18
objective of, 23
opportunities, identification of, 19
pocket margin band, 37, 39, 41
pocket margin waterfall, 37, 40,
248–252
pocket price band, 25, 27–29, 41,
224–225
pocket price waterfall, 24–27, 41, 56,
123, 194–195, 200, 239–247
postmerger, 135–137
significance of, 41–42

Transaction optimization software, 172
Transparent prices, 81–82, 181
Transparent rationale, 81–82

U.S. banking industry, 133–134
U.S. pricing law:
  EU pricing law compared with,
      261–262
  predatory pricing, 260
  price discrimination, 257–258
  price encouragement, 254–256
  price fixing, 254–256
  price signaling, 256–257
  price squeezing, 260
  promotional discrimination, 258–259
  vertical nonprice restrictions, 259–260
Upscale consumers, 98–99

Value-added resellers (VARs), 53
Value-advantaged position, 46–47,
      57–59, 65, 67, 69, 118
Value-disadvantaged position, 47, 69
Value equivalence line (VEL):
  blank space, 68–69
  cutting off customers, 69
  defined, 46
  implications of, 46–47, 59–60
  misjudgments, 149–150
  moving off the, 62–64
  postmerger pricing, 133
  price floor, determination of, 103, 106
  repositioning along, 60–62
  volume distribution, 69

Value maps:
  benefit perceptions, 47–54
  benefits, types of, 49
  case illustrations, 47–60
  changes in, 56–67
  customers on, 67–69
  drawing guidelines, 45–47
  price/benefit tradeoffs, 148
  price perceptions, 54–56
  price wars and, 153–154
  significance of, 73
  value equivalence line (VEL), *see*
      Value equivalence line (VEL)
Value pricing, 44
Value repositioning, 60–62, 201
Variable costs, 4, 6, 152
Vertical nonprice restrictions, U.S.
      pricing law, 259–260
Vertical price fixing, 179, 186
Visibility, in price leadership, 80–82
Volume discounts, 47
Volume loss, 67

Wal-Mart, 8
Workflow tools, pricing approval,
      167
Workshops, 215

X-Act Copy, 136

Zone of credibility, 55, 103
Zone of indifference, 54–55, 69, 108,
      163, 229